AHEAD
OF THE
MARKET

The Zacks Method for Spotting
Stocks Early—In Any Economy

Mitch Zacks

HarperBusiness
An Imprint of HarperCollins *Publishers*

FIRST EDITION

Designed by Pete Lippincott, D&G Limited, LLC

Library of Congress Cataloging-in-Publication Data

Zacks, Mitch.
    Ahead of the market : the Zacks method for spotting stocks early—in any economy / Mitch Zacks.
      p. cm.
    Includes bibliographical references and index.
    ISBN 0-06-009968-2
1. Stocks—United States. 2. Investments—United States. I. Title.

HG4910 .Z32 2003
332.63'22—dc21   2002192235

03 04 05 06 07   10 9 8 7 6 5 4 3 2 1

To my Father

Table of Contents

Acknowledgements

I'D LIKE TO THANK THOSE whose contributions made this book possible: Dan Miller, the business editor at *The Chicago Sun-Times*, who first gave me the opportunity several years ago to write a weekly column, for which I will always be eternally grateful; David Conti, my editor at HarperCollins, who was an absolute pleasure to work with and was instrumental in helping me make the book accessible to any reader (David's editorial comments as well as those of his assistant Knox Huston were dead-on and extremely useful—I was lucky to have such a talented editorial team dedicated to the book); Lisa Berkowitz for her assistance in marketing as well as Carie Freimuth for believing in the book; Daniel Greenberg, an extraordinary agent without whom this book would not have been possible; Ben Zacks, for teaching me about the markets; Rebecca Zacks, for teaching me about life; Rayna, Danielle, Len, and Francine; and most importantly Laura, my wife.

Introduction

RIGHT NOW, THE MARKETS FACE A CRISIS OF TRUST. The conventional wisdom is that the people at the top of the U.S. corporate structure are benefiting themselves while disregarding the interests of their workers and their shareholders.

For many very good reasons, most of you do not trust your broker, you likely do not trust the CEOs of corporate America, and if you have read the newspaper recently you also do not trust the analysts.

After having spent my entire professional career reading and analyzing brokerage research reports and using the data produced by analysts to manage portfolios, I can tell you without any shadow of doubt that your suspicions regarding analysts are absolutely correct. It is a mistake to take the research produced by analysts at face value.

Brokerage firms collectively pay thousands of stock research analysts over $1 billion a year to write research reports on stocks. However, if you had followed the advice of these analysts and purchased the stocks that were the most highly recommended by them, you would have lost an incredible 47% over the past two and a half years while those stocks least recommended by analysts fell only 11% over the same time period.

This does not mean, though, that you can not use the research produced by analysts to make money. Despite recent criticisms, analysts actually provide a wealth of market-moving information that, if interpreted correctly, can get you ahead of the market. It is simply a matter of focusing on the information produced by analysts that is important and profitable while ignoring the information that is misleading and manipulative.

This book teaches you how to do just that: *Ahead of the Market* shows you how to profit from the $1 billion being spent each year by Wall Street firms on stock analysts and avoid being taken for a ride by Wall Street's research machine.

The cornerstone of *Ahead of the Market* is an emphasis on several independent, time-tested investment strategies that are currently used by professional portfolio managers, but until now have remained unknown to most individual investors. If implemented correctly, these strategies—which focus on the profitable use of analyst research—will generate market-beating returns in any market environment.

Although Wall Street research is now ubiquitous, most individual investors are actually harming their portfolios by using the research improperly. This book teaches you how to sift through the noise contained in analysts' research and focus on precisely what information should be acted upon and what information should be ignored.

Although hundreds of professional money managers implement the methods contained in this book, no one has yet explained the methodologies to individual investors.

Ahead of the Market provides this explanation in a straightforward, simple manner.

If you take the time to read, digest, and understand the concepts in this book, I am confident that with discipline and determination you can dramatically improve your investment performance in both bull and bear markets, as well as any market in between.

What Does Zacks Investment Research Do?

On a daily basis, Zacks Investment Research processes and analyzes thousands of research reports written by over 3,000 equity analysts employed at over 250 brokerage firms across the United States and Canada.

For the past twenty years, we have been going through the research produced by Wall Street brokerage firms with a fine-tooth comb. Along the way we have been credited with changing the way people view and use the research coming out of Wall Street.

- We were the first firm in the country to start tracking the buy/sell/hold recommendations made by analysts.

- We developed the concept of the quarterly consensus earnings estimate.

- We created the consensus recommendation score.

- We invented the "quarterly earnings surprise."

- We were the first firm to rank analysts based on their accuracy in predicting earnings and making stock recommendations.

Through twenty years of intensive research, we have determined that *the most important driver of stock prices is revisions to analysts' earnings estimates.*

Zacks has used this knowledge to create two proprietary quantitative models that predict price movement ten days and ninety days into the future. These models are currently used by institutional clients to manage over $100 billion in assets. The model that predicts the price movement of stocks over the next ninety days is known as the Zacks Rank.

For the past twenty years we have published the Zacks Rank on a monthly basis. Over that time period, this unbiased stock ranking system has generated extraordinary returns. Excluding transaction costs, a monthly rebalanced portfolio consisting of Zacks #1 Ranked stocks produced an average annualized return of 31.8% over the period from January 1980 through September 2002, as compared to a 12.6% annualized return for the S&P 500.

If you had religiously followed the Zacks Rank during the last few years, you would be substantially better off than if you had listened to analysts' recommendations. In fact, while the S&P 500 fell 9.1% in 2000, 11.9% in 2001, and 28.2% through September of 2002, the Zacks #1 Ranked stock portfolio rose 16.2% in 2000, was up 18.7% in 2001, and was down only 5.9% through September of 2002. In this book, I explain the methodology behind the Zacks Rank, why it works, and how you can make it work for you.

The Strategies

Ahead of the Market provides you with objective, independent advice, a road map to understanding and profiting from the brokerage research that is now readily available. The advice I detail in this book is based on roughly twenty years of painstaking quantitative research and analysis combined with my practical experience implementing the strategies described. Unlike other investment book authors, I am not going to talk in vague generalities or give you war stories about stocks I have purchased that have doubled in price. Instead, each chapter of *Ahead of the Market* provides you with actionable advice based on extensive statistical analysis concerning the historical reaction of stocks to analyst activity.

This book is not a history book. It is not a piece of journalism explaining what has gone wrong with the markets. It is not a biography.

Rather, this book is about how you can effectively use analyst research to make money.

Ultimately, *Ahead of the Market* is designed to be a handbook for interpreting and profiting from analyst research. The central point of this book is that a single analyst's recommendation and earnings estimates, in and of themselves, are useless. What is important is the following:

- What *all* the analysts say about a given stock

- How those views change over time

When you combine the two you have what has proven to be one of the best ways of finding stocks that will outperform the market.

What Will You Learn in this Book ?

The most profitable uses of the research produced by Wall Street research analysts are not widely known. Instead, most individual investors continue to focus on the elements of the research produced by Wall Street analysts that are the most misleading, and so by definition the most useless.

By the end of this book you should know the following:

- Why analysts' earnings estimate revisions occur incrementally over time and how you can profit from this phenomenon

- How you can avoid being misled by analysts' buy/hold/sell recommendations

- How you can employ the methodologies used by several large hedge fund managers to predict earnings surprises

- How to avoid being overwhelmed by the amount of stock recommendation data available online and in the financial media by instead focusing on the important analyst-related data that you can use to make a profit

For example:

- You will learn whether you should buy a stock after the stock's price has dramatically reacted to an analyst's recommendation upgrade. Is it too late, or do even more significant moves follow?

- Similarly, you will learn whether you should buy a company's stock after the company reports earnings worse than analysts' expectations. Is the stock likely to bounce, or sink further?

- And more importantly, you will find out if you should even look at brokerage firm recommendations, or if analyst research contains a more powerful piece of information that can help you make money.

How the Book Is Organized

I have read many investing books and know the frustration a reader feels as, chapter after chapter, the author slowly moves toward a conclusion, setting up strategies made of straw only to knock them down.

So, instead, I summarize in Chapter One the key ideas that you need to understand. After Chapter One, you should be better able to use the research produced by analysts to improve your portfolio performance, especially after reviewing the section that tells you exactly what analyst-related data you need to focus on in order to generate returns.

Chapter Two takes a step back and explains exactly who analysts are and what role they play in the financial markets. Chapter Two also contains a thorough overview of the structure of the investment industry, which helps explain why analysts are unlikely to issue sell recommendations and why they are less than straightforward in their analysis due to conflicts with investment banking. Chapter Two also answers the question of whether there are, in fact, exceptional analysts whose recommendations should be followed.

Chapter Three examines a sample brokerage research report and identifies which of the items contained in analyst research are useful and which items should be ignored. By understanding the individual parts of an analyst's research report and how those parts are put together to create consensus data, the stage is set for an investor to better understand the ratios presented later in the book.

Chapters Four and Five focus on analysts' earnings estimates—the most important and powerful item in a brokerage research report. Chapter Four explains why earnings estimates are so important to stock valuations and why changes in earnings estimates can be used to predict stock price movement. Chapter Four also illustrates a phenomenon called "analyst creep" and explains why the phenomenon exists.

Chapter Five details a six-step process for effectively using earnings estimate revisions to pick winning stocks. Additionally, in Chapter Five I explain exactly which specific data items you should focus on in order to predict future earnings estimate revisions.

Chapter Six explains what an earnings surprise is and why some earnings surprises cause greater price impacts than others. Additionally, Chapter Six details five accounting games companies play with their earnings and what you can do about them.

Chapter Seven shows how you should and should not use earnings surprises in your investment process, including the three steps you should take before reacting to any earnings surprise. The chapter describes the "cockroach effect" and "post–earnings announcement drift." Chapter Seven also explains how and why you should begin focusing attention on a new metric called a Sales Surprise™ in addition to an earnings surprise. Chapter Seven ends with a description of the strategies that several large hedge funds use to predict earnings surprises.

Chapter Eight presents an overview of the Zacks Rank, explains why it works so well, answers some frequently asked questions about the Rank, and details the primary factors used in constructing the Rank. In Chapter Eight, we also see the Zacks Rank in action and learn how it helps you to pick winners and avoid losers.

Chapter Nine contains specific instructions on how various classes of investors can implement the Zacks Rank. Chapter Nine ends with the six-step method that details how exactly to implement the Zacks Rank in an investment process.

Chapter Ten presents some new research on the performance of analyst recommendations that helps explain why stocks that have been highly recommended by analysts have underperformed in the market over the past two years. Many people believe the underperformance is due to the conflict between investment banking and analyst research, but there is something far more fundamental going on of which you should be aware. Chapter Ten also illustrates exactly how using analyst research incorrectly can harm your portfolio and how you should use analyst recommendations in your investment process.

Chapters Eleven and Twelve investigate some lesser-known uses of analyst data such as valuation metrics, neglect analysis, and earnings uncertainty, as well as how to use the long-term earnings growth rate produced by analysts to determine which stocks to avoid.

Additionally, the appendixes contain very valuable information. One appendix that you should definitely not skip is Appendix I which offers a free one-month subscription to zacksadvisor.com, the most popular subscription-based investment newsletter on the Internet. The subscription also provides you with daily access to both the Zacks Rank and the Zacks Focus List.

Final Words

Some words of advice or caution: This book contains no magic formulas that will make you wealthy beyond your dreams. The book does, however, include methodologies and strategies that, if implemented properly (and I will show you how), will generate market-beating returns in both bull and bear markets.

Some of the results in this book are counterintuitive, some are even controversial. In fact, you may be surprised to find that our analysis indicates that the recommendations issued by many brokerage firms are not worth the paper they are printed on. However, the underlying message of all the research points toward one simple conclusion:

You should buy stocks that receive upward earnings estimate revisions and avoid stocks that receive downward earnings estimate revisions.

I explain all this and more in the pages ahead.

This book teaches you how to rely on yourself in a world where it's not clear whom you can trust or what the market will hold.

Let's get started.

## Chapter One

The Main Themes

What's ahead in this chapter?

- Meet the Analyst and His Research Report
- Analysts and Sell Recommendations
- Analysts and Buy Recommendations
- Analysts and Earnings Estimates

THIS BOOK IS DESIGNED TO TEACH YOU how to implement several investment strategies that enable you to use the research produced by Wall Street stock analysts profitably.

These investment strategies will provide you with independent, time-tested advice and are currently used extensively by professional investors. The strategies are based on over twenty years of research by Zacks into how an investor can most effectively use analyst research.

If used correctly, these strategies will generate market-beating returns in both bull and bear markets.

The purpose of this first chapter is simple. I want to present you with a basic introduction on how to use analyst research, which became publicly available over the Internet for the first time in the mid–1990s.

Meet the Analyst and His Research Report

To begin our journey, we must first understand the enigmatic and recently much maligned Wall Street analyst. Yes, analysts suffer from entrenched problems due to the system that they operate in, and yes, analysts are lousy stock pickers; but analysts and the research that they produce can be incredibly useful—you just need to know how to correctly interpret analysts' research reports and the data that is generated from them.

Wall Street brokerage firms collectively employ over 3,000 analysts. These analysts are paid to tell the brokerage firms' customers which stocks to buy and sell. Analysts serve two types of customers: large institutional clients such as mutual funds, pension funds, and hedge funds, and individuals ranging from people saving for their children's education or their personal retirement, to wealthy individuals with several million dollars to invest.

Analysts are collectively paid well over $1 billion a year to write research reports explaining their opinions on particular stocks or groups of stocks to the clients of their brokerage firms.

These research reports contain a tremendous amount of data, but the two most important components in the research reports are the analysts' recommendations and their earnings estimates.

The recommendation refers to whether an analyst thinks you should buy or sell a stock while the earnings estimate is the analyst's prediction of what he thinks a company is going to earn, on a per-share basis, in the next couple of quarters and the next few fiscal years.

Up until the mid-1990s, the research reports produced by analysts and the data created from the analysts' reports were, for the most part, not available unless you were a professional investor or had a very large account at a full-service brokerage firm.

Today, all the information produced by brokerage firm analysts—their earnings estimates, their recommendations, and even their research reports—is available to almost any investor.

Unfortunately, most investors are using this newly available information incorrectly and their portfolios are suffering as a result.

It Pays to Focus on Earnings Estimates

Individual investors seem to be fixated on the most biased parts of analyst research—the recommendations—while ignoring the unbiased information that professional investors have been using for years, which is contained in the earnings estimates.

In order to use analyst research in the right way you must learn exactly what information produced by analysts you should be focusing on and what information you should be ignoring. The answer is to focus on revisions to analysts' earnings estimates as well as earnings surprises.

Let's start by examining the buy/hold/sell recommendations and the earnings per share (EPS) estimates, both of which are contained in an analyst's research report.

The Recommendation

At the top of every analyst's research report the recommendation is prominently displayed. Recommendations come in a variety of flavors. Each brokerage firm has its own classification of recommendations that its analysts can issue. Some firms have had, at one time, as many as twenty-four possible recommendations that can be issued while other firms have only five possible recommendations that their analysts can issue: "Strong Buy," "Buy," "Hold," "Sell," or "Strong Sell."

Beginning in late 2001, many large brokerage firms started to simplify their recommendation classifications in response to the public outcry regarding the lack of sell recommendations industrywide.

As a result of these recent changes, most major brokerage firms seem to be migrating toward specifically using "Over-Weight," "Equal-Weight," and "Under-Weight."

Most of the major brokerage firms, in addition to issuing a recommendation on a stock, also provide a recommendation on the stock's industry. For instance, Microsoft might receive an "Over-Weight" recommendation and in the same research report, Microsoft's industry of "Computer Software" might receive an "Equal-Weight" recommendation. With three possible recommendations on the stock, and three possible recommendations on the stock's industry, most brokerage firms are moving toward nine possible recommendations available to an analyst.

An analyst's recommendation is supposed to boil all his research down into one simple actionable piece of advice, the answer to the question, "Nice ten-page report, but what should I do about the stock?"

Not surprisingly, the recommendation is probably the most widely used piece of information contained in the analysts' research reports simply because it is, at face value, easy to understand and appears to be straight-forward. Do not be fooled. An analyst's recommendation is a wolf in sheep's clothing.

It *is* simple.

It *is* straightforward.

And invariably it is *wrong*.

In fact, if you had bought those stocks that were the most highly recommended by analysts over the two-and-a-half-year period from April 2000 to September 2002, you would have lost a phenomenal 47%.

KEY POINT   Following analysts' recommendations will lead to poor investment performance. Although the recommendation is the most widely used component of the analyst's research report, it should not be—it is misleading to investors.

Analysts and Sell Recommendations

One big problem with listening to analysts' recommendations is that analysts have historically been very reluctant to issue sell recommendations. This has been the case since Zacks began tracking analysts' recommendations in the mid-1980s. Today sell recommendations are still uncommon, and this will likely be true in the future even if the various reforms currently being discussed are enacted. Why? Because, as we shall see in the next chapter, the reasons for analysts not issuing sell recommendations are endemic to the system.

For now, just accept this: Currently, analysts are collectively over ten times more likely to issue a buy or hold recommendation than a sell recommendation.

If you have been following the news, the collective reluctance of analysts to issue sell recommendations should not surprise you. Eliot Spitzer, the attorney general of New York, led an investigation which ended in December of 2002 that brought the dearth of sell recommendations to the public's attention. Since the summer of 2001, analysts have been publicly eviscerated. Jack Grubman has been blamed for the woes of WorldCom, and Henry Blodget was made the fall guy for the Internet bubble. Analysts as a group have been blamed for the "loss of investor confidence" that afflicted the market following the meltdown of technology stocks that began in the first quarter of 2000.

The reluctance of analysts to issue sell recommendations has been offered as one reason why individual investors lost a tremendous amount of money. You may have seen pundits and politicians parading themselves on the nightly news indicating that the nefarious analysts are responsible for the infectious greed that brought on the bear market like a fulfillment of biblical prophecy.

The Reluctance to Issue Sell Recommendations Is Nothing New

Yes, analysts are reluctant to issue sell recommendations, but this is nothing new to the institutional investors who have used analyst research since the dawn of Wall Street. And the whole tech fiasco was not caused by individuals trading stocks online; large institutions bear far more of the blame. The problem is not that analysts are biased; the problem is that no one let individuals in on the secret or told them how to effectively ignore the hype contained in analyst recommendations.

Compounding the problem, the Internet gave individuals access to analysts' recommendations and research without the requisite education on how to use the data, so they understandably took analysts' recommendations at face value.

When an analyst says "hold," most individuals unfortunately still do not realize that this means "sell," simply because analysts almost never issue negative recommendations.

As Spitzer's investigation showed there is an inherent conflict between a brokerage firm's research and its investment banking division. This influences what an analyst is willing to publish in his research reports. Obviously, analysts are reluctant to issue negative research reports on clients of their brokerage firm.

Here's why.

Investment bankers want to do business with companies—take them public, help them sell additional shares through secondary offerings, advise them on deals—and the last thing investment bankers need is one of their firm's research analysts telling the world that the company they want to do business with is a dog.

The problem is that high-profile analysts like Jack Grubman compromised the integrity of their research in order to generate investment banking revenue. With WorldCom a voracious acquirer, the argument is that Grubman issued overly optimistic research reports to boost WorldCom's stock price so that WorldCom could make even more acquisitions and generate more fees for his firm.

There is definitely some truth to this, but what is not readily known is that even before such conflicts of interest began to appear, analysts always had a bias against issuing negative recommendations. The problem is structural in nature.

In fact, the distribution of analyst recommendations has proven to be fairly constant over time. Of the roughly 30,000 individual analyst recommendations that Zacks tracks on over 4,500 individual stocks, currently 8.3% of all analyst recommendations are some form of sell (either a "sell" or "strong sell") and this is the highest the level has been within the last ten years. For most of the past decade, the percentage of all analysts' recommendations that are some form of sell has remained pitifully low.

Starting around mid-2001, due to a combination of the bear market (analysts are more likely to issue sell recommendations in a bear market) and the political pressures being placed on analysts to issue more sell recommendations, there has been a slight increase in the number of sell recommendations. However, despite these pressures and a string of slick new ads for brokerage firms in which they herald the independence of their analysts, I would not expect the distribution of analysts' recommendations to change dramatically in the coming months and years. If the distribution does change I would expect the change to be temporary. Why?

Because once analysts and their recommendations fade from the regulatory spotlight, brokerage firms, as we shall see, will always have everything to lose but nothing to gain by issuing a "sell" recommendation.

KEY POINT   Regardless of the structural changes made, analysts will continue to be reluctant to issue sell recommendations. This reluctance is endemic to the system. In addition, analysts' recommendations move markets. As long as this is the case, analysts' recommendations will likely be manipulated or at least influenced by investment bankers.

Analysts and Buy Recommendations

So, waiting for an analyst to flat-out tell you to sell a stock is a modern-day financial version of *Waiting for Godot*.

Still, you may be wondering whether analysts' buy recommendations can make you money. This question will be examined thoroughly later on, but for now let's skip to the chase:

The answer, unfortunately, is "not readily."

The simplest way to see this is to look at the performance of what are called "brokerage firm buy lists."

Brokerage Firm Buy Lists

Most brokerage firms create a "buy list" or "core list" that generally comprises anywhere between fifteen and thirty stocks representing a well-balanced portfolio of the firm's top stock picks taken from all the analysts working at the firm. Some firms even offer their buy lists as an actual portfolio that investors can invest in. These buy lists are thus usually screened for diversification concerns to ensure the entire list is a reasonable portfolio that can be bought in its entirety.

At Zacks we have been tracking the performance of every brokerage firm's buy list for over ten years, and their performance is not as exceptional as you might be led to believe. The results for fifteen large brokerage firms are given in Figure 1-1.

Ever since we have been monitoring the performance of brokerage firms' buy lists, over almost any period examined, roughly half of the brokerage firm buy lists beat the S&P 500 and half of the brokerage firm buy lists under-perform the S&P 500. In other words, the best picks of the top analysts at the top brokerage firms are no better than those selected by the typical mutual fund manager, which also under-perform the S&P 500 about half of the time.

The moral is clear: Analysts and the data they produce may be good for many things, but telling you when to buy or sell is definitely not one of them. You need to rely on other information.

KEY POINT   Analysts are not exceptional stock pickers. This is apparent when you investigate the returns of the buy lists created by brokerage firms.

Figure 1-1 Brokerage houses' stock-picking prowess.

Estimated performance of stocks on the recommended lists of fifteen major brokerage houses through June 30, 2002. Figures include price changes, dividends, and hypothetical trading commissions of 1%.

	Return		
	Last Quarter	**One-Year**	**Five-Year**
Raymond James	3.4%	3.8%	41.5%
Bear Stearns	−4.1%	2.3%	59.4%
Bank of America	−5.1%	N.A.	N.A.
Prudential Sec.	−9.5%	−8.5%	22.0%
Merrill Lynch	−9.9%	−10.1%	43.6%
Credit Suisse F.B.	−12.7%	−19.6%	26.8%
RBC Dain Rauscher	−12.9%	−24.1%	N.A.
J. P. Morgan Sec.	−13.2%	−8.1%	N.A.
Morgan Stanley	−14.3%	−17.5%	11.1%
Lehman Bros.	−15.1%	−21.0%	1.9%
Edward Jones	−15.8%	−14.7%	33.0%
A.G. Edwards	−15.8%	−18.9%	2.7%
Goldman Sachs	−17.9%	−33.1%	21.0%
U.S. Bancorp	−23.3%	−33.9%	−6.5%
Salomon S.B.	−26.5%	−33.4%	−23.1%
S&P 500 Index	−13.4 %	−18.0%	19.7%

Source: Wall Street Journal/Zacks 8/22/02.

Although you can not easily use an analyst's recommendation to tell you when to buy and sell a stock, the analysts do produce a piece of information that will help you: their earnings estimates. Because a company actually reports earnings each and every quarter, analysts' earnings estimates are tied to reality and are less subjective in nature. As a result, analysts' earnings estimates are far more pure than analysts' recommendations.

KEY POINT   Focus on analysts' earnings estimates rather than their recommendations because the earnings estimates are less subjective and thus contain more information for the investor.

Importance of Predicting Analysts' Behavior

The best way to use analyst research is to try to anticipate what an analyst is going to do in the future instead of simply responding to the information contained in an individual analyst's research report.

You need to understand the distinction. At the most basic level, the recommendation contained in an individual analyst's research report is likely to already be reflected in the price of a stock—especially if the research report is more than a month or two old.

If a Morgan Stanley analyst issues a recommendation saying that buying General Electric (GE) stock at current levels is the best opportunity the analyst has seen in the last decade, GE's stock price is going to almost immediately soar to reflect this information. Invariably, by the time you act on what is in the analyst's research report, it will be too late. GE's stock will have already made its move.

You want to buy—in the case of upgrades—or sell—in the case of downgrades—before the analyst issues his recommendation change, not after.

This is relatively hard to do with recommendation changes, but as we shall see later on, it can be done; stocks for which multiple analysts have upgraded their recommendations tend to exhibit strength over the next month, while stocks for which multiple analysts have downgraded their recommendations tend to exhibit weakness over the next month. We will address this in Chapter Ten when I discuss a statistic called the consensus recommendation score.

While it is difficult to predict whether an analyst will upgrade or downgrade a stock, it is far easier to anticipate if an analyst will change his earnings estimates.

By buying stocks whose earnings estimates have recently been revised upward and selling stocks whose earnings estimates have been revised downward, you can effectively anticipate the future actions of both analysts and the large institutional investors whose behavior moves stock prices. This enables you to be able to buy or sell a stock "ahead of the market."

KEY POINT   By combining the research produced by multiple analysts and looking for changes over time in the revisions to analysts' earnings estimates, you can predict what analysts will likely do in the future.

Analysts and Earnings Estimates

There is a whole chapter in this book (Chapter 4) devoted to why analysts' earnings estimates are one of the most important determinants of a stock's price. But, for now, I want to explain *how* you can find stocks for which analysts are raising their earnings estimates. These are the stocks you should be buying.

In order to determine which stocks are receiving upward earnings estimate revisions from analysts, you need to condense all the earnings estimates issued by all the analysts following a stock into a statistic called the consensus earnings estimate.

The next step is to then track changes to the consensus earnings estimate over time and buy stocks for which the consensus earnings estimate is increasing over time.

A consensus earnings estimate sounds rather exotic but in reality is rather mundane. The consensus earnings estimate is simply the average value of all the earnings estimates issued by all the analysts following a specific stock.

Here's how we determine it at Zacks. Right below the recommendation in an analyst's research report are the analyst's earnings estimates. These earnings estimates are what the analyst feels the company he is covering is going to report in earnings on a per share basis in the coming quarters and the coming and next fiscal year. To create the consensus earnings estimate, we take the earnings estimates issued by all the analysts following a stock and average them.

In Figure 1-2 is a sample of the research Zacks provides to Quicken.com, which is available free to anyone who has access to the Internet. (To find several websites that contain the following data or similar data, please see Appendix III.)

Figure 1-2 Quicken.com analyst data for Sears (S).

Analyst Ratings	Today	1 month ago	2 months ago	3 months ago
1 - Strong Buy	2	3	3	3
2 – Buy	1	1	1	1
3 – Hold	5	4	6	5
4 – Sell	0	0	0	0
5 - Strong Sell	0	0	0	0
*** Average Rating ***	2.38	2.13	2.23	2.14

A.) Analyst Estimates	This Qtr 12/2002	Next Qtr 03/2003	This Fiscal Year 12/2002	Next Fiscal Year 12/2003
Date of Earnings Release	01/09/2003	04/17/2003	01/09/2003	N/A
Average Earnings Estimate	$2.06	$0.99	$5.09	$5.66
# of Analysts	8	5	8	8
Low Estimate	$1.97	$0.95	$4.80	$5.30
High Estimate	$2.12	$1.05	$5.17	$5.95

See S's 5-year projected growth rate compared to historical earnings

Figure 1-2 (*cont.*)

B.) Analyst Estimates Trend	This Qtr 12/2002	Next Qtr 03/2003	This Fiscal Year 12/2002	Next Fiscal Year 12/2003
Current	$2.06	$0.99	$5.09	$5.66
7 days ago	$2.12	$0.99	$5.16	$5.80
30 days ago	$2.19	$1.00	$5.31	$5.84
60 days ago	$2.17	$1.02	$5.25	$5.85
90 days ago	$2.15	$1.06	$5.26	$5.81

Qtrly EPS History	09/2001	12/2001	03/2002	06/2002	09/2002
Estimate EPS	$0.80	$1.97	$0.93	$1.14	$0.82
Actual EPS	$0.80	$2.02	$0.93	$1.31	$0.59
Difference	$0.00	$0.05	$0.00	$0.17	-$0.23
% Surprise	0.0%	2.5%	0.0%	14.9%	-28.1%

Earnings Growth	Last 5 years	This Fiscal Year	Next Fiscal Year	Ave Est Next 5 years	P/E (FY 2002)	PEG ratio
S Industry Rank: 2 of 4	5.2%	20.6% (12/2002)	11.2% (12/2003)	10.0%	4.75	0.47
Industry| (retail-mjr dep)	-9.0%	13.6%	27.1%	10.8%	11.34	1.04
Sector (retail/wholesale)	14.8%	61.3%	15.2%	17.8%	20.45	1.31
S&P 500	-1.1%	30.2%	12.4%	8.0%	17.49	2.19

Covering Analysts

Argus Research

Edward D. Jones

Fahnestock and Company, Incorporated

Goldman Sachs and Company

H & R Block Financial Advisors

Merrill Lynch and Company

Morgan Stanley, Dean Witter and Company

Prudential Securities, Incorporated

UBS Warburg

W.R. Hambrecht & Co. LLC

Data as of 10/19/2002.

All the data that is in bold is consensus data. That list of brokers at the end of the report is the list of brokers from which the consensus data is calculated.

Look at section A in Figure 1-2. This section shows the current consensus earnings estimate for Sears (S). At the time this page was printed off of the Internet, eight analysts were issuing earnings estimates for Sears for the coming quarter. Of these eight analysts, their earnings estimates ranged from a low of $1.97 to a high of $2.12, with an average, or consensus, of $2.06.

Armed with that information, you should then employ a strategy that is well known to professional investors: Look for changes to the consensus earnings estimate over time.

To do this, identify section B of the report, labeled "Analyst Estimates Trend." In this case we note that for Sears, the consensus earnings estimate for the current and next fiscal year has decreased over the past thirty days. This means that over the last month, some of the analysts have lowered their earnings estimates for Sears. This is a bearish sign and indicates that Sears should be avoided in the immediate future because other analysts will likely be lowering their earnings estimates and, additionally, the market will take some time in reacting to the already lowered earnings estimates.

KEY POINT   The simplest and best way to use analyst research is to focus on revisions to analysts' earnings estimates. An excellent way to accomplish this is to watch for changes to the consensus earnings estimate over time.

Does Focusing on Analysts' Earnings Estimates Actually Work?

Of the roughly 9,000 U.S. stocks that you could buy through a discount brokerage account, about 3,300 of them have a market capitalization of more than $100 million and also have at least one analyst who follows the stock and issues earnings estimates.[1]

To see the effect of tracking changes in the consensus, each and every month let's divide the 3,300 largest stocks into roughly five portfolios, each containing an equal number of stocks based on the degree to which analysts have revised their earnings estimates over the past month.

We'll call the first portfolio the "Earnings Estimates Slashed" portfolio. This portfolio contains the 660 stocks for which the consensus earnings estimate decreased by the greatest percentage over the last month. The fact that the consensus earnings estimate decreased over the past months means that some if not all of the analysts following the company lowered their earnings estimates over the past month. In order to be in the "Earnings Estimates Slashed" portfolio, a stock's consensus earnings estimate must have decreased by greater than 3% over the past month.

Let's call the fifth portfolio the "Earnings Estimates Dramatically Raised" portfolio. This portfolio contains those 660 stocks that had the highest percent change in the consensus earnings estimate over the last month. These are the stocks for which analysts raised their earnings estimates; thus the consensus earnings estimate increased. Over the full time period, in order to be in the "Earnings Estimates Dramatically Raised" portfolio, a stock's consensus earnings estimate must have increased, on average, by greater than 1% over the past month. This value is lower than what was necessary to be included in the "Earnings Estimates Slashed" portfolio because large negative earnings estimate revisions are more common than large positive earnings estimate revisions.

If we put an equal amount of money into each portfolio and track the returns each month, what do we find?

Well, if we track the performance of these portfolios over the fifteen years from October 1987 through September 2002, what we discover is that the "Earnings Estimates Slashed" portfolio fell at an annualized rate of 4.2% over the full time period.

On the other hand, the "Earnings Estimates Dramatically Raised" portfolio rose at an annualized average rate of 20.1% over the full time period. The annualized returns of the five portfolios are given in Figure 1-3.

These annualized returns do not factor in transaction costs or commissions; if you are not careful, you may go broke from the huge commissions due to the high turnover in your portfolio.

Nevertheless, the results are quite compelling. What we see is that stocks that are receiving upward earnings estimate revisions tend to increase in value over the next month, while stocks receiving downward estimate revisions tend to be weak over the next month.

Figure 1-3 Annualized return of portfolios based on percent change over the past month in the current consensus earnings estimate (October 1987 to September 2002).

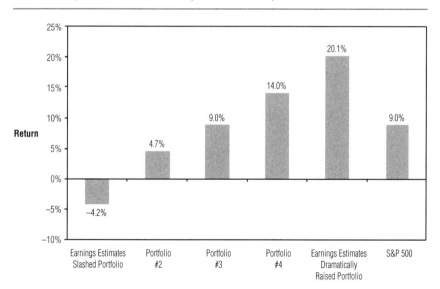

KEY POINT   Changes in the consensus earnings estimate are a far stronger signal of future price movement than analysts' buy/hold/sell recommendations.

How do you put all this information to work for you? It is clear that you should do the following:

- Buy stocks that are receiving upward earnings estimate revisions.

- Buy stocks whose consensus recommendation score has substantially increased over the past month. (We will see more proof of this later on.)

- Sell stocks that are receiving downward earnings estimate revisions.

- Sell stocks whose consensus recommendation score has decreased substantially over the past month.

All of this makes it sound as if interpreting analysts' data is a bit of an art—and it is. I will show you how to use analyst research profitably in the next several chapters, paying particular attention to revisions to analysts' earnings estimates, earnings surprises and changes in analysts' recommendations.

Summary

- Analysts are biased in their recommendations and are not exceptional stock pickers. You should, for the most part, never use analysts' recommendations to tell you when to buy or sell a stock.

- In order to use analyst research effectively, it is necessary to combine the research from multiple analysts and focus on how this combined data changes over time. By doing this, you can anticipate analyst activity and determine which analyst actions will result in a price response that lasts over a period of time.

- The piece of combined data that is the most important to focus on is revisions to analysts' earnings estimates.

- Revisions to analysts' earnings estimates are reflected in changes to the consensus earnings estimate over time. Thus you want to buy stocks for which the consensus earnings estimate is increasing and sell stocks for which the consensus earnings estimate is decreasing.

Endnotes

[1] The database used for all the studies in the book has been adjusted to remove any survivorship or look-ahead bias. What this means is that in the studies it is possible to buy any stock even if the stock later goes bankrupt or is acquired—the database does *not* consist of only surviving companies.

Chapter Two

How the Analyst Got His Bias

What's ahead in this chapter?

- The Analyst
- Why Do Analysts Exist?
- How Analysts Are Biased—Two Main Ways
- How Is an Analyst Paid for Research?
- Why Does an Analyst's Prestige Generate Revenue?
- Are There Exceptional Analysts?
- A Trap to Avoid
- Will the Regulation of Analysts Eliminate Bias?

The Analyst

A WELL-RESPECTED ANALYST—WHO, AS WE WILL SEE SHORTLY, is very different from a good or accurate analyst—makes well over ten times what the average stockbroker earns. Analysts with salaries of over $1 million are not uncommon—and the superstar analysts who can generate millions in investment banking revenue can frequently make five times that.

In exchange for these jaw-breaking salaries, an analyst strives to become the world's expert on the companies he or she follows. The analyst's goal is to be on the short list of individuals whom large and powerful institutional investors will call when they have questions regarding a company. Essentially, the analyst strives for influence over the largest and most powerful portfolio managers. The more influential an analyst is, the greater the power his research has to move markets and the more money the analyst is paid.

Because analysts are always striving to gain influence, it should not be surprising to learn that analysts only spend roughly half of their time actually researching companies. The rest of an analyst's time is spent selling his investment ideas to institutional investors (and traveling from city to city to meet and interview the managers of the companies that he covers).

Now, an analyst does not sell his research ideas in the literal sense. An analyst does not pick up a phone and ask for credit card numbers from mutual fund managers. Instead, analysts are constantly selling in the sense that they are always trying to get the people who read their reports to act on their ideas. The reason is simple: the more large money managers listen to the analyst's ideas, the more power the analyst will wield over the markets and the higher his salary will be.

An analyst's research can extract money from investors because he is perceived to be an expert on the companies he covers and thus his views are deemed to have value.

The reports an analyst writes are distributed by his employer—the brokerage firm—to investors. Institutional investors such as pension funds, hedge funds, bank trust departments, insurance companies and mutual funds are provided with the research almost as soon as the reports are written. Individual investors have access to the analyst's research only if they have an account with the brokerage firm issuing the research report.

However, you must always remember that the clients whom the analyst cares the most about are the institutional investors for whom he primarily writes the research reports and whose level of respect determines his salary. For most analysts, individual investors represent at best, a distraction, and at worst, a potential lawsuit for bad advice.

KEY POINT   The analyst seeks to gain influence with large institutional investors, namely, portfolio managers. The more influence the analyst attains, the more power he has to move markets, and the more money he gets paid.

Despite this, analysts are still integral to the way brokerage firms work. How important is an analyst? At some firms, brokers that cater to individuals are not even allowed to recommend stocks that have not been cleared by the firm's analysts.

Why Do Analysts Exist?

With all the news about the bias in analysts' recommendations, and in light of data that shows analysts' stock-picking ability is rather weak, you may be asking the very reasonable question, "Why does the market even need analysts?"

Analysts evolved to meet the needs of institutional investors. There are three simple reasons why institutional investors need analysts:

- There are many stocks out there.

- It would cost a great deal of money to hire enough independent analysts to follow all the stocks.

- It is more efficient for the function to be centralized.

Money managers who invest in small-caps, for example, have roughly 2,000 stocks they could potentially buy. A mutual fund money manager who invests in large-cap and mid-cap stocks has around 1,000 stocks he could buy.

Assuming an individual employed by a money management firm as an analyst could cover, on average, twenty stocks, each money management firm would need to hire 150 independent stock analysts to effectively cover the full universe of potential investments. And the money management industry is fairly fragmented, meaning that thousands of money management firms are out there.

It makes a lot more sense for a brokerage firm to hire those 150 analysts and then distribute the research produced by them to thousands of money management firms.

Many money managers pride themselves on performing independent research. But to a large extent they use the research produced by the brokerage firm analysts as their starting point.

Some read the brokerage reports in an attempt to glean specific information that will assist them in their independent analysis. Others simply take the analysts' earnings estimates and use them as the input to a valuation model. Even money management firms that have the size to employ a large number of independent analysts are very much aware of, and influenced by, the research done by analysts at the brokerage firms.

KEY POINT   Analysts originated in order to serve the needs of institutional investors. By centralizing analysts at a brokerage, each money management firm does not have to hire over one hundred analysts.

How Analysts Are Biased—Two Main Ways

We are going to dissect and analyze the typical research report in the next chapter. But before we do that, we need to spend some time on the entire issue of an analyst's credibility. Even the casual reader of the business press knows that Wall Street firms paid hundreds of millions of dollars in fines in 2003 as a result of providing investors with biased research.

But not everyone is clear on exactly on how that bias became institutionalized and why the bias is built into the system.

When I say analysts are biased, I am likely not going to get much of a disagreement. But we really need to be more specific. Analysts' bias is expressed in two major ways:

- Analysts are very reluctant to issue sell recommendations.

- Analysts are influenced by investment banking concerns from revealing their true views in their research reports.

KEY POINT   Analysts' bias can be broken down into two factors: their reluctance to say "sell" and the influence that investment banking wields over them.

Reasons for Analysts' Historical Reluctance to Issue Sell Recommendations

The reluctance to issue sell recommendations is not entirely due to conflicts with investment bankers. In fact, the reluctance of analysts to issue sell recommendations was present even when brokerage firms generated most of their revenue from executing trades—handling the buy and sell orders that come in from clients—rather than engaging in investment banking. This historical reluctance to issue sell recommendations was, and is, due primarily to the following three reasons that cannot be eliminated regardless of the reforms enacted:

- Analysts do not want to upset the management of the companies they are covering by issuing sell recommendations, for fear of being cut off from the company's management. Unhappy management can limit an analyst's access, putting the analyst at an informational disadvantage relative to other analysts covering the company. Essentially, analysts do not want to upset their suppliers.

- Analysts also do not want to upset their consumers. Sell recommendations bother professional portfolio managers. A sell recommendation that is widely and fairly distributed is like yelling "fire" in a crowded theater. Everyone, especially the portfolio managers who have large positions in the stock, gets crushed—in this case financially—in the rush to sell. To keep from alienating their clients, what usually happens is that an analyst mentions to a few of his firm's biggest accounts that a stock is a dog. They leave the theater (sell) and then when all of the analyst's best clients are out (have sold the stock), he shouts "fire" (or more accurately, "sell"). No one—especially important customers—likes to be burnt, and no one likes an analyst who is always lighting theaters on fire. It makes one very unpopular when portfolio managers are asked to rank the best analysts in the annual *Institutional Investor* magazine survey.

- There are more potential clients looking for a (good) buy than there are looking to sell a stock. Almost any investor is interested in buying a stock that will make them money, but besides the relatively few short-sellers out there, the only investors interested in sell recommendations are those investors who already own the shares being sold. A buy recommendation has more value to a brokerage firm because it gets the brokers on the phone selling stocks to new clients and opening new accounts.

KEY POINT   Analysts' reluctance to issue sell recommendations is due to three basic structural reasons: (1) Analysts don't want to upset the managers of the companies they are covering; (2) analysts don't want to upset their customers, namely, the professional portfolio managers; (3) there are more clients looking for a "buy" than a "sell," so a buy recommendation has more value to a brokerage firm.

Ever since Zacks began tracking analyst recommendations in the mid-1980s, analysts have been extremely reluctant to publicly issue a "sell" on one of the companies they follow. So, the fact that analysts do not issue sell recommendations, although only recently publicized in the media, is in reality nothing new.

In fact, the percentage of sell recommendations has been under 8% for the past decade. Figure 2-1 shows the distribution of analysts' recommendations over the past twelve years.

As of the later half of 2002, under tremendous regulatory pressure, the number of sell recommendations has been steadily increasing, back to levels not seen since the early 1990s. According to Zacks data, as of October 20, 2002, the number of sell recommendations is at the highest level it has been in several years, hovering above 8%. However, it should not surprise you that brokerage firms remain very reluctant to issue sell recommendations on their investment banking clients.

In fact, according to a recent article in the *Wall Street Journal*, for every twenty-five companies that Merrill Lynch rates as a "sell," only one is a

Figure 2-1 Percent distribution of analyst recommendations 1985–2002.

	% Strong Buy	% Buy	% Hold	% Sell	% Strong Sell
2002	28.00%	22.66%	41.08%	3.53%	4.73%
2000	32.49%	38.87%	27.74%	0.52%	0.38%
1995	29.42%	25.11%	40.87%	2.46%	2.14%
1990	23.66%	21.14%	45.79%	6.36%	3.05%

client of the firm—this implies that the vast majority of Merrill's sell ratings are on rival banks' clients—while Merrill has a banking relationship with six out of ten of the companies it rates as a "buy."[1]

This problem is not unique to Merrill. At practically every brokerage firm, analysts have historically been more reluctant to issue sell recommendations on banking clients than on nonbanking clients.

Analysts Are Influenced by Investment Banking Concerns

When New York Attorney General Eliot Spitzer began investigating the analysts, one of the biggest problems revealed to the public was that analysts were less than honest in their research. Spitzer uncovered what many institutional investors have known about for quite some time—namely that it is not uncommon for an analyst to think a stock is a "dog" but to recommend the stock as a "hold" or even a "market outperform" and to indicate that the stock represents a "good long-term opportunity." I have witnessed this several times in contacting analysts directly who will indicate that "although the research report is neutral the stock should be avoided."

Why Analysts Sometimes Believe One Thing and Say Another

If an analyst uses his influence and his brokerage firm's distribution channels to convince investors to avoid a given stock, that company's management will likely be livid with not only the analyst but also the brokerage firm where the analyst works.

Hell hath no fury like a CEO who has lost several million dollars due to some smart-aleck analyst. You can bet that for the next several years—and perhaps for as long as that CEO is in power—that the aggrieved company is not going to do any business with the brokerage firm where the pessimistic analyst works (and it's also possible that the analyst will be fired). While most investors may forget about the sell recommendation in a couple of months, corporate management tends to have a much longer memory. When you lose several million dollars worth of stock options—as the CEO of a downgraded firm will attest—you tend to take it very personally.

Also, investment banking relationships are worth tens if not hundreds of millions of dollars to a brokerage firm. The relationships are under constant attack from rival brokerage firms—who would like to have favored investment bank status—and the entire business of generating and maintaining investment banking relationships is intensely competitive. The easiest way an analyst can get himself fired on Wall Street is to destroy or sour an existing investment banking relationship.

The desire to preserve investment banking relationships is part of the reason that analysts are not likely to fully express their negative views. Instead of issuing a negative research report, analysts instead simply tend to not say anything positive.

KEY POINT   Analysts' desire to maintain valuable investment banking relationships and to not annoy the management of the companies they follow (which would cause the companies to stop doing business with the analysts' brokerage firms) leads them to refrain from expressing their negative views.

Follow the Money

Like Woodward and Bernstein, if you really want to understand why these two analyst biases exist, you have to follow the money. If analysts worked exclusively at independent research firms these problems would be lessened. However, analysts for the most part work at investment banks and as crazy as it sounds, investment banks make their money not through issuing good advice to investors but rather by generating banking deals.

How Is an Analyst Paid for Research?

Analysts are basically paid a salary and a bonus. Like practically all Wall Street professionals, the majority of an analyst's compensation comes in the form of a bonus.

Traditionally an analyst's bonus is determined by one or more of six factors: performance of the analyst's stock recommendations; trading commissions generated in the stocks that the analyst follows; assistance in generating banking revenue; general impression made on bankers, brokers, and institutional sales people at the firm, or internal reputation; general impression made on institutional portfolio managers, or external reputation; and the standing of the analyst in *Institutional Investor* and Zacks Rankings.

Although these six characteristics determine an analyst's bonus, the two most important are the banking fees the analyst helps generate and the trading commissions the analyst's research generates.

These two elements are not at all necessarily related to how accurate the analyst's recommendations have been.

Trading Commissions

Portfolio managers are willing to pay for research because they do not spend their own dollars. Instead, professional portfolio managers spend their clients' dollars by directing the trading arm of the brokerage firms that employ the analysts to execute trades for them.

Currently, most large institutional brokerage firms charge portfolio managers commissions that range anywhere from three to four times the commissions that the portfolio manager would be charged if the trading was executed through an electronic order entry system.

Essentially, the whole stock research function of Wall Street evolved as a means of justifying commission rates and competing for the trading business of institutional money managers.

This system of paying Paul to please Peter worked extraordinarily well for about two decades. Investors were happy to receive analysts' research reports and brokerage firms were happy to make money executing trades for clients. A prestigious or prescient analyst would work hard to develop a following among portfolio managers and, in return, the portfolio managers would execute their trades at the brokerage firm where that analyst worked. The more respected the analyst, the more money the analyst could make for the firm where he worked, and the more money the analyst would be paid in bonuses.

Over the last two decades the rules of the game have changed, primarily due to two trends: falling commission rates and an increase in investment banking revenue.

First of all, the commission rates that brokerage firms charge for executing trades have decreased dramatically over the last twenty-five years. Second, concurrent with the falling commission rates there has been an absolute explosion in the IPO market and in the money an investment bank can make through merger and acquisition activity.

In 1975, the U.S. Securities and Exchange Commission eliminated fixed prices on trades, so firms are free to charge whatever they want to handle a buy or sell order. This led to the creation of discount brokers and pricing pressure on commissions. The improvement in information technology over the last decade has also dramatically reduced the price of handling a trade.

These increasing competitive pressures have reduced the commission rate charged by a brokerage firm to an institutional investor down to an average of around $0.05 per share. As a result, the profit margins for brokerage firms on pure trade executions are down dramatically. Today, at all the major investment banks, trading commissions generated by analysts cover only, at most, half of the expenses borne by a firm's research department. As a result, most major brokerage firms currently lose money on their analyst research departments, if only trading revenue is examined. That, however, is only half of the story.

Investment Banking Revenue

With falling commission rates, the way that an investment bank extracts payment for the research its analysts produce has shifted from the trading side toward the investment banking side. Whereas historically an investment bank made money on the research its analysts produced by executing trades for clients who used the research, now an investment bank makes most of its money by using the analysts to exercise influence over a certain sector of stocks and using this influence to compete for the extensive investment banking fees being generated by publicly traded companies in the sector.

Currently, according to recent congressional testimony, for most major brokerage firms the profit ratio of investment banking services to trading services is about four to one. Two decades ago, this ratio was one to one.

However, there remains a direct relationship between the amount of investment banking revenue an analyst can generate and the analyst's reputation among large professional money managers.

As an analyst, the more you can control or influence a stock's price with your research, the more you will be paid. The reason is simple— the more control or influence you are perceived to have over a group of stocks, the more investment banking business your firm will win among these stocks. But in order to control or influence a stock's price, people who control tremendous amounts of money must invest based on your research and opinions. This will not occur if you are perceived to be a tool of the bankers or inaccurate—it will happen only if you have a stellar reputation among large institutional investors.

It is important to remember that the reason Grubman was so influential over the price of telecom stocks and the reason he was able to generate massive investment banking revenue for Salomon in the telecom sector was because almost every large portfolio manager and mutual fund manager in the country read, and more importantly acted upon, the research Grubman wrote. The only reason this occurred was because, for a variety of reasons, investors truly believed that Grubman would make them money.

Even in this new era of influence-based compensation, analysts are still ultimately concerned about their reputation among institutional portfolio managers. But the net result is that when an analyst is being paid based on the investment banking revenue he helps generate, there is much more pressure on the analyst to please investment bankers with his research.

KEY POINT   An investment bank now makes most of its money by using analysts to exercise influence over stocks and thereby compete for investment banking fees. As a result, analysts are paid in relation to how much investment banking revenue they can generate. Therefore, there is tremendous pressure on analysts to curry favor with investment bankers.

Regardless of what legislation is passed trying to divorce analysts' compensation from the investment banking revenue they generate, the market will find a creative way of getting around it. Think of it this way: Chances are that analysts who generate more revenue for the brokerage firms where they work will be paid more money. This is why it will always be important to discount the recommendations issued by analysts.

Why Does an Analyst's Prestige Generate Investment Banking Revenue?

Imagine you are a CEO about to make a tricky or questionable acquisition. As the CEO, you don't need help negotiating the deal; what you really need more than anything else is for your company's stock price not to tank after you make the acquisition. Companies engaging in acquisitions see their stock price fall for a variety of reasons, the most common being that the acquirer almost always overpays.

As the CEO, the best way to guarantee that investors don't flee your stock when you decide on an acquisition (for example, if you absolutely must acquire a movie studio in order to realize synergies with your industrial manufacturing business) is to make sure that the one man on Wall Street who is trusted to predict your stock's future price supports the merger.

The best way to accomplish this is by paying the investment banking division of the brokerage firm that employs this top analyst tens of millions of dollars in fees. This may not assure you a "pound the table" buy recommendation, but it guarantees that you will receive a better recommendation than you otherwise would.

The following account will give you an idea of how all this plays out in practice.

Analyst Bias in Action

Narrator: The following, while fiction, is based unfortunately on fact.

The Scene: Miller & Company, a preeminent investment bank in New York. Behind a large mahogany desk adorned with Lucite tombstones of successful banking transactions his firm has done, bank CEO Danforth Miller III gestures for newly hired analyst Ned Newman to have a seat.

Miller: Ned, glad to have you on board. I see from your resume that you are one sharp cookie, top of your class at Wharton. We always need talent here at Miller & Company, and as you know, our employees are our most important resource.

Ned: It's an honor to be here, sir.

Miller: Ned, we have hired you to be an equity research analyst. It's a great, interesting, and lucrative position, but you need to be willing to travel.

Ned: Where will I have to go?

Miller: Well, seeing that you are assigned to cover semiconductor companies, specifically Intel, you will probably make a couple trips a year to Silicon Valley, head over to Asia every once in a while—since that is where many of the semiconductors are actually made.

Ned: Fine, sir.

Miller: We expect you to work long, hard hours and produce research reports for our institutional trading clients on firms like Intel. Get to know everything about the company, from how many chips they expect to sell to what morale is like in their R&D department. Then create a valuation model and write some research reports that we can deliver to the mutual funds, pension funds, hedge funds, and the foundations that buy and sell Intel shares through us.

You should try very hard to develop a relationship with Intel's CEO and upper management so that your research will reflect what is actually going on in the company.

Ned: I see. So, the more trading activity I can generate through my research reports, the more money I can make for Miller & Company, and the higher my compensation will be?

Miller: Not so fast, Ned. Fees from trading activity are generally pretty low. Executing trades is really a commodity business these days. Our clients can buy and sell shares at pretty much the same cost with any firm at one of ten electronic trading platforms. So, yes, your research reports will generate some revenues for us. Firms will steer some business our way, as a quid pro quo for receiving your research. But while we are glad to have the revenue, that's not where the big money is.

Ned: Where do we get that, sir?

Miller: Well, the way Miller & Company makes the largest portion of its fees is through our investment banking services. When Intel's management wants to raise money by issuing more of its stock, they will hire the investment bank that they have what they call the "best relationship" with, or the bank that can "most cost-effectively raise the funds among the most desirable investor base."

This is all code-speak for the investment bank that has helped the company stock the most over time, or that they believe will support the stock in the future, should the firm ever run into trouble.

Generally, Intel will give its banking business to the firm whose analyst has the most influence over Intel's stock price in the market.

And that, of course, can have ripple effects. Other firms will see what we've done for Intel and will want us to do the same for them. For example, if that new start-up, BBQ-Nanochips, that's in today's *Wall Street Journal,* is successful, the partners in the venture capital firm that backed it will want to hire the investment bank that has the most respected semiconductor analyst to take them public. That's why we want you to write and establish your reputation.

Ned: I see.

Miller: Good. So, don't forget to send your reports to all the newspapers, business magazines, and especially the electronic media. They're an excellent way to boost your reputation. They are always looking for sound bites and they don't delve too deeply.

Ned: So, in order to generate investment banking fees, I need to develop a reputation as an industry expert.

Miller: Yes. And, Ned, one last thing, whatever you do, do not upset Intel's management. Our lifeblood depends on establishing a relationship with them. If they become mad at us, not only will they not use us in the future when they need to raise money, but we will likely not see any advisory fees from acquisitions that they engage in, and a follow-up equity or debt offering is also out the window.

Ned: What could I do that might upset them?

Miller: By issuing a sell recommendation. A decade ago, we had an analyst who issued a sell recommendation on McDonald's Corporation. The analysis and recommendation was dead on. The analyst accurately predicted that all the talk about "mad cow disease" would hurt McDonald's sales substantially. It was one of the most brilliant pieces of research ever issued. The piece predicted the slide in McDonald's share price months before it happened. Money managers who followed his advice saved their clients millions.

Ned, do you know what the analyst who wrote the report is doing today?

Ned: I'll bet that analyst is you, Mr. Miller!

Miller: Get a grip, Ned. I fired him on the spot. That moron cost us tens of millions by making us miss out in leading the debt offering when McDonald's raised money to buy all of their McFlurry machines.

Narrator: While what you just heard was obviously fiction, it is based on actual events. The names have been changed to protect the innocent and the guilty.

Hopefully, this exchange between Ned and Danforth Miller explains why strong sell recommendations are rare and how conflicts with investment banking arise.

At the most basic level, you should always remember that analysts work for brokerage firms and brokerage firms make money by selling stocks. Whether the brokerage firm sells stocks to you through a broker, to mutual funds through an open market purchase, to a hedge fund through an IPO, or to a corporation through an M&A transaction, the goal is the same: The entire brokerage industry is structured to sell the most amount of stock as efficiently and cheaply as possible.

Everyone and anyone is fair game for a brokerage firm and everyone includes you, the individual investor.

Are There Exceptional Analysts?

Analysts are not that great at issuing individual recommendations and are lousy at telling you how much you should be willing to pay for a stock. However, analysts are quite good at providing fundamental research such as earnings estimates on the companies that they cover.

The reason for this apparent contradiction is fairly clear: It is easier for a brokerage firm to sell stock if the analysts are always optimistic and telling clients that on the whole stocks are worth more than their current prices.

However, when multiple analysts are suddenly saying that a stock is worth $30–$40, when just a while ago the same analysts were saying the stock was worth only $16, it means that the stock is likely going to be rising in price immediately and likely over the next month.

This, in a nutshell, is the reason that you should never use analysts' recommendations at face value, but should instead focus on the *changes* to analyst recommendations over time.

There are a handful of analysts who reach that conclusion faster than their peers and have exhibited historical skill in valuing companies. The question is, where can you find them?

How to Find Exceptional Analysts

The oldest two studies of analyst ability are conducted by Zacks Investment Research and *Institutional Investor* magazine.

The *II* annual ranking is basically a survey of professional portfolio managers who vote for their favorite analyst. Those who get the most votes are deemed *II* top-ranked analysts.

Although the *II* survey is extremely important in setting an analyst's compensation, it is at root a popularity contest. The *II* survey tells you which analyst has the greatest influence on stock prices by virtue of being the most popular among institutional managers, but the survey will not tell you which analyst is the most accurate in making stock recommendations.

Additionally, the top *II* analysts are often more likely to be tempted to compromise their research by the prospect of banking revenue. This is because a well-respected analyst can influence mergers while an unknown analyst lacks the prestige and power to influence the markets. Top *II* analysts also tend to be more conservative and less willing to take risks in their recommendations and earnings estimates than other analysts simply because they have more to lose by making a bad call. A far more worthwhile means of identifying exceptional analysts is to determine which analysts' recommendations actually made investors money.

Zacks All Star Analysts

As we shall see later on, if you buy those stocks that are the most highly recommended by many analysts, you do not generate good returns. But, research has shown that if instead you follow the recommendations of those analysts who have historically been the best at issuing stock recommendations, you actually do perform well.

In fact, *Fortune* magazine used Zacks' ranking of analyst accuracy as the starting point to select a team of all-star analysts in 2001. These all-stars' stock picks for 2001-2002 were up an impressive 13% as of when the June 10th baseline edition of *Fortune* went to press, compared with a drop of 13% for the S&P 500 over the same time period.

Since 1993, Zacks has been ranking all the analysts in the United States based on how quantitatively accurate they are in projecting earnings and making stock recommendations. What we have found is that certain analysts tend to consistently perform well over time in both making earnings estimates and issuing recommendations.

Sometimes, Zacks All Star Analysts are the same analysts who are the most widely respected, but often the analyst with the best historical track record is neither the analyst who is the highest paid nor the analyst who has the best reputation among institutional investors. In many cases, the analyst who is most accurate in making stock recommendations comes from a regional brokerage firm and sometimes the analyst is relatively unknown.

Just as you do not give your money to a mutual fund manager who has had a terrible track record, you should not follow the recommendations of analysts who have historically lost investors money. That's why you want to draw a distinction between the analysts who are most popular and the analysts who are most accurate.

A Trap to Avoid

Do not let a broker use analyst recommendations to get you to generate commissions.

> "Jim, it's your broker over here at EF Stanley; I want to give you a heads-up. Betty Donahue, our macro investment strategist who works here at Stanley, has increased the weighting of stocks in her model portfolio from 70% to 85%. She also indicated investors should significantly overweight retail stocks. That's why the retailers rallied today. I am thinking we should start putting more of your cash to work. Specifically, we should be buying some retail stocks for you."

Many brokers use analyst recommendations to convince you to make trades. Specifically, brokers often try to get their clients to adjust their asset allocation on the advice of an analyst who focuses on broad macro trends.

One of the biggest and most correctible mistakes you can make using analyst recommendations is to allow the recommendations to serve as a means by which brokers can sell you a stock.

You may not fully realize that the more you trade, the more money your brokerage firm makes, and that your broker personally pockets between 25–50% of the fees that you generate for your broker's firm.

As a general rule of thumb, you should be wary of any broker who actively tries to induce you to trade. If you are using a full-service broker to buy and sell stocks, most likely you are being sold down the river. I can say this without knowing anything about your broker, your relationship with your broker, your returns, the commissions you are paying or any one of another ten variables. The reason you are likely being taken advantage of is that the majority of brokers are still paid through commissions, and this is a problem—a big problem.

Fixing this problem is easy. You should find a way of paying a flat asset-based fee to your brokerage firm instead of paying for each transaction.

You should absolutely demand that your broker allow you to pay fees based on how much money you have invested with the firm, as opposed to commissions. It is your money and if your broker does not want to charge you a fixed fee based on assets under management, there are many firms out there that will. As an investor at a full-service brokerage firm, you should be able to negotiate a fee that is less than 2% of your assets under management. The more money you have, or even more importantly, the more money the brokerage firm thinks you may have, the lower your fees should be. If you have more than $1 million at a brokerage firm, your total fees should absolutely be under 1.5%.

Under a fixed-fee scenario, you pay the brokerage firm a flat fee that covers all trading costs. Because you are paying a fee regardless of the number of trades you make, your broker has no incentive to take advantage of your account by churning it through many different stocks.

Most importantly, because you are being charged a fee instead of paying a commission, you and your broker will have similar interests— namely, increasing the value of your account.

Accounts managed by brokers also tend to try to time the market, because under the auspices of trying to pick winners and losers, or of providing a good "asset mix," the broker can easily persuade you to do a lot of trading. Every time the market swoons and you feel fear in the pit of your belly, you will likely receive a call from your broker advocating a change in your asset mix. The research produced by macro strategists can take up reams of paper, or generate endless sound bites, but ultimately it is of no value for this simple reason: No one, not me, not the analysts, not even Warren Buffet, has the ability to time the market.

So, when you get that call, it could appear that your broker is diligently watching out for your interests. But, in reality, your broker has found a rather sophisticated way to persuade you to generate trades and thus line his pockets with commissions.

KEY POINT   In order to avoid excessive transaction costs you should pay a flat asset-based fee to your brokerage firm. If your brokerage firm won't do this, find one that will.

This is also the main reason that analysts who work as broad market strategists, (analysts who try to tell clients what percentage of their assets should be in the market) tend to change their asset allocations regularly. The new asset allocation provides the firm's brokerage force with a reason to call clients and to induce them to make trades. If you are going to use analyst research to help you make your buy and sell decisions, your attention needs to be on analysts who follow individual companies, and not on a brokerage firm's chief equity strategist.

Will the Regulation of Analysts Eliminate Bias?

It is not likely.

Analysts' recommendations are definitely biased—that much any casual reader of the business section of the paper would be able to tell you.

Politicians and regulators were initially made aware of the two types of bias in analyst recommendations through an article written by Gretchen Morgenson in *The New York Times* on December 31, 2001 that quoted Zacks data. The article primarily focused on the reluctance of an analyst to issue sell recommendations, but the article hinted at the fact that analysts are concerned about offending investment banking relationships. In the article I was quoted as saying that the "way an analyst can get fired is to damage an existing investment banking relationship with a company or sour a future investment banking relationship. The way you do that as an analyst is coming out and telling people to sell a stock."

A year later, e-mails continue to surface in which prominent and powerful stock analysts indicate that they could not fully express themselves in their research reports for fear of upsetting banking clients of the brokerage firms that employ the analysts.

Immediately following the article in *The New York Times*, I began to get calls from various senate investigative committees that wanted me to come down to Washington and reveal how analysts are downright evil. After talking to various staffers, I quickly realized that to them the conflict-of-interest issue of the analysts was just the flavor of the day. For the most part, the staffers had no real understanding of what was truly going on. The whole thing started to reek like some modern-day financial version of "The Crucible."

In the markets, as in life, things are not black and white.

Analyst bias is endemic to Wall Street, and will require tremendous regulatory changes to eliminate. No matter what reforms are enacted, analysts will continue to help generate investment banking revenue.

The market will find some way to pay more money to those analysts who help generate more investment banking revenue regardless of whether there is a division erected between banking and investment research.

Summary

- Analysts exist because of institutional investors.
  - There are many stocks out there.
  - It would cost a lot of money to hire enough independent analysts to follow all the stocks.
  - It is more efficient for the function to be centralized.

- Analysts are paid based on their ability to exercise influence over the markets. For this reason an analyst is primarily concerned about his prestige among institutional investors. The more prestigious an analyst is considered to be by institutional investors, the more trading commissions and banking revenue the analyst will be able to generate, and the bigger the analyst's bonus.

- Analysts suffer from the following two major problems:
  - Analysts are very reluctant to issue sell recommendations.
  - Analysts are influenced by investment banking concerns to not reveal their true views in their research reports.
- Because of these two problems you should, for the most part, discount individual analyst recommendations.
  - It is possible to identify exceptional analysts. Instead of listening to the analysts who are the highest paid (because they generate the most investment banking revenue), you should focus on those analysts who have historically been accurate in their recommendations.
  - Be careful of falling into the trap of allowing a macro analyst to cause you to make asset allocation trades at a brokerage firm and incur commission costs. As a general rule of thumb, you should try to get your broker to switch from a commission-based fee schedule to an assets-under-management-based fee schedule.

Endnotes

1 *Wall Street Journal*, 9/13/02.

Chapter Three

Dissecting the Analyst's Report

What's ahead in this chapter?

What Makes Analyst Research So Special?

WRITING EQUITY RESEARCH REPORTS is far from rocket science. Although a research report may seem like a complicated treatise to an investor who is not used to reading annual reports, the average research report is in reality not all that sophisticated.

In fact, the number crunching that is done by Wall Street analysts does not differ that much from the analysis that is taught in any one of the hundreds of business schools across the country. Every one of the MBAs minted in the United States each year is capable of producing the same accounting models that the analysts churn out on a daily basis.

The hard part of the analyst's job is having the right data to input into the accounting model, so that the results generated provide some degree of insight.

When you actually pull away all the trappings of the analyst reports produced by prestigious Wall Street brokerage firms, the fundamental difference between the research they produce and the research generated internally by analysts working for mutual fund managers is that the reports issued by Wall Street analysts both move prices and are public.

If a newsletter writer, a financial journalist, or a portfolio manager appearing on *Wall Street Week* makes an articulate, well-researched stock recommendation there is usually very little impact on a stock's price. However, when an analyst who works at Goldman Sachs changes his recommendation in a research report—and it does not matter how well written, deep, or accurate the information backing his decision is—the market responds immediately.

KEY POINT   What makes analysts' research special is that it impacts stock prices, because large institutional investors act on the contents of the research report.

Regulation FD and Its Effect

It used to be that analysts who worked at brokerage firms had an informational advantage over other investors because they had unique access to the people running the companies that they were writing research reports on. If prospects at a company were improving or deteriorating, the Wall Street analyst was one of the first people to be told the news by the company's management.

All this changed in late 2000 when the SEC enacted Regulation Fair Disclosure (Reg FD):

> *The regulation provides that when an issuer, or person citing on its behalf, discloses material nonpublic information to certain enumerated persons (in general, securities market professionals and holders of the issuer's securities who may well trade on the basis of the information), it must make public disclosure of that information. The timing of the*

required public disclosure depends on whether the selective disclosure was intentional or non-intentional; for an intentional selective disclosure, the issuer must make public disclosure simultaneously; for a non-intentional disclosure, the issuer must make public disclosure promptly."

Source: U.S. Securities and Exchange Commission

Essentially, Reg FD makes it illegal for a public company to selectively disclose "material information"—which is defined as anything that could potentially move stock prices—to one party, such as a brokerage research analyst, without making it available to everyone.

Today, material changes in a company's potential fortunes are given to the market via press releases, as opposed to being leaked to selective, friendly analysts, as was done in the past.

Reg FD is an excellent piece of legislation that should effectively level the playing field. It ensures individual investors get the same information at the same time as money managers at Janus, Fidelity, and other large firms. Equally important, Reg FD puts you and the stock analysts on an equal footing. You both now have access to the same information at exactly the same time.

The SEC's action took a tremendous amount of political courage, especially in the face of intense lobbying against the ban by almost every large brokerage and money management firm. It appears this is a rare case of the government acting in the best interests of the citizens as opposed to the best interests of the lobbyists.

The smaller and less powerful an investor, the more they generally like Reg FD.

Be Careful What You Wish For

However, while the SEC ban on selective disclosure makes access to information eminently fair, the result may not be as intended. Most likely, institutional investors will be brought down to the informational level of individual investors, rather than the reverse.

We are seeing that already. A ban on selective disclosure, while accomplishing its stated policy goal, unfortunately reaches that goal by reducing the flow of information. In their concern not to violate the regulation, companies are disclosing the absolute minimum amount of information to investors.

KEY POINT   Ironically, Reg FD will have a contrary result than what legislators intended. Instead of allowing individual investors to get more material information, institutional investors will have less access to such information. However, in this way, by restricting everyone's access to information, Reg FD will level the playing field.

Thus, in my mind, the desirability of the ban is questionable because it will probably decrease the overall efficiency of the market. Markets are most efficient when all information is disclosed. Because of Reg FD there will be less disclosure, and therefore less efficiency.

Who cares?

Well, less efficiency means that the market may experience greater uncertainty, which is economist-speak for indicating that stock prices will bounce around more than they should. The more information out there, the more certainty. The more certainty, the less market volatility.

It is important to note that Reg FD applies only to information provided by corporate management. The regulation in no way prevents brokerage analysts from selectively revealing information or opinions to their best clients before everyone else. While it would be illegal for an analyst to tell a client he is changing his recommendation before he actually does, nothing prevents the analyst from indicating in general terms he is turning more optimistic or pessimistic on a stock.

The net effect of Reg FD is that the information that is used to construct an analyst's research report is not proprietary. The only thing unique about the report is how the analyst puts it together, and why he chooses one conclusion over another.

Clearly, if you understand an analyst's biases, you can avoid being misled by Wall Street. Additionally, if you further examine the research produced by analysts, you will find that some of the research they produce can be turned into a very profitable investment strategy. But before we can figure out how to take advantage of the value contained within an analyst's report, we need to understand the report itself.

Pulling Apart the Analyst's Research Report

Figure 3-1 shows a sample of a research report. Although no two research reports are identical, at the most basic level, an analyst's research report contains a recommendation for the stock, as well as estimates of what the company will earn on a per-share basis over the next four quarters and the next two fiscal years.

Most research reports also contain what is called a long-term growth estimate. The long-term growth estimate is the rate at which the analyst believes earnings per share will grow annually over the next three to five years.

Finally, any research report worth its salt will explain the reasoning behind the investment recommendation and the earnings estimates, and will contain a target price. The target price is the price the analyst expects the stock to hit over the next twelve months.

I will go into each section of the research report in depth in a minute, but let me make this point here, so you know where you should focus your attention: *The most important information contained in an analyst's research report is the analyst's earnings estimates.*

However, the earnings estimates from any one individual analyst are not all that useful; what is useful is to track how the earnings estimates change over time and across multiple analysts.

At the most basic level, stocks that receive upward earnings estimate revisions from multiple analysts generally will perform well over the next one to three months, while stocks that receive downward earnings estimate revisions from multiple analysts will be weak over the next one to three months.

If you stopped ten individual investors at random, at least nine of them—and very possibly all ten—would tell you that the recommendation (buy, sell, or hold) condenses all the information contained within the research report into one piece of advice you should act on when making an investment decision. As we have seen, nothing could be further from the truth.

Recommendations, although useful, can be—as we saw in the mythical exchange between the head of the investment bank and his new analyst in the last chapter—severely biased.

Target prices can also be wide off the mark for exactly the same reason: Analysts don't want to upset potential investment banking customers

Figure 3-1 Sample research report.

INVESTMENT RESEARCH

October 15, 2002

Rating: 1-BUY
Multi-Industry

General Electric Company

(GE - NYSE)

Third Quarter Earnings Up 15% Excluding Gain on Asset Sale

		December Fiscal Year*	2001	2002E	2003E
Recent Price	$24.35	Diluted Earnings Per Share	$1.41	$1.62	$1.75
52-Week High Price	$41.84	P/E Multiple	17.3x	15.0x	13.9x
52-Week Low Price	$21.40	Return on Equity (2001)			27%
12-Month Target Price	$36.00	LT Debt/Total Cap. (6/02)			1.4%
Indicated Dividend	$0.72	Est. 3 Year EPS Growth Rate			10%-15%
Dividend Yield	3.0%	Insider/Institutional Ownership			1%/63%
Market Value (millions)	$241,279				

*Figures exclude non-recurring items.

Company Description: GE is a diversified industrial and financial services concern. About $68 billion in 2001 revenues came from the industrial area, including aircraft engines, appliances, broadcasting, plastics, power systems, and medical equipment. GE Capital, with interests in real estate lending, retailer financing, asset management, and reinsurance, among others, contributed approximately $58 billion to 2001 consolidated revenues.

- **General Electric reported third quarter earnings of $.41 per share, up 25% from $.33 in the third quarter of 2001.** Figures from a year ago were depressed by significant losses in the reinsurance business related to the September 11 terrorist attacks. Results for the current quarter benefited from a gain on the sale of a business partially offset by a restructuring charge in Power Systems. Excluding these items, third quarter EPS were $.38 versus $.33, up 15%.

- **Third quarter consolidated revenue rose 11% to $32.6 billion.** GE Capital revenue was up 13%, rebounding from lower levels a year ago. Sales of non-financial goods and services rose 6%, which we view as fairly strong in the current economic environment. NBC reported the strongest revenue growth, up 31% due to acquisitions, a stronger advertising market, and weak comparisons with last year.

- **Earnings growth will be difficult to achieve in 2003.** GE management reaffirmed its expectation for 2002 EPS of $1.65, which would be $1.62 excluding gains. However, results next year will depend on improvement in more economically sensitive businesses that can offset the coming decline in Power Systems.

- **We feel that GE is performing well in a challenging economic environment.** The company has so far avoided the earnings shortfall experienced by other large industrial entities. The GE business model where long cycle businesses and growth in the financial unit help smooth out variations in more cyclical areas has worked well so far. However, continued sluggishness in the U.S. economy could lead to only modest growth in 2003.

See disclosures at end of document.

• May Lose Value
• No Bank Guarantee

The information herein has been obtained from sources we believe to be reliable but is not guaranteed and does not purport to be a complete statement of all material factors. This report is for informational purposes and is not a solicitation of orders to purchase or sell securities.

by pointing out that their shares are not going to appreciate over the next twelve months.

Although reading the entire analyst report can be enlightening, focus on revisions in earnings estimates. Otherwise, the report may simply reinforce your preconceived ideas about a stock. For instance, if you are holding a burned-out dot-com retailer you might decide to hold on to it, even in the face of estimates being lowered, if the text says the stock still has long-term potential.

KEY POINT   The most valuable part of the research report is revisions in analysts' earnings estimates.

The earnings estimates, not the verbiage, are the secret to decoding an analyst's research report. We will talk more about this when we get to the earnings estimate section of the analyst's report further on.

The Recommendation

The most basic part of any research report is the investment recommendation. It's how the analyst differentiates the companies he covers. A "strong buy" issued on Ford by an auto analyst means that Ford is one of the most attractive auto stocks that the analyst is following. Recommendations are always relative to the other stocks that an analyst is covering.

The analyst's recommendation is supposed to be what the entire research report leads up to. It answers the question, "What should I do about the stock?"

Is It Useful?

As I explained in the last chapter, the advice contained in the recommendation is almost always biased. So taking the recommendation at face value is akin to believing that your neighbor really did catch a two-foot long whitefish on Lake Okanawa during his vacation.

The upshot? Despite the attention they receive in the media—"John Q. Smith of MegaBrokerageCo reiterated a buy on ExxonMobil" you hear reported breathlessly on CNBC's *Squawkbox*—the recommendation is one of the least useful parts of an analyst's research report.

Part of the reason is analysts' reluctance to issue sell recommendations and analysts' inability to say what they actually think due to the need to generate investment banking revenue. As a result, analysts employ euphemisms. Instead of saying "I wouldn't go anywhere near this stock," an analyst will write, "short-term, the company will be under severe market pressure," and give the stock a hold recommendation.

But there is another, more subtle reason. Institutional investors realize that, for the most part, current recommendations are already reflected in a stock's price. Professional investors know that when 10 of the 12 analysts following a stock rate it a "strong buy," this information has already moved the stock price higher.

The important question is not what the outstanding recommendations are for a given stock but whether any of the outstanding recommendations have recently changed.

KEY POINT   Analysts' recommendations in and of themselves are of little value to you. Instead, look at changes in analysts' recommendations over time.

How Should I Use Recommendations?

- The best way to use analyst recommendations is to engage in a strategy of piggybacking. This strategy basically entails buying stocks for which multiple analysts recently upgraded their recommendation.

- Do not wait for an analyst to tell you to sell a stock. If you wait until an analyst issues a sell recommendation, chances are you will have waited far too long and will have lost quite a bit of money.

- The older the recommendation, the less useful it is. Market conditions change much too quickly for you to rely on recommendations that are older than four months.

- The buy, sell, or hold recommendations are interesting. But, as always, you want to focus on the changes—if any—to the earning estimates, which can be found later in the report.

- Focus on changes in recommendations made by analysts with good historical track records, that is, those analysts who in the past have proven to be accurate in their recommendations. Do not simply focus on recommendations that come out of the most prestigious brokerage firms—sometimes the least accurate analysts work at these firms.

- A "strong buy" or "over-weight" recommendation should be seen as a positive recommendation. A "buy," "equal weight," or "market outperform" recommendation should be seen as a neutral recommendation. "Under-weight," "market-perform," "hold," "sell," and "strong sell" recommendations are effectively negative recommendations. For those firms that have gone to three levels of recommendations, only the highest recommendation issued by the firm should be considered a positive recommendation.

Earnings Estimates

Earnings estimates are the most valuable piece of information contained in an analyst's research report.

Practically every research report contains a projected income statement, which is an educated guess by the analyst as to what a company will earn over the next couple of quarters and the current and next fiscal year. To calculate the projected income statement, the analyst starts with revenue projections, deducts expected expenses, and eventually boils everything down to future income.

An earnings estimate is essentially this projected income divided by the number of shares in the company. Thus an earnings estimate is what the analyst expects the company will earn on a per-share basis in the future.

It gets a little more complicated than this in practice, in that analysts often project earnings that exclude nonrecurring items—"We bought a competitor and had lots of legal fees"—as well as extraordinary accounting charges—"we declared a one-time charge due to the new accounting rules," but take into account the "fully diluted" number of shares (how many shares would be outstanding if everyone exercised their stock options).

But the basic approach remains the same, and generally analysts issue both quarterly and fiscal-year earnings estimates; in some cases, they may even project earnings further out beyond that.

Because earnings are tethered to reality on a quarterly basis, when a company must actually report its earnings, the analysts' earnings estimates tend to be the least biased piece of information in the report.

Although any analyst can make a reasonable argument for a recommendation that indicates a stock is 30% overvalued or 30% undervalued, the analyst has no real qualitative leeway in predicting what a company is going to earn on a per-share basis in the coming quarter.

The Consensus Earnings Estimate

Zacks was one of the first companies to take the earnings-per-share estimates issued by all the analysts following a given stock and create a consensus earnings estimate. The consensus earnings estimate is essentially an average of all the earnings estimates issued by all the analysts who cover a given stock.

However, the consensus earnings estimate in itself, like the recommendation, is not that valuable. The fact that analysts in the aggregate project a company will earn $1.10 per share this year and $1.35 per share next year is of little use to you, as this information is most likely already reflected in the stock's price.

When analysts change their earnings estimates, it means that a stock's price should change as well: Analysts revise their earnings estimates upward? Then the stock should climb. Downward revisions to the consensus earnings estimate? Then the share price should fall.

This indicates that it is important to focus on changes to the individual analyst's earnings estimates and thus changes to the consensus earnings estimate over time.

Long-Term Earnings Growth Estimate

In addition to making a recommendation and projecting earnings for the immediate future, an analyst often includes a long-term earnings growth estimate in his research report. The meaning of "long-term" varies somewhat from analyst to analyst but is almost always three to five years out. The long-term earnings growth estimate is the rate at which the analyst anticipates the company's earnings will grow on a per-year basis over the next three to five years. In contrast to the earnings estimates, which are forecasts of dollars per share for a quarterly or annual fiscal period, the long-term growth estimate is a forecast of percent growth per year.

A consensus long-term growth estimate is calculated by taking an average of all the individual analysts' long-term growth estimates.

Is It Useful?

It can be useful, but misleading.

Most importantly, what is misleading is that those companies with the highest projected long-term earnings growth estimates by multiple analysts actually tend to under-perform over time.

Additionally, because the long-term earnings growth estimate is an average of what the analyst expects to happen over the next three to five years, an analyst can often avoid having to lower the long-term earnings growth estimate even in the face of several recent quarters of poor performance.

KEY POINT   The long-term earnings growth estimate is a misleading metric. In fact, companies with very high projected long-term growth rates tend to under-perform the market over time.

Generally, analysts tend to be more reluctant to lower a company's long-term earnings growth estimate than they are to raise it. As a result, many a stock has gone to its grave with a double-digit long-term earnings growth estimate.

PEG Ratio

The relationship between the projected long-term earnings growth rate and the P/E of a stock is the basis for the price/earnings to growth (PEG) ratio, which is used by many investors as a rule of thumb regarding valuation.

A PEG ratio is an attempt to measure and uncover value. To calculate the PEG ratio, divide a company's P/E ratio by the consensus long-term growth estimate. For example, in late 2002 Hewlett-Packard Co. (HPQ) trades around $14, or roughly 17.9 times projected earnings for the current year. Analysts on average have a long-term earnings growth rate for Hewlett of 10% per year over the next five years. Doing the math (17.9 ÷ 10), we see that HPQ has a forward PEG ratio of 1.79.

A high PEG ratio indicates that the market—which awards the company its P/E—is significantly more enthused about the growth prospects of a company than are analysts, the folks responsible for the growth estimate.

A low PEG ratio indicates analysts are more enthused about the company's growth prospects than the market.

If you believe the growth estimates of the analysts are correct, then it makes sense to buy stocks that have low PEG ratios. The reason is that these stocks may be slightly underpriced, since they are trading for less than what analysts believe they are worth. Conversely, a very high PEG ratio indicates that the market is far more enthused about the stock's prospects than are analysts. As analysts are generally quick to point out potential growth where it exists, this may mean the stock has come under the grip of irrational exuberance.

KEY POINT   The PEG ratio is the most valuable use of the long-term growth estimate. If you think analysts' growth estimates are accurate, you should buy stocks with low PEG ratios and sell stocks with very high PEG ratios.

The Moral of All This?

- Use the long-term earnings growth rate to calculate a PEG ratio. Look for stocks with PEG ratios lower than their industry's average to find firms that may be undervalued.

- You are much more likely to encounter a change in an analyst's quarterly earnings estimate than you are to encounter a change in an analyst's long-term growth estimate. (The reason is that although quarterly earnings bounce around based on temporary shocks to near-term earnings, analysts reserve changes in the long-term growth rate for permanent and lasting changes in earnings prospects. Often an analyst will wait for several blow-out quarters before raising a company's long-term earnings growth rate.)

- Changes in the long-term earnings growth estimates often signal a fundamental or permanent change in a company's earnings prospects. Analysts for the most part do not like to change their long-term earnings growth estimate that often—the reason is because the long-term earnings growth estimate is supposed to reflect the fundamental long-term earnings prospects for a business. Theoretically these prospects should not change even if a company has a few bad quarters. As a result, analysts change their long-term growth estimates only when it is very clear that the business has changed to such a degree that previous long-term earnings assumptions are no longer accurate.

- Analysts are reluctant to lower long-term growth estimates, so be wary of companies that have declined in price and have unusually low PEG ratios. Often, an abnormally low PEG ratio is the result of stale long-term growth rates and the company should be avoided.

Target Prices

The Meaninglessness of Target Prices

In December 1998, an unknown analyst, Henry Blodget, secured a promotion at Merrill Lynch by issuing a $400 price target for online bookseller Amazon. For many individual investors and quite a few institutional investors, Blodget's price target sounded a clarion call to buy. Millions of individuals bought Amazon with an almost religious fervor.

Like lemmings marching over a cliff, investors followed Blodget's stratospherically high target price into Amazon oblivious of all risks. Although quite a few institutional managers were swept up in the mania pervasive at the time, in this particular instance many institutional investors were able to avoid Blodget's siren call.

By keeping their eyes on analysts' earnings estimates, some institutional investors effectively avoided being bamboozled by Blodget's, and other analysts', overly optimistic price targets.

What many retail investors failed to realize is that when Blodget raised his price target to not only be the highest for Amazon, but also the highest price target of practically any stock ever, he failed to raise his earnings estimates by a similar magnitude. The reason for the discrepancy between target prices and earnings estimates is simple: Unlike price targets, which tend to be qualitative valuation calls and about as useful as sunspot activity and hemlines in predicting stock prices, earnings estimates are strongly tethered to reality.

Many institutions saw the high price target for what it was—a means of self-promotion—and while many investors were caught up in the game of "Greater Fool," for the most part many institutions sold into the frenzy.

Nuts and Bolts of a Target Price

A target price is an extremely qualitative and nebulous number that attempts to provide a rough estimate as to what a stock's price will be in a year's time.

You probably are better off picking numbers out of a hat than taking an analyst's target price seriously. Here's why: Analysts generate price targets in a two-step process. The first step is to make a projection of future earnings, which under the best of circumstances is a Herculean task. The second step entails slapping a subjective P/E multiple on these future earnings. It is this second step that is the killer.

A stock's P/E level is totally based on how popular the stock and sector have become. In wars, for example, defense stocks and consumer staple stocks become popular; in recessions, medical stocks become trendy. When an industry comes into vogue, its average P/E level can easily exceed historical norms and rationality.

The difficulty in projecting future P/E levels is what makes the target price such a crude number. Blodget was able to justify such a high price target for Amazon because he looked at other Internet stocks to justify the high P/E level he was placing on earnings projected far into the future. Target prices do not help you avoid manias because the P/E level used in calculating a target price is totally relative and arbitrary.

KEY POINT   Analysts create price targets in two steps. First, analysts make a projection of future earnings, and second, analysts add a subjective P/E multiple to these future earnings. What makes the target price such a meaningless number is the arbitrariness of calculating future P/E levels.

At some level, the target price is a feeble attempt to differentiate between the company and the market. For instance, an analyst covering steel companies might have one company rated as a strong buy and another company rated as a hold. This signals that an analyst feels the first steel company will outperform the second. That's fine. But the target price of all the steel companies might not be that dramatically different from the prices at which the companies are currently trading. This would indicate that the analyst feels that the entire steel industry is not likely to outperform the market.

How Should I Use it?

Don't.

Depending on the analyst and when the target price is issued, a target price can run the gamut from being deceptive to being downright dangerous. The target price often provides you with a false sense of security. If an analyst says the target price of a stock you own, one that has seen its consensus earnings estimate fall, is substantially higher, you may be likely to hold on to it. However, the right course of action, in light of the downward earnings revisions, would be to sell.

Additionally, in the aggregate, target prices tend to be far too optimistic. The reason boils down to the simple fact that it is easier for an institutional salesman to sell a money manager a stock if the analyst provides a high target price.

Target prices are probably the least reliable source of information coming out of an analyst's research report. If you insist on taking the target price into account when you are thinking about buying a stock—and I don't think you should—remember it conveys how the analyst expects the stock to perform relative to the market, while the recommendation indicates how the stock should perform relative to its peers. For this reason, if you use target prices, always use them in conjunction with recommendations. Use an analyst's target prices to compare stock picks across industries. Use recommendations to compare stocks within the same industry.

KEY POINT   My advice is to avoid using target prices as part of your investment strategy. However, if you do consult target prices, use them
along with analyst recommendations.

Text

The text of an analyst's research report is the narrative. It can be as short as one page or, in the case of research reports that cover entire industries, as long as one hundred pages. This is where the analyst explains the reasoning behind the other elements of his research report.

Is It Useful?

It should not surprise you to hear that most of the language in an analyst's research report tends to be optimistic. Analysts tend to follow the maxim your mother probably taught you: "If you don't have something nice to say, don't say anything at all."

As a result, some of the most negative research reports tend to be the shortest, consisting of downward earnings estimate revisions and a brief note commenting on short-term earnings difficulties.

As I said in the recommendation section, investors reading analyst research reports should recognize that any comment that is not inherently optimistic is a *de facto* pessimistic comment. That's an important point. Many individual investors hold onto losing positions for too long because of neutral comments in a brokerage research report.

KEY POINT   When reading the text of the research report, as you should do
when reading the recommendation, realize that any statement that
is not optimistic is actually a negative comment on the stock.

You must remember that analysts work at brokerage firms, and brokerage firms, for the most part, make money by selling stocks to institutional and individual investors.

For this reason, analysts often find good things to say about almost any stock out there.

As a result, it is not uncommon to find negative comments couched in neutral tones such as

"In the short term, IBM may have some difficulties, but the long-term prospects look bright."

"There is no positive catalyst in the immediate future for Philip Morris, but the shares remain a core holding."

"Microsoft, while continuing to execute well, remains fully valued."

These comments should be seen for what they are, namely extremely negative sentiment on the part of the analyst writing the research report.

Is there any time I would read the body of an analyst's research report? Yes, I can think of two situations:

- To determine why an analyst revised his earnings estimates

- To examine whether the revisions to the earnings estimates are the result of accounting changes, cost savings, top-line revenue growth, or acquisitions

How Should I Use it?

I would suggest that you read the text in an analyst's research report the same way I do (see the preceding discussion) or the way that many portfolio managers who run a less quantitative investment process do.

Portfolio managers are often looking for the following two things in reading the research reports issued by analysts:

- They are looking for earnings estimates in a research report that they can use as part of their proprietary valuation models for a stock.

- They are looking for answers to specific questions about issues such as margins, R&D expense, segment demand, and the other numbers associated with running a business.

Additionally, when you approach the text in an analyst's research report, always try to keep the following points in mind:

- Be on the lookout for neutral statements. Any statement that is not overtly positive in a research report should be interpreted by you as a negative comment.

- Don't let an analyst's comments steer you away from focusing on the revisions to earnings estimates. No matter what the analyst says, following changes in the earnings estimates is the way to make money from analysts' research reports.

- Use the text of the research report to determine the reason behind any estimate revision changes. Upward earnings estimate revisions due to top-line revenue growth are the most desirable. Upward earnings estimate revisions due to cost savings are okay. Upward earnings estimate revisions due to acquisitions should be severely discounted. Upward earnings estimate revisions due to accounting changes should be ignored.

The Net Result? Analysts Can Move Markets

There really are three ways by which an analyst's research impacts a stock's price.

1. Large money managers listen to what the analyst writes and act on his guidance.

2. The institutional sales force that works for the brokerage firm where the analyst is employed begins calling money managers to pitch them the analyst's ideas.

3. The retail brokerage force at the firm that employs the analyst starts selling the analyst's ideas to individual investors.

So, the analyst's reputation, his report, and the brokerage firm marketing apparatus work together to move the market.

If you think there is a bit of circular reasoning at work here, you're right. To some degree, investors—both institutional and individual—listen to what an analyst writes because they know that an analyst's comments will move a stock's price.

The more power that an analyst holds over a stock, that is, the more power an analyst has over and beyond that offered by the brokerage firm's sales force, the more the analyst is going to be paid.

"Well, that is all fine and good, Mitch," I hear you say. "Analysts don't issue sell recommendations and as a result I should not wait for an analyst to tell me when to sell a stock. That is just common sense. And they move markets. Tell me something I don't know."

"But you are missing the point, Mitch," you continue. "These analysts are biased and therefore what they produce—and everything they say—is worthless. Want proof? These analysts lost all my friends lots of money in the big technology boom. These analysts are a bunch of crooks and the worst type of crook is a crook that wears a suit and is interviewed on CNBC. The only way an individual can effectively pick stocks is to do their own homework and to be greedy when everyone is fearful and fearful when everyone is greedy. You only make money by being a contrarian."

I would agree with you on many of those points. Yes, the recommendations issued by analysts are biased; yes, it almost always pays to do your own research; and yes, I fervently believe there is a very strong kernel of truth in the old Wall Street adage that it pays to be a contrarian.

But I would strongly disagree with the statement that says, "because the recommendations the analysts issue are biased, all the research they produce is totally useless."

If I analyze the data, or if academic researchers analyze the data, we both come to the same conclusion—there are several ways that analysts' research can be used properly and profitably.

How?

That is the subject of the rest of the book.

Summary

- Analysts can move markets with their research reports.

- Regulation FD has reduced analysts' informational advantage over other market participants. The less powerful an investor is the more he generally likes the regulation.

- Analysts' research reports consist of five parts: a recommendation, an earnings estimate, a long-term earnings growth estimate, a target price, and the text of the report.

- Although the entire analyst report is interesting and useful in gleaning specific information, you should pay the most attention to changes in the analyst's earnings estimates.

- The long-term earnings growth estimate can be useful but is often misleading, and the target price and recommendations contained in a research report tend to be the least useful elements.

- Read the text of a research report to figure out why an analyst revised his earnings estimates. When reading the text, you should interpret any statement that is not overtly optimistic as negative, and not let any of the analyst's statements prevent you from focusing on the revisions to earnings estimates. In addition, use the text of the research report to determine the reason behind any earnings estimate revision changes.

Chapter Four

The Importance of Earnings and Earnings Estimate Revisions

What's ahead in this chapter?

- Why Are Revisions to Analysts' Earnings Estimates Important?
- Why Do Earnings Matter?
- Greater Fools and Dividend Payments
- Who Are Institutional Investors?
- Revisions to Earnings Estimates
- Making Money Using Revisions to Analysts' Earnings Estimates
- The Quick and the Dead: Responding to Analysts' Earnings Estimate Revisions
- Anticipating What Analysts Will Do: "Analyst Creep"
- Why Does Analyst Creep Exist?
- Basic Strategy of the Zacks Method

Why Are Revisions to Analysts' Earnings Estimates Important?

IN ORDER TO ANSWER THIS QUESTION, it is first necessary to understand why earnings are so important to a company's stock price.

Let me concede up front that talking about the importance of earnings seems dull. It is far sexier to wax on in an erudite fashion about barriers to entry, strategic competitive advantage, the signaling properties of insider trading, how to identify and buy companies that are leaders in their field, or even how to pick a great stock by independently measuring the demand for their products.

But the fact is that in the end, earnings trump everything else out there in terms of importance when it comes to figuring out which stocks will rise and fall in price.

And that makes earnings "sexy," indeed.

If a company cannot deliver earnings to its shareholders, it is irrelevant how great the company's products are, or how fast the company's revenues are growing.

Earnings are the most important driver of a stock's price. If a company is able to steadily grow earnings, the company's stock price will eventually rise over time. However, if a company cannot grow earnings or generate a profit, the company's stock price will eventually collapse, regardless of whether the company is in vogue.

Investors learned this lesson in the aftermath of the great Internet bubble. As any market observer can tell you, tuition for this lesson was extremely expensive.

From March of 2000 to August 2002, the "Internet Sector," as measured by the Philadelphia Stock Exchange's Internet index, fell 94%. To put this in perspective, $1,000 invested in a diversified group of Internet stocks in March of 2000 was worth just $60 two scant years later.

The major reason why practically every Internet stock fell so far, so fast, is that the "new economy" stocks had been bid up to unrealistic levels by a mania, an asset bubble, in which the prices investors paid for stocks bore no tether to reality and were instead inflated with hot air and hype. During the time the "Internet" bubble was being inflated, earnings ceased to matter with respect to valuations.

That is never a good thing. Eventually, investors realized earnings do matter and those companies that could not grow earnings—or even generate positive earnings (which was the case for most of the companies in the Philadelphia Stock Exchange's Internet index)—were severely punished.

Why Do Earnings Matter?

An example will show you why earnings are so important. But the message is plain—as an investor in the stock of a company, earnings are the only thing that you can eat.

Say you decide to purchase a 20% stake in a local convenience store called Qwik-E-Mart. Which of the following pieces of information is most pertinent to you in trying to figure out how much you should pay for your stake?

A. The number of people who visited the Qwik-E-Mart during the last quarter.

B. The number of employees Mr. Hooper, the Qwik-E-Mart founder, owner, and manager, has hired to work in the store.

C. The fact that Qwik-E-Mart spent $22,000 this past quarter to build a website that has sold $2,000 worth of Twinkies online.

D. Your share of the Qwik-E-Mart's future earnings. And what those earnings are likely to be.

While A, B, and C are interesting, and they give you some idea about how the business is run, D is what should matter the most to you as an investor.

Item D provides you with the best indication of how much money you will likely make as a result of your Qwik-E-Mart investment. In this case, the amount of money Mr. Hooper will pay you in the future is going to have a huge influence over how much you might be able to sell your stake for (if you decide to get out), and how much your Qwik-E-Mart stake is worth to you while you are still an owner.

The amount of money that you are entitled to as a result of your partial ownership in the Qwik-E-Mart is, in essence, your proportional share of the Qwik-E-Mart's quarterly earnings.

That's why earnings are so important. Earnings are an indication of how much money the company is potentially generating for share-holders. If a company does not earn anything—if it sells goods for less than it costs to produce them—then the company is worthless. It may take some time—Internet stocks were bid up to ridiculous heights for a while—but eventually investors always return to earnings.

Now, Mr. Hooper doesn't necessarily have to pay your share of the Qwik-E-Mart's earnings in cash. You may agree to plow your share of the profits back into the business.

For example, Mr. Hooper could come to you at the end of the year to tell you the store had been very profitable over the last 12 months, but instead of paying you in cash he wants to invest both his and your share of the earnings in a Slurpee machine. You may go along with the proposal because you believe a new Slurpee machine will increase profits, meaning that Mr. Hooper will pay you even more money in the future.

The point is this: In valuing your Qwik-E-Mart stake, what is important is not whether Mr. Hooper actually gives you an envelope full of cash every quarter, but rather whether Mr. Hooper's business has the *capacity* to provide you with an envelope of cash on a regular basis.

It is the size of these theoretical envelopes of cash that will determine how much your stake in the Qwik-E-Mart is worth.

Another investor could always buy your stake, hire a lawyer, and demand that Mr. Hooper pay him cash as opposed to wasting it on Slurpee machines that are always breaking down. But the amount this other investor would be willing to pay for your stake is going to be determined by the size of the cash payments Mr. Hooper could potentially pay to you now and in the future.

KEY POINT   It doesn't matter how big the company is—be it ExxonMobil or Mr. Hooper's corner grocery store—or whether it is public. The only thing that ultimately determines how much a company is worth is what it earns for its shareholders.

As it is with the Qwik-E-Mart, so is it with every publicly traded company. Earnings, and only earnings, determine a company's true value.

Greater Fools and Dividend Payments

About the same time Enron was defrauding investors in what was one of the biggest accounting and investment scandals in history, the company's corporate communications department saw fit to use investors' money to create an absolutely thrilling commercial in which a man lumbered around in some sort of iron straitjacket while the narrator, in an annoying nasal voice, droned on and on asking the question, "Why?" The message, I guess, was that Enron was a company that always dug deeply. The point of the commercial, which ran continually, was obvious: the commercial was designed to cause people to buy Enron's stock by portraying the image that the company was full of bright inquisitive minds always searching for answers. It is always a bad sign when a corporation that does not sell consumer products starts buying massive amounts of television advertising.

Whenever I saw the spot, I mentally rewrote it to bring out the company's real intent.

Here's how my version went:

> Charlie, I just bought this great energy stock called Enron!
>
> *Why?*
>
> Well, I am going to make a killing on it!
>
> *Why?*
>
> Enron's price is going to definitely break $200, I am sure of it!
>
> *Why?*
>
> Enron is revolutionizing this new energy trading business. These people are very smart. Once Enron dominates the energy trading business, everyone will want to own the stock.
>
> *Why (does this matter)?*
>
> Well, once Enron dominates this new business, more people are going to want to own the stock and then the stock's price will go up!
>
> *Why?*
>
> Charlie, you sound like a broken record, just buy the stock! Come on, you know the company. You remember their awesome commercial!

The point is that there has to be a reason to buy a stock. Yes, investors buy stocks in order to sell them later at a higher price to other investors, but ultimately there has to be a fundamental reason to buy in the first place. The whole game cannot be one of buying and finding a greater fool to whom to sell. If that were the case, the market would collapse like a house of cards.

Well, if you dig deep enough, what you eventually discover is that dividend payments—a shareholder's proportionate cash payments as a result of owning a stock—are what chain stock prices to reality. The reason earnings per share (EPS) are so important for publicly traded companies is because earnings serve as a proxy for what a stock can potentially deliver each quarter as a cash dividend payment—a dividend that can be given to you explicitly in the form of cash, or implicitly in the form of capital appreciation when you sell your shares to another investor for more than what you paid for them.

Now, just as in our example with Mr. Hooper and the Qwik-E-Mart, you may not actually receive a dividend. Over the past fifty years, publicly traded companies have become increasingly more likely to keep the money they generate in earnings and reinvest it in their business as opposed to paying actual cash dividends.

If you asked a CEO why his company does not pay dividends, he'd probably say that the investment opportunities available to the company are greater than those available to investors. (What the CEO likely will not tell you is he would rather run a company with 10,000 employees than one with 1,000 employees because the CEOs of larger companies are usually paid more money. Plowing what would have been dividends back into the business gives him a source of funding to expand his firm.)

If you asked the company's lawyer why the firm is reluctant to pay dividends, she might respond by saying the firm is just trying to keep from having its earnings taxed twice. The company is taxed on the money it earns. And then when you, the shareholder, receive the dividend check, those same earnings are taxed again. Given that, she will tell you, it does not make much sense for companies to pay dividends.

Regardless of the reason, the fact remains that the number of companies that pay dividends has been steadily decreasing over the past two decades. In 1978, roughly 66.5% of all companies paid some sort of dividend. In 1998, only 20.7% of all companies paid a cash dividend to shareholders.[1] There has been some talk recently of reducing or even eliminating the double taxation of dividends. If this occurs, most likely the percentage of companies paying a dividend will definitely rise. Even if a company pays you a dividend, the question you should be asking is not how much am I receiving, but rather how much can I potentially receive in the future. Earnings serve as a proxy for the potential dividends that a company can pay, and this is what gives a stock its true worth.

KEY POINT   Earnings are important because they serve as an indication of what a company could potentially pay as a dividend. Dividend payments, and thus earnings, provide a stock with inherent value.

Without earnings, stocks are simply impressive-looking pieces of paper with nice watermarks.

With all this by way of background, let's return to the Qwik-E-Mart example for a minute. Remember, the key question in determining the value of your stake in the Qwik-E-Mart is not how much Mr. Hooper would have paid you in the past, but rather how much money he is likely to give you in the future.

Mr. Hooper might have paid you tens of thousands of dollars over the last couple of years since you are a partial owner of the Qwik-E-Mart. You may be very confident about Mr. Hooper's capabilities as a manager and think of him as your friend. All that is fine, but the value of your Qwik-E-Mart stake is going to be determined by how much money the person who buys your Qwik-E-Mart shares expects to receive from Mr. Hooper in the future.

How the Qwik-E-Mart has performed in the past is interesting in that it might provide the potential buyer of your stake with an estimate of how the Qwik-E-Mart will perform in the future. But ultimately the buyer only cares about how much money he will receive from Mr. Hooper in the future.

What is true for you—and the potential buyer of your stake—is true of the stock market as a whole. Stock prices are determined by investors' views of future earnings. Analysts' earnings estimates are so important because they quantify what the company is expected to earn in the future.

KEY POINT   The important question in determining the price of any stock is not how much the company has earned in the past, but how much the company will likely earn in the future. This is why analysts' estimates of future earnings are so important.

Even though they are secondhand data—the information is not coming directly from the company, but rather from someone who is trying to interpret what the company's earnings prospects are—analysts' earnings estimates are the only publicly available information that indicates what a company is expected to earn in the future.

Analysts' earnings estimates are the means by which investors determine the size of the potential envelopes of cash that they are entitled to as a shareholder in the company.

Those earnings forecasts are also the basis for the valuation models used by institutional investors.

Who Are Institutional Investors?

Why should you care how much institutional investors think a stock is worth? Institutional investors are the professionals who manage the trillions of dollars invested by mutual funds, pension plans, insurance companies, and hedge funds. ("Individual investor" is the term Wall Street uses to refer to all the John Q. Publics of the world who independently invest for their own private accounts, either through full-service brokerage firms or online through a discount brokerage firm.) Institutional investors, who come to the market ready to trade hundreds of millions of dollars on any given day, are the people who really set and move stock prices.

When you understand the power institutional investors wield over the markets, then the next step is to try to understand what motivates institutional buy/sell decisions.

Most institutional investors attended business schools where they were taught a number of classical financial models to use in calculating the "true" or "fair" value of a company and its shares. The "fair" value for a company is a nebulous concept, but it basically means the price a company's stock *should* trade at, as opposed to the price that a company's stock actually does trade at in the market. Almost without exception, these valuation models focus on the future earnings generated by a company.

KEY POINT   Because institutional investors oversee such vast sums of money, the buy and sell decisions of these institutional investors are what truly impact and move stock prices. Most institutional investors make their buy and sell decisions based on models keyed to the future expected earnings of a company.

Until someone invents a time machine, the only way to run a model based on future earnings is through the use of analysts' earnings estimates.

On the simplest level, the higher the earnings estimates used in the model (the input), the higher the "true" (or "fair") value for the company and its stock (the output).

Revisions to Earnings Estimates

A given company has anywhere from one to more than thirty Wall Street analysts following its stock and issuing earnings estimates.

At Zacks, we create a consensus, or average, earnings estimate from all the individual earnings estimates. To make a long story short, there is no reason to rely on the estimate of just one analyst when you can combine the intelligence of the whole analyst community by creating an average earnings estimate.

Various research conducted by professors of accounting in business schools has shown that consensus earnings estimates are more accurate than the earnings estimates issued by any one individual analyst. Additionally, the consensus earnings estimate is a better gauge of what a company is going to earn in the future than you can get simply by looking for a trend in a company's historical earnings.

At Zacks, we calculate the consensus earnings estimate for each of the next four fiscal quarters, and each of the next three fiscal years, based on extensive data. We receive daily electronic files from over 250 brokerage firms in the U.S. and Canada and during an average week we record over 25,000 earnings estimate revisions made by the 3,000 brokerage analysts at these firms.

It is these earnings estimate changes or revisions—as opposed to the initial estimates themselves—that have a tremendous impact on stock prices.

Here's why. The fact that analysts collectively expect a company to earn $1.25 per share this year is likely already reflected in the stock's price. As an investor, what you are really concerned about is not why a stock is trading at $10 per share or $50 per share; you want to know what will happen to its price in the future.

KEY POINT   What analysts expect a company to earn in the coming quarter or year is likely already reflected in a company's stock price. What is important is not how much analysts expect a company to earn, but rather how these expectations have recently changed.

This is where changes to the consensus earnings estimate come in. The cause and effect is clear: Upward revisions in earnings estimates almost always cause a stock to climb; downward revisions in earnings estimates almost always cause a stock to fall.

Why Do Revisions Cause Stock Price Changes?

In order to understand why upward earnings estimate revisions cause a stock's price to rise and downward revisions cause it to fall, it is important to realize that at the end of the day, stock prices change because of supply and demand. If investors want to buy—for whatever reason—more shares of a stock than there are shares available, then the price of a stock will rise in order to induce more people to sell. End of story.

Again, it doesn't matter why they want to buy: because they believe the company is undervalued, because the company's product is hot, because they heard someone who heard someone say the company is for sale, because they think they can flip the shares following an IPO, because a respected analyst has recommended the shares, whatever.

If more investors want to buy than sell, the price goes up; if more people want to sell than buy, a stock's price goes down.

When analysts raise their earnings estimates, institutional demand for a company's stock increases. Why? It goes back to the institutional manager's valuation model. Higher earnings estimates directly lead to a greater "fair value" price for a stock that an analyst is following. Since the institutional manager now expects the share price to go higher (because his model indicates a higher "fair value"), the institutional investor buys the stock.

KEY POINT   Essentially, when analysts raise their earnings estimates, it is an indication that the envelopes of cash investors are entitled to (in the form of dividends) will probably contain more money in the future then previously believed. That increased expectation drives the share price higher.

At the most basic level, stock prices respond to upward earnings estimate revisions because the changes represent positive information regarding the future earnings potential of a company. Whenever a company's future earnings look like they are going to improve, a company's stock price should rise as well.

You are probably wondering if you can benefit from these changes. That is the subject of our next section.

Making Money Using Revisions to Analysts' Earnings Estimates

One of the best ways to find out whether you can make money is to calculate how much you would have made if you had possessed the ability to predict analysts' behavior perfectly.

To find out what such precognitive abilities would have earned you, let's divide the universe of the 3,300 largest stocks that have at least one analyst following them into five separate, equally weighted portfolios, each containing 660 stocks.[2]

Using our crystal ball, we find out how much the consensus earnings estimate for the coming fiscal year is going to change over the next month for each stock. Starting in 1987, for 15 years, we'll rebalance the portfolios every month so that Portfolio #1 always has the 660 stocks whose consensus earnings estimates will decrease the most over the next month, and Portfolio #5 contains those 660 stocks whose consensus earnings estimates will increase the most over the next month. Now remember, this portfolio construction is done as if you had the ability to predict the future but your predictive ability was limited to knowing how much the consensus earnings estimate was going to change over the next month.

The point is, we are trying to determine what sort of returns you could have generated if you could have predicted analysts' earnings estimate revisions and thus changes in a stock's consensus earnings estimate with 100% accuracy.

(The three remaining portfolios will be in the middle, with Portfolio 4 being closest to 5 in terms of positive earnings estimate revisions and Portfolio 2 being closest to 1.)

Figure 4-1 contains the results of the experiment. It shows you the returns you could have generated if you had had the ability to predict analysts' earnings estimates.

As you can see, Portfolio #1 returned on average a negative 30.6% per year over the fifteen-year period. In contrast, Portfolio #5 produced a positive 53.0% annualized return, substantially above the S&P 500, which returned on average 9.0% per year.

Figure 4-1 Annualized returns with a crystal ball that predicted earnings estimate revisions (October 1987 through September 2002).

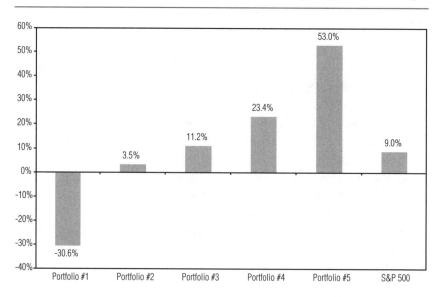

KEY POINT It is clear that if you had the ability to perfectly predict changes to analysts' earnings estimates, you could generate phenomenal returns.

As impressive as the returns of Portfolio #5 are, don't rush out, take out a second mortgage on your house, and deposit the money in your discount brokerage account just yet. The reason is that no one has a true crystal ball, and the preceding returns are based on perfect foresight. However, the data clearly shows that if you could predict analysts' earnings estimate revisions with some degree of accuracy, excess returns could be generated.

What Have We Learned?

Figure 4-1 shows that if you know ahead of time that analysts are going to raise their earnings estimates on a stock, you can make substantial profits. The big problem is, of course, that no one has this kind of information.

In the absence of a crystal ball, there are two ways that you can use analysts' earnings estimates to make money in the market. You must try to do the following:

- Respond as quickly as possible to analysts' earnings estimate revisions.

- Anticipate which stocks are likely to receive upward earnings estimate revisions in the future by analyzing analysts' recent actions.

KEY POINT The two ways to effectively use analysts' earnings estimates are to quickly react to earnings estimate revisions and to try to determine which stocks are likely to receive upward earnings estimate revisions in the future.

The Quick and the Dead: Responding to Analysts' Earnings Estimate Revisions

In general, the stock market is very efficient. That is economist-speak for the fact that new information is quickly reflected in a stock's price.

However, revisions to earnings estimates are a bit of an exception to the efficiency rule. When analysts revise their earnings estimates it takes some time for the change to be totally factored into a stock's price.

Why? Well, remember what we said before about institutional investors. Because they buy billions and billions of dollars worth of equities, it is the institutional investors who really determine a stock's price. And once they receive the revised earnings estimates, it takes these large organizations a while to react.

Instead of immediately jumping in and buying shares when a stock receives upward earnings estimate revisions, or selling on downward earnings estimate revisions, the portfolio managers at the mutual and pension funds review the stock more extensively, read the research report, and see if the analysts' reasoning agrees with their own views.

Some institutional investors select stocks only after building agreement across multiple portfolio managers and internal researchers, which adds even more time to the process. Additionally, many institutional portfolio managers oversee billions of dollars worth of stocks, which makes it impractical for them to quickly move into and out of individual stocks. Instead, after analyzing the earnings estimates, the large institutional investors begin buying stocks over the next several days or even weeks.

The net effect is a brief delay in the market's response to earnings estimate revisions, and this gives an aggressive investor the opportunity to earn substantial returns by quickly buying in the face of upward earnings estimate revisions.

KEY POINT   There is a delay in the market's reaction to revisions to analysts' earnings estimates. Because of their size and the way they select stocks, it takes most institutional investors a bit of time to respond to the earnings estimate revisions.

What happens if you can't move quickly? That brings us to the second and far more important point—how you anticipate what analysts are going to do in the future.

Anticipating What Analysts Will Do: "Analyst Creep"

It turns out you can predict what analysts are likely to do in the future. How? By looking at what they have done in the recent past.

If you examine the data, what you find is that stocks that have received earnings estimate revisions last month are more likely to receive earnings estimate revisions in the same direction in the next month.

In order to understand why this is the case, it makes sense to look at a phenomenon called "analyst creep." Let's start with the data contained in Figure 4-2.

If we examine all the earnings estimate revisions that analysts made from 1987 to 2002, in aggregate we find that over the entire time period, analysts were more likely to lower earnings estimates than raise them. Why? Analysts have historically tended to be overly optimistic in their initial earnings projections.

In fact, when we examine all the earnings estimate revisions issued by analysts on a monthly basis since 1987, we find that among the

Figure 4-2 All stocks followed by analysts—3,320 stocks on average (1987 to 2002).

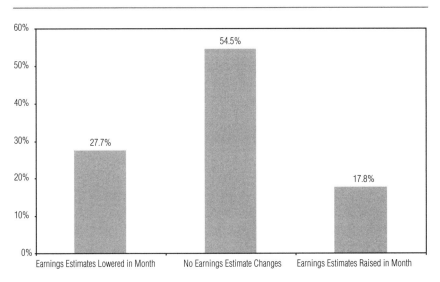

largest stocks followed by analysts, in a given month, analysts on average lowered their earnings estimates on 28% of the stocks and raised their earnings estimates on 18% of the stocks (with 54% of the stocks receiving no material change in analysts' earnings estimates).

But that is not the end of the story. If, instead of selecting from all the stocks covered by analysts, we chose only from those stocks that received upward earnings estimate revisions during the previous month, we find something very interesting: *Analysts are far more likely to revise earnings estimates in the same direction as they did in the previous month.*

KEY POINT   If analysts raised their earnings estimates on a stock over the last month, there is a good chance that they are going to revise earnings estimates up in the next month.

This tendency for analysts' earnings estimates in aggregate to be revised in the same direction month after month is called analyst creep.

In fact, a stock that received an upward earnings estimate revision last month has a 33% chance of receiving additional upward earnings estimate revisions this month. Essentially, this means that by buying stocks that received upward earnings estimate revisions last month, you are roughly twice as likely to select stocks that will receive upward earnings estimate revisions this month. Figure 4-3 shows the chance that a stock which received upward earnings estimate revisions last month will receive upward earnings estimate revisions this month.

The reverse also appears to be true. Stocks that received downward earnings estimate revisions last month are more likely to receive downward earnings estimates this month. This is readily apparent in Figure 4-4.

All this data points to a phenomenon that is not widely known to investors but that you can use to make money: Revisions to analyst earnings estimates are serially correlated over time. This sentence is a mouthful, but what it means is that analysts as a group tend to revise their earnings estimates incrementally over time.

The result is that one of the best predictors of what analysts are going to do in the next month is to look at what they did the previous one. By being able to predict revisions to analysts' earnings estimates you can begin to predict price movement over the next few months.

Figure 4-3 Stocks for which analysts raised their earnings estimates in the previous month—595 stocks on average (1987 to 2002).

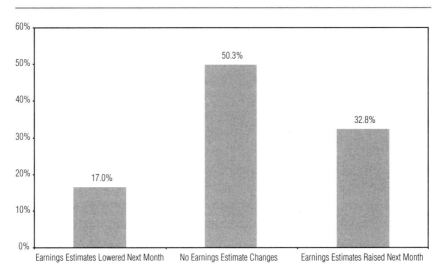

Figure 4-4 Stocks for which analysts lowered their earnings estimates in the previous month—919 stocks on average (1987 to 2002).

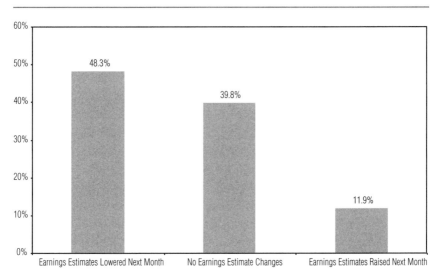

KEY POINT   By buying stocks that have received upward earnings estimate revisions last month you are purchasing stocks that are more likely to receive upward earnings estimate revisions this month. Similarly, you should sell stocks that receive downward earnings estimate revisions, as these stocks are more likely to receive further downward earnings estimate revisions in the next month.

Why Does Analyst Creep Exist?

Herd Behavior

In order to understand why analyst creep exists, it is necessary to walk a mile in the analyst's shoes.

Imagine an analyst, Andrew, who actively covers and writes research reports on Dell (DELL), Apple (AAPL), Gateway (GTW), Ingram Micro (IM), Smartdisk (SMDK), and Tech Data (TECD).

After some new data was released Wednesday showing an increase in corporate information technology spending, Andrew spends the rest of the week, and all of the weekend, trying to figure out what this new information means for the potential demand for Dell's laptops.

Based on a combination of the new IT spending data, very crude econometrical modeling, some empirical channel checks, a few talks with management at various PC retailers, sporadic monitoring of the traffic to Dell's direct sales website, some information gleaned from reading several articles regarding the new Dell laptop in trade publications, and his own intuition, Andrew concludes that Dell is likely to have an absolutely terrific coming quarter due to accelerating laptop sales.

The twenty-two other analysts covering Dell expect that the company will earn anywhere from $0.16 to $0.20 per share this quarter, with the average, or consensus estimate, being $0.17. Based on Andrew's research he thinks Dell is going to earn $0.23 per share.

That difference may not seem like much. But when a move of a couple of cents either way can send a stock soaring or plunging, six cents is a huge amount of money.

The gap is so large that the first thing Andrew does is double-check his assumptions and his forecasting model. "How could everyone be so off?" Andrew wonders. The next thing Andrew does is review his last research report on Dell, and he finds that he predicted Dell to earn $0.16 per share, before the new information came out.

His math checks out, and he still can't figure out why everyone else has missed the boat.

What does Andrew do next?

Most likely, he raises his earnings estimate from $0.16 to around $0.19 per share.

Why doesn't he go to $0.23 per share?

He is worried about being wrong.

If Andrew worked as a day trader and he was wrong, it might cost him a couple thousand dollars. But Andrew is a highly respected equity analyst and if he is wrong enough times, it might cost him his high-priced job.

Now the worst-case scenario for Andrew would be if he is wrong and all alone. If out of twenty-three analysts, Andrew has the highest earnings estimate of $0.23 and Dell actually reports a disappointing quarter of $0.15 per share, Andrew's mistake is going to stick out like a sore thumb. If Andrew makes mistakes like this a couple more times, he will be known as the former analyst who had rose-colored glasses.

If, however, Andrew issues an estimate of $0.19 per share and Dell reports $0.15, Andrew will be wrong, but he will have quite a bit of company. In the brokerage community there is definitely safety in numbers.

"Look, Jerry," Andrew will say, "I realize I lost your mutual fund $20 million with my recent optimistic Dell research report, but hell, Dell's poor quarter really took everyone by surprise; management was very deceptive. They misled everyone on the street."

As a cold, calculating Wall Street professional, it makes a lot more sense for Andrew to hedge his bets.

As a result of his desire to stick with the herd, Andrew issues the $0.19 earnings estimate and will likely raise his earnings estimate in the future if he witnesses other analysts raising their estimates as well. Very early on, analysts learn that the herd provides safety.

Despite all of an analyst's research, the fact of the matter is that analysts do not know with any real certainty what a company is going to earn in the coming quarter. Therefore, it makes more sense in almost every case for an analyst to play it safe and stick with the herd, as opposed to sticking his neck out.

KEY POINT   Analysts tend to "herd" with other analysts when making changes
to their earnings estimates. The analyst does this in order to protect his job. As a result, revisions to analysts' earnings estimates
tend to be serially correlated over time.

Generating Prestige

In addition to their desire to hold onto their jobs, there is another reason that analysts are predictable. They want to gain the respect of large
institutional money managers. (We talked about why that is so important in Chapter Two.)

Consistency often spells respect for analysts. To understand why, let's
take a look at doctors. Very few patients would respect a doctor who
constantly revised her diagnosis.

Say you are feeling sick and you visit a doctor. She takes a blood
sample, but tells you based on your fever and chills that you likely just
have a bad case of the stomach flu that is going around. The doctor rec-
ommends rest.

You go home and load up on chicken soup, but are disturbed twelve
hours later by a call from your physician. Apparently, after analyzing the
results of your blood test, she has concluded you may have a rare Asian
virus and that you should immediately come in for further tests.

The next day the doctor performs extensive tests and comes to the
conclusion that her two initial diagnoses were off and that you likely
are suffering from a severe bacterial infection.

If this hypothetical scenario actually happened, you would likely
find a new doctor, convinced your current one is either incompetent
or a nut, or perhaps both.

Even if at each stage of the diagnosis more information were
revealed to the doctor, by constantly changing her diagnosis the doctor
creates the perception of incompetence.

White-collar workers in almost any professional field tend to be the
same way—reluctant to admit mistakes or reverse their opinions.
Analysts, in this regard, are no different from other professionals. In
order to maintain their prestige in the eyes of the money managers to
whom they provide research, analysts are often conservative in their
pronouncements and don't like to say that they were wrong.

For this reason, once an analyst has committed to a certain earnings per share estimate, he is reluctant to revise it.

When an analyst revises his earnings estimates he is effectively admitting that his previous earnings estimate was wrong. If he aggressively changes his earnings estimates every couple of weeks, he loses face significantly in front of portfolio managers. As a result, analysts make changes to their earnings estimates incrementally and slowly.

KEY POINT   Large and frequent moves in an analyst's earnings estimates that are not accompanied by other analysts moving their estimates in the same direction may lead investors to believe that the analyst making the changes does not have a good grasp of what is really going on at a company. As a result, analysts make changes to their earnings estimates incrementally, in small steps.

Basic Strategy of the Zacks Method

These behaviors—the herding, the conservative nature of analysts, and the incremental way that analysts tend to make changes to their earnings estimates—result in the trends I just illustrated. Instead of making one dramatic revision up or down, most analysts will do what tech analyst Andrew did and revise their earnings estimates incrementally. The net effect? If an analyst revised his earnings estimates upward last month, the analyst will likely revise his earnings estimates this month, and additional analysts are also likely to revise their earnings estimates this month as well.

So, look at what we have discovered:

- Prices respond to earnings estimate revisions.

- Stocks that received upward earnings estimate revisions by analysts last month are more likely to receive upward earnings estimate revisions this month.

The result of both? *It is profitable to buy stocks following upward earnings estimate revisions by analysts.*

An analyst's initial upward earnings estimate revision serves as a signal of future upward earnings estimate revisions by other analysts following the stock as well as a sign that the initial analyst will likely raise
his own earnings estimates in the future. As we have seen, if an analyst
has revised his earnings estimate once, he is likely to revise it again in
the same direction. The basic process is detailed in Figure 4-5, which
shows how changes to earnings estimates are related over time.

Upward earnings estimate revisions result in an initial, but somewhat delayed, price response (A). However, these initial earnings estimate revisions also signal an increased likelihood of future earnings
estimate revisions (B). The future earnings estimate revisions result in
future price movements (C).

So, by buying at the first sign of upward earnings estimate revisions,
an investor is effectively anticipating future upward revisions and a
future increase in the stock's price. This is shown by line (D) in Figure
4-5.

Figure 4-5 Earnings estimate revisions over time.

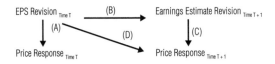

What About Changes in the Analyst's Recommendation to Buy, Hold, or Sell a Stock?

We have all seen dramatic moves upwards when an analyst says "buy." And conversely, we have seen stocks plummet on sell recommendations.

But, to be honest, we don't see those kinds of dramatic reactions to revisions in earnings estimates.

To a novice investor, this may be proof that recommendation changes are more powerful than earnings estimate revisions in terms of predicting future stock price movements.

The reality is, in fact, the opposite.

Although the immediate price response to analyst recommendation change is dramatically stronger than the price response to an earnings estimate revision, recommendation changes are not as correlated over time as earnings estimate revisions.

What this means is that if Andrew upgrades his buy/hold/sell recommendation on Dell to a "strong buy," then Bob—a different analyst—is not significantly more likely to upgrade his recommendation in the coming month. This means that future broker recommendation changes—either up or down—are harder to predict than earnings estimate revisions.

Additionally, most institutional investors realize that recommendations are usually issued for the benefit of the brokerage firm's retail customers and the recommendations are often used to hype stocks. For the most part, institutional investors acknowledge that earnings estimates are far more useful than brokerage recommendations and many professional portfolio managers actually tend to ignore brokerage recommendations entirely.

An analyst can effectively make incremental moves over time for earnings estimates, but the nature of the recommendation process doesn't allow him to do that.

For this reason, when it comes to investing, I generally prefer to use analysts' earnings estimate revisions rather than broker recommendation changes. With broker recommendation changes you have only the institutional delay to the change in the recommendation working for you, while with earnings estimate revisions you have both the institutional delay and the correlation of the analysts' earnings estimate revisions over time working in your favor.

Exactly *how* you implement earnings estimate revisions to make money is the subject of the next chapter.

Summary

- Earnings matter because at the end of the day, earnings are what give a stock its intrinsic value.

- What is important in evaluating the earnings of a company is not what the company has earned historically, but rather, what the company will earn in the future. This is why analysts' earnings expectations are so important.

- What is important to focus on is changes to analysts' earnings estimates over time.

- Because of analyst creep, if a stock received upward earnings estimate revisions last month, it is likely to receive upward earnings estimate revisions in the next month. Likewise, if a stock received downward earnings estimate revisions last month, the stock is likely to receive downward earnings estimate revisions in the next month.

- Since stock prices respond to earnings estimate revisions and stocks that received upward earnings estimate revisions by analysts last month are more likely to receive upward earnings estimate revisions this month, it is a profitable strategy to buy stocks as soon as possible following upward earnings estimate revisions.

- By quickly buying stocks that are receiving upward earnings estimate revisions, you profit from the slight delay of institutional investors in reacting to the estimate revisions. More importantly, you are buying stocks that are likely to receive *future* upward earnings estimate revisions. As a result, stocks that receive upward earnings estimate revisions tend to outperform over the next one to three months.

Endnotes

[1] Source: "Disappearing Dividends." March 1999, Fama/French working paper.

[2] There are roughly 4,500 companies that have at least one analyst issuing a recommendation and 4,300 companies that have at least one analyst issuing earnings estimates. In this study, I limited the universe to 3,300 in order to avoid the problem of stale prices that occurs with very small-cap stocks.

Chapter Five

How to Use Earnings Estimates to Pick Stocks Profitably

What's ahead in this chapter?

- Implementing a Stock Selection Strategy
- The 30-day Consensus Estimate
- What Is an Earnings Estimate Histogram?
- What Returns Can Be Expected from Focusing on Changes to the Consensus Earnings Estimate over Time?
- When Wouldn't Prices Respond to Estimate Revisions?
- Using Earnings Estimate Revisions to Manage Your Portfolio

Implementing a Stock Selection Strategy

THE PREVIOUS CHAPTER EXAMINED why focusing on revisions to analysts' earnings estimates is a very profitable investment strategy to use. In this chapter, I continue to examine an estimate revision stock selection strategy, but while the previous chapter focused on explaining why such a strategy works, this chapter focuses on explaining how to implement such a strategy. The first step to implementing such an earnings estimate revision strategy is finding the correct earnings estimate data to focus on.

Step One: Find the Right Data to Focus On

Figure 5-1 shows exactly how the consensus earnings estimates for Blockbuster (BBI)—the video rental store—has changed over the past

Figure 5-1 Consensus earnings estimates trends—Blockbuster (BBI).

	This Quarter Sep-02	Next Quarter Dec-02	This Year Dec-02	Next Year Dec-03
Current	$ 0.30	$ 0.42	$ 1.30	$ 1.52
7 Days Ago	$ 0.30	$ 0.42	$ 1.30	$ 1.52
30 Days Ago	$ 0.30	$ 0.40	$ 1.27	$ 1.51
60 Days Ago	$ 0.29	$ 0.40	$ 1.16	$ 1.38
90 Days Ago	$ 0.29	$ 0.40	$ 1.16	$ 1.36

few months. The table in Figure 5-1 was taken off the Internet from the Zacks.com free investment site, but the table and several others like it is available at any one of several free investment sites. This table contains all of the data necessary to implement an earnings estimate revision strategy.

Remember, the consensus is the average of all the earnings estimates issued by analysts. If the consensus goes up over time, it means that analysts are revising their estimates upward. If the consensus earnings estimate declines, it means that analysts are revising their earnings estimates downward.

The first thing that you may notice in this table is that consensus earnings estimates are displayed for the current quarter, the next quarter, the current fiscal year, and the next fiscal year.

Our analysis indicates that changes in the current fiscal year consensus estimate have the greatest value.

An explanation for this finding is that the near-term earnings for the coming fiscal year are the earnings most likely to have an impact on a stock's price. These earnings are more likely to be accurately predicted than earnings for the next fiscal year and the earnings usually span over several quarters.

Quarterly earnings estimates are important, but it is not unheard of for analysts to lower earnings estimates for the coming quarter while raising earnings estimates for the year, due to cyclical seasonal factors or a one-time weak quarter that is unlikely to repeat.

Therefore, you really should focus on column three in Figure 5-1. This column, which is highlighted, indicates how the consensus earnings estimate for the current fiscal year has changed over time. In this instance we see that currently the consensus earnings estimate for Blockbuster is $1.30 a share, but thirty days ago it was $1.27. This means that earnings estimates are being revised upward.

KEY POINT   You want to buy stocks for which the consensus earnings estimate for the current fiscal year has been increasing over time. These stocks are receiving upward earnings estimate revisions.

The question is, of course, has the consensus earnings estimate for the current fiscal year increased sufficiently for you to buy the stock?

There are several additional steps to follow in order to help you answer this question.

Step Two: Only Buy a Company that Analysts Expect to Generate a Profit

A good rule of thumb is to only buy a company that is expected to turn a profit. Very simply, do not buy a stock unless analysts project that the company will generate positive earnings per share in the current and next fiscal year. Do not worry about five years from now, do not believe stories of incredible earnings three years out, do not even wait a year and a half for positive earnings. A bird in the hand is worth two in the bush—make sure the consensus earnings estimate for the coming and next fiscal year is positive.

Seeing This Step in Action

This simple bias towards profitable companies would have helped you dramatically lessen losses in 2000 through 2002.

In order to create Figure 5-2, at the beginning of each month from October 1987 to September 2002, I checked every stock's consensus earnings estimate for the current year.

If the consensus earnings estimate for the coming year was less than or equal to zero, I put the stock into the "Profit-less portfolio." The "Profit-less portfolio" is the home for companies projected by analysts to lose money on a per-share basis in the coming year.

If the consensus earnings estimate is greater than zero I placed the stock in the "Profitable portfolio": these companies are projected by analysts to generate a profit at the end of the current fiscal year.

For Blockbuster (BBI), the consensus earnings estimate for the current year is $1.30. All those late fees add up—Blockbuster is projected to generate positive earnings per share and thus in this case would be placed in the "Profitable portfolio."

Each of the two portfolios is then equal-weighted and we measure the performance of each portfolio for a full month. At the end of the month we re-balance the portfolios, making sure the portfolios remain equal-weighted and that every stock is in the appropriate portfolio.

What you find after doing this sorting each and every month is that over the past fifteen years, on average, the "Profit-less portfolio" consisted of roughly 10% of the 3,300 largest companies that are followed by analysts, while the "Profitable portfolio" made up the rest. This means 10% of the 3,300 largest stocks that are followed by at least one analyst are projected to not make any money on a per-share basis.

Figure 5-2 shows the annualized returns of the two portfolios, and the results demonstrate just how important it is to make sure that the stocks you buy are projected to generate a profit in the coming year. As Figure 5-2 shows, over the past fifteen years a portfolio consisting of the stocks of companies that analysts expected to generate positive earnings per share outperformed a portfolio consisting of companies that analysts expected to generate negative earnings per share—by an annualized amount of about 20%.

What Does This All Mean?

KEY POINT   Stocks that are projected to generate a profit have historically out-performed stocks that are expected to generate a loss—you should avoid stocks that are not projected by analysts to generate positive earnings in the coming and next fiscal years.

The fact that the stocks of companies that are expected to lose money under-perform the stocks of companies that are expected to make money is not surprising. However, what is interesting is that

Figure 5-2 Annualized returns of stocks based on whether consensus earnings estimate is positive (October 1987 to September 2002).

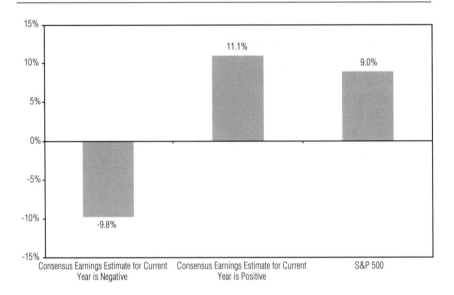

this phenomenon does not occur every year and that there are periods in which the stocks of companies that analysts expect to lose money outperform stocks that analysts project to make money.

In fact, during 1995, 1998, and 1999, the "Profit-less portfolio" outperformed the "Profitable portfolio." These years are periods in which investors tended to be looking far into the future—they were years when growth was the mantra of the day.

While there are periods when unprofitable companies outperform profitable companies, over the long haul the odds are substantially better that the reverse will occur.

KEY POINT   There are some times when it makes sense to buy a company that is losing money—in these cases, you usually want to see that analysts are raising their earnings estimates so that profitability is expected within a two-year time frame. Still, these instances are the exception rather than the rule. For the most part, you want to stick with companies that are in fact generating a profit.

What this study clearly suggests is that it is not a good idea to invest in a company that is expected to lose money in the current year, and that it is definitely a bad idea to invest in a company that is projected to lose money over the next two years.

The best way to ensure that the stocks you buy are expected by analysts to generate a profit is to check to see that the consensus earnings estimates for the current and next fiscal year are positive. This means that you should always make sure that the numbers in the "current" row in columns three and four, as in Figure 5-1, are greater than zero.

In the BBI example, analysts on average estimate that Blockbuster is going to earn $1.30 per share this year and $1.52 next year. Since both these numbers are positive, BBI passes the first test and it is on to step three.

Step Three: Calculate the Percentage Change in the Current Year's Consensus Estimate over the Last Thirty Days

This is a brief step, but it is also the most important. The way you get ahead of the market is to buy stocks that receive upward earnings estimate revisions.

The question is, how do you determine if a given stock is receiving substantial upward earnings estimate revisions? Well, there is a very straightforward way to determine this.

The key is to focus on how the consensus earnings estimate has changed over time.

Let's take a look at the important consensus earnings estimate trend table for another stock: Autozone (AZO). Autozone is a specialty retailer of automotive parts and accessories, primarily focusing on do-it-yourself customers. What is interesting to me about AZO is not that you can buy car parts fairly inexpensively there, but rather that analysts are raising their earnings estimates on the stock.

Figure 5-3 contains the earnings estimates trend table for AZO taken from Yahoo Finance, which basically has the same format as the trend table displayed for Blockbuster (Figure 5-1) that was taken from Zacks.com.

The consensus earnings estimate for the current year for Autozone has been increasing over the past ninety days. Sixty days ago the consensus

Figure 5-3 Earnings estimates trends and revisions—Autozone (AZO).

	This Quarter (Nov 02)	Next Quarter (Feb 03)	This Year (Aug 03)	Next Year (Aug 04)
Analysts' earnings estimates trend				
Current	0.95	0.77	4.80	5.44
7 Days Ago	0.95	0.77	4.78	5.44
30 Days Ago	0.90	0.77	4.34	N/A
60 Days Ago	0.90	0.77	4.34	N/A
90 Days Ago	0.90	0.73	4.32	N/A

earnings estimate for the fiscal year ending August 2003 was $4.34; the consensus earnings estimate went up to $4.78 seven days ago and currently stands at $4.80. Clearly analysts are raising earnings estimates.

But beyond just seeing an upward trend, how do you determine whether the change in the consensus earnings estimate is substantial? The way you do this is to calculate the percentage change in the consensus earnings estimate over the last thirty days. Again, you want to focus on the consensus earnings estimate for the current year, which would be column three.

In order to do this, plug the values from Figure 5-3 into the following equation:

$$\frac{CC-MAC}{MAC} \times 100 \quad (1)$$

where

CC = The consensus earnings estimate for the coming fiscal year (highlighted in dark grey in Figure 5-3)

MAC = The consensus earnings estimate for the coming fiscal year as of one month or thirty days ago (highlighted in light grey in Figure 5-3)

For AZO this would work out to be $(4.80-4.34)/4.34 \times 100 = 10.6\%$.

For BBI we have $(1.30 - 1.27)/1.27 \times 100 = 2.4\%$

The next question is whether 10.6% is a good-enough value to merit a buy decision on AZO, and similarly, is 2.4% enough of an increase to merit a buy decision on BBI?

KEY POINT : When determining whether a stock has been receiving upward earnings estimate revisions, you should focus on the percentage change to the current year's consensus earnings estimate over the past thirty days. The more positive the percentage change is, the stronger the "buy" signal.

To answer that question we must turn our attention to step four.

Step Four: Check Whether the Percentage Change over the Last Thirty Days in the Current Year's Consensus Earnings Estimate Is above the Threshold Buy Level

Generally, you want to buy stocks that have a percentage change in the current year's consensus earnings estimate over the past thirty days that puts the stock in the top 10% of all stocks that are followed by analysts.

Now, the cutoff or threshold level that is necessary to be in the top 10% of all stocks changes over time, depending on whether analysts on the whole are optimistic or pessimistic about future earnings.

The current threshold level as well as the historical threshold levels are given in Figure 5-4.

Over the last ten years, the threshold level has ranged from a low of around 1.9% to a high of just above 5.0%, and it currently stands at around 3.0%.

For AZO, the consensus earnings estimate for the current year has increased roughly 10.6% over the last month, so it would be considered a buy candidate.

For BBI, which has seen its consensus earnings estimate for the coming year increase by only 2.4% over the past thirty days, the increase is not large enough to reach the current threshold level of 3.0%. As a result, although BBI is receiving upward earnings estimate revisions, the stock would not be considered a buy candidate.

Figure 5-4 Current and historical threshold buy levels.

Year	Threshold Level in Percent
1987	3.7
1988	4.5
1989	3.5
1990	2.5
1991	2.3
1992	2.9
1993	2.7
1994	2.7
1995	2.8
1996	2.5
1997	2.6
1998	1.9
1999	3.1
2000	5.1
2001	2.9
2002	3.0

The break points for the preceding strategy are updated daily on the zacksadvisor.com website (as explained in Appendix I), but looking at historical values, the threshold level averages around 3%. This means, for the most part, that you want the consensus earnings estimate for the coming year to increase by at least 3% over the past thirty days.

KEY POINT   Generally, you want to buy stocks for which the change in the current year's consensus earnings estimate over the past thirty days is at least 3%.

So far, so good; it looks like AZO is a potential buy candidate. But before you buy, there are a couple of things you must check for, which brings us to step five.

Step Five: Before Buying a Stock, Make Sure the Earnings Estimate Revisions Are Not Due to Accounting Gimmickry or an Acquisition

Before you pull the trigger and buy AZO, you want to make sure that the earnings estimate revisions are "organic." No, you do not have to make sure the earnings estimate revisions are available at your local vegetarian restaurant. Rather, organic earnings estimate revisions are those that are due to top-line revenue growth. This means that analysts project the company to grow both revenues and earnings.

Making sure the earnings estimate revisions are organic signifies that the company's core business is growing, as opposed to the company simply playing financial games, such as when earnings estimate revisions are due to accounting changes or, in some cases, acquisitions.

The best way to ensure that earnings estimate revisions are organic is to identify which analysts are responsible for raising earnings estimates, then actually obtain the research reports written by these analysts.

KEY POINT   Before buying the stock and committing hundreds if not thousands of dollars to a position, you should obtain a couple of the analysts' recent research reports and make sure that earnings estimates were revised upward because business prospects and top-line revenue are improving. Avoid stocks that analysts raised earnings estimates on simply for accounting reasons.

By reading analysts' research reports, it will be apparent whether the estimate revisions are due to changes in top-line revenue growth or not. In this case, I pulled a research report for Autozone written by SunTrust Robinson Humphrey, which reads as follows:

> AZO delivered another impressive quarter, showing significant upside to estimates driven by gross margin expansion, *commercial comps driving top line,* and share repurchase.[2] (emphasis added)

Another report, written by Morgan Stanley, yields similar information, as follows:

> We are raising our FY 2003 EPS estimate from $4.24 to $4.80
> due to our expectation of *slightly faster sales growth,* additional store
> openings and continued margin expansion.[3] (emphasis added)

As you can see, the research report indicates that the upward earnings estimate revisions are due to greater than previously expected organic top-line growth—thus AZO is a go.

The next step is determining when to sell AZO.

Step Six—Know When to Sell

In an estimate revision strategy you purchase stocks because you anticipate that the stock that you are buying will receive upward earnings estimate revisions by analysts in the immediate future and you expect the stock to be strong in the immediate future as large institutions react to the recent earnings estimate revisions. But, once you have bought a stock like AZO, you need to know when to sell.

The short answer: You want to sell once it becomes clear that analysts are not going to raise earnings estimates further. There are two sure-fire signs to look out for that indicate analysts are not going to raise their earnings estimates in the future:

- Analysts are actually lowering their earnings estimates.

- The company reports earnings weaker than what analysts are expecting or issues negative guidance.

If you are not tracking analysts' individual earnings estimate revisions, the best way to determine whether a stock has received downward earnings estimate revisions is to focus on changes to the consensus earnings estimate over time. If the consensus earnings estimate for the current fiscal year falls below the level it was at when you bought the stocks, you should sell.

KEY POINT   As a general rule of thumb, you should sell a stock if the consensus earnings estimate for the current fiscal year has fallen over the past thirty days.

You must be wary, though, of transaction costs. Because the earnings estimate revision strategy that I outline here will result in an above-average amount of trading, the strategy will generate a high level of commissions. These commissions can be a real killer if not managed properly.

For this reason, it pays to have your account at a deep discount brokerage firm. Only trade through a full-service brokerage firm if you have negotiated a flat fee (something that is usually associated with a "wrap account," where you pay the brokerage firm a fixed percentage of the assets you have with the firm, and all brokerage transactions are included).

What Else to Watch For?

In addition to calculating the percentage change over the past month in the consensus earnings estimate—as suggested in the previous steps—you should also be on the look-out for stocks for which the most recent analysts' earnings estimates are above the consensus earnings estimate.

It is generally a bullish signal if the most recent analysts' earnings estimates are above the consensus estimate, while it is a bearish sign if the most recent analysts' earnings estimates are less than the consensus estimate.

These are the two ways to determine where the most recent analysts' earnings estimates are relative to the consensus earnings estimates:

- Examine a table that includes a 30-day consensus estimate.

- Examine a graphical representation of earnings estimates: a histogram.

Let's go over examples of both.

The 30-Day Consensus Estimate

Figure 5-5 shows the detailed earnings estimates for Allstate (ALL) as of mid-December 2002, as taken from the Zacks.com free website. From the data in Figure 5-5, you can determine where the most recent analysts' earnings estimates are relative to the standard consensus.

Figure 5-5 Zacks detailed analyst estimates for: Allstate.

Ticker Symbol: ALL | Cusip: 020002101 | Fiscal Year End: December
Updated: 12/10/02

Broker	Recommendation	Fiscal Year EPS Estimates 12/02	12/03	Quarter EPS Estimates 12/02	03/03	5 year Growth Est(%)	Estimate Date
Insttn'l Broker	1.0 Strong Buy	2.81	3.10	0.76	—	10.00	11/29/02
Regional Broker	2.0 Moderate Buy	2.80	3.35	0.63	0.77	—	11/27/02
Insttn'l Broker	3.0 Hold	2.95	3.40	0.77	—	12.00	11/20/02
Insttn'l Broker	3.0 Hold	2.81	3.30	0.76	—	10.00	11/14/02
Regional Broker	3.0 Hold	2.84	3.40	0.79	—	12.00	11/14/02
Regional Broker	1.0 Strong Buy	2.86	3.35	0.81	—	9.00	11/14/02
National Broker	3.0 Hold	2.80	—	0.72	—	10.00	11/13/02
Regional Broker	6.0 N/A	2.90	2.95	—	—	—	11/08/02
Regional Broker	1.0 Strong Buy	2.85	3.35	—	—	—	11/08/02
National Broker	5.0 Strong Sell	2.75	3.15	—	—	9.00	11/07/02
Regional Broker	3.0 Hold	2.90	3.15	—	—	—	10/21/02
Regional Broker	1.0 Strong Buy	3.00	3.50	—	—	—	10/18/02
Regional Broker	3.0 Hold	2.94	3.33	—	—	—	10/17/02
Regional Broker	2.0 Moderate Buy	2.75	3.25	—	—	10.00	10/08/02

30-Day Consensus

Low Estimate	2.80	3.10	0.63	0.77	9.00	
*Mean / Consensus Estimate	2.85	3.32	0.75	0.77	10.50	
High Estimate	2.95	3.40	0.81	0.77	12.00	
Number of Estimates	10	6	7	1	6	

Broker	Recommendation	Fiscal Year EPS Estimates 12/02 12/03		Quarter EPS Estimates 12/02 03/03		5 year Growth Est(%)	Estimate Date
120-Day Consensus (All Estimates)							
Low Estimate		2.75	2.95	0.63	0.70	7.00	
*Mean / Consensus Estimate		2.85	3.26	0.72	0.74	10.090	
High Estimate		3.00	3.50	0.81	0.77	12.00	
Number of Estimates		19	18	11	2	11	

Total Number of Reporting Brokers: 19

NOTE: Earnings estimates are for diluted earnings per share from continuing operations before extraordinary earnings adjustments & discontinued operations.

NOTE: Quarterly estimates roll over 45 days after the quarter. Fiscal year estimates roll over 60 days after the fiscal year.

In analyzing Figure 5-5, the focus should be on earnings estimates for 12/03. This is because the detailed estimates for Allstate (ALL) is as of December 10, 2002, and the fiscal year ending December of 2002 is only half a month away. For the fiscal year ending December 2003, there are eighteen analysts issuing earnings estimates for Allstate (ALL).

For the 2003 fiscal year, the analysts' earnings estimates range from a low of $2.95 per share to a high of $3.50, with the average or consensus at $3.26 per share.

In Figure 5-5, two types of consensus earnings estimates are displayed: the "standard" or "full" consensus estimate (a standard Zacks created) and the 30-day consensus estimate.

The difference between the two is straightforward. The standard consensus contains all the individual analyst earnings estimates issued within the last 120 trading days while the 30-day consensus consists of all the individual analyst earnings estimates issued in the last 30 trading days.

For Allstate, of the eighteen analysts issuing earnings estimates for 2003, six of them have issued earnings estimates within the last thirty days, with the average of all earnings estimates issued being $3.32 per share. This is higher than the standard consensus, consisting of all eighteen analysts, of $3.26.

When the 30-day consensus estimate is higher than the standard consensus, it is usually a bullish sign. Not only does it mean that the most recent analysts' earnings estimates are coming in above older projections, it is a signal that these older estimates are likely to be revised higher in the immediate future.

In this example, the consensus or average earnings estimate from the nine analysts issuing estimates within the last thirty days is $0.06 higher than the standard consensus. This is a bullish sign for Allstate.

KEY POINT   One means of determining whether analysts are raising their earnings estimates on a stock is to check if the 30-day consensus earnings estimate is greater than the standard consensus earnings estimate.

What Is an Earnings Estimate Histogram?

Another, more intuitive, means of determining how recent analysts' earnings estimates compare to the standard consensus earnings estimate is to look at what is called an earnings estimate histogram. These earnings estimate histograms are available for free from the Zacks.com website (see Appendix III on how to access them).

An earnings estimate histogram sounds sophisticated but it is really just a graphical representation of the values at which analysts are issuing their earnings estimates.

The histogram, as we will see in a moment, consists of a whole bunch of Xs and Os arranged along a horizontal line. Each X and O represents an individual analyst's earnings estimate. The Xs represent older analyst earnings estimates and the Os represent the three most recent analyst earnings estimates.

Figure 5-6, for instance, is the earnings estimate histogram of Coca-Cola Enterprise, a bottling company.

By looking at the histogram you get a very nice graphical representation of exactly where the most recent earnings estimates are relative to the analyst "herd."

When the Os are to the right of the Xs, it means that analysts are revising their earnings estimates upward. Conversely, when the Os are to the left of the Xs, it means that analysts are revising their earnings estimates downward. The histogram for CCE is bullish, as the most recent analysts' earnings estimates are coming in above the analyst herd for the fiscal year ending 12/02, and for the fiscal year ending 12/03 the highest earnings estimate is one of the most recent estimates.

KEY POINT   In using the earnings estimate histograms, you want to buy stocks when the Os are to the right of the Xs, and sell stocks when the Os are to the left of the Xs. The bigger the difference between the Os and the Xs, the more powerful the signal.

Figure 5-6 Distribution of EPS estimates histogram as of 10/20/02.

```
                    COCA-COLA ENTRP

        FY End - 12/02              FY End - 12/03
          15 ESTS.                    14 ESTS.




              0
       X X    0 X                X  0   X      0
       XX XX    XXX 0X0          XXOX  XXX X   X      0
       !-----!-----!-----!-----!     !-----!-----!-----!-----!
       0.92  0.97  1.02  1.07  1.12  1.09  1.14  1.19  1.24  1.29
       "X" = EPS ESTIMATE ($)        "0" =  MOST RECENT ESTS.
```

Figure 5-7 contains a bullish earnings estimate histogram for Aetna (AET).

Figure 5-8 contains a bearish earnings estimate histogram for Interpublic Group (IPG).

Figure 5-7 Distribution of EPS estimates histogram as of 10/20/02.

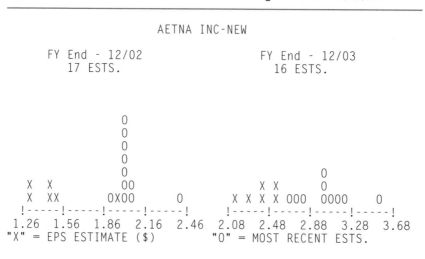

```
                        AETNA INC-NEW

        FY End - 12/02                  FY End - 12/03
           17 ESTS.                        16 ESTS.



                       0
                       0
                       0
                       0
                       0                          0
     X   X            00               X X        0
     X  XX          0X00         0     X X X X 000   0000      0
     !-----!-----!-----!-----!         !-----!-----!-----!-----!
     1.26  1.56  1.86  2.16  2.46      2.08  2.48  2.88  3.28  3.68
     "X" = EPS ESTIMATE ($)            "0" = MOST RECENT ESTS.
```

Figure 5-8 Distribution of EPS estimates histogram as of 10/20/02.

```
                       INTERPUBLIC GRP

        FY End - 12/02                  FY End - 12/03
           12 ESTS.                        11 ESTS.




     0
     0
     0
     0              X                       00
     XO         X X XX        X         0 00X    XX  X       XX
     !-----!-----!-----!-----!           !-----!-----!-----!-----!
     0.84  1.04  1.24  1.44  1.64       0.96  1.16  1.36  1.56  1.76
     "X" = EPS ESTIMATE ($)             "0" = MOST RECENT ESTS.
```

What Returns Can Be Expected from Focusing on Changes to the Consensus Earnings Estimate over Time?

As I have said before, there are roughly 3,300 stocks that have a market capitalization above $100 million and have at least one analyst who follows the stock and issues earnings estimates for the coming fiscal year.

At the end of each month from October 1987 to September 2002, in order to generate the returns included in Figure 5-9, we took all the stocks that were followed by at least one analyst and created three portfolios based on the degree to which the consensus earnings estimates changed over the past month.

- Portfolio #1 was made up of those stocks for which the consensus earnings estimate for the current year *fell* by over 1% during the last month.

- Portfolio #2 consisted of those stocks for which there was *no change* in the consensus earnings estimate over the last month.

- Portfolio #3 comprised those stocks for which the consensus earnings estimate for the current year *rose* by greater than 1% over the last month.

Here's how the study worked.

For each portfolio, an equal dollar amount was put into every stock and then the portfolio was held for the entire month. At the end of the month the percentage change in the consensus earnings estimate for each and every stock was measured.

Then the 3,300 stocks were sorted into the three portfolios and performance was measured for the next month. This process was repeated every month for a full fifteen years.

What did the study find? The results are given in Figure 5-9.

KEY POINT   An analysis of the data clearly shows that a portfolio consisting of stocks whose consensus earnings estimate for the current year has increased over the past month substantially outperforms over time.

Portfolio #1, which contained those stocks for which analysts lowered their earnings estimates over the previous month, rose at an

Figure 5-9 Annualized return based on change in consensus earnings estimate over the past month (October 1987 to September 2002).

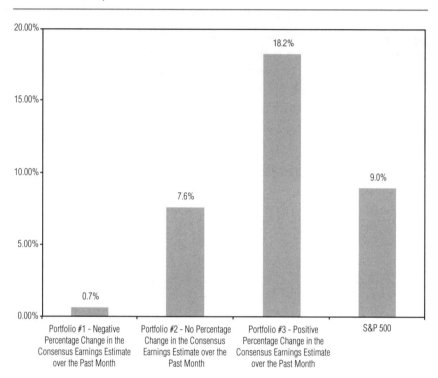

annualized average rate of only 0.7% per year over the fifteen-year time period.

On the other hand, Portfolio #3, which contained those stocks for which analysts raised their earnings estimates the greatest degree, climbed at an annualized average rate of 18.2% per year over that same time period. Portfolio #3 significantly outperformed Portfolio #2, which consisted of those stocks for which analysts did not substantially change their earnings estimates at all over the past month, as well as the S&P 500, which rose at an annualized rate of roughly 9% per year over the past fifteen years.

These annualized returns do not factor in transaction costs, which would be substantial in this case. Nevertheless, the results are quite compelling: *Basically, stocks that receive upward earnings estimate revisions tend to substantially outperform over time.*

When Wouldn't Prices Respond to Estimate Revisions?

One final thought about an earnings estimate revision strategy.

I do not want you to think that focusing on earnings estimate revisions is some panacea. True, the majority of the time, upward revisions to analysts' earnings estimates result in an increasing stock price. However, there are some periods in which earnings estimates being revised upward will not result in a stock's price going higher.

Our historical analysis at Zacks shows that these periods coincide with broad economic shocks and periods, such as the recent tech bubble, in which price movements become driven by concerns other than earnings.

The reason that earnings estimate revisions do not work when the market is seized by manias is fairly self-evident. When investors take leave of their senses, they tend to ignore earnings and fundamentals, and as a result, what comes to dominate a stock's price is how the stock is related to whatever is driving the bubble. In the 1998–2000 period several large but relatively simple industrial stocks that received downward earnings estimate revisions soared in price because they announced they were going to create some sort of Internet-based purchasing platform.

It takes a little bit more explanation to understand the effect of economic cycles on earnings estimate revision strategies.

When the economy is exiting a recessionary environment, immediate future earnings—that is, earnings that are going to be reported in the coming fiscal year—are not nearly as important in determining the price of a stock as the earnings that a company will generate once a full economic recovery is underway.

When exiting a recession, investors actually start buying companies that receive downward earnings estimate revisions with the anticipation that these companies will benefit the most from an anticipated economic recovery. In this kind of economic environment, stock prices respond to anticipated major macroeconomic changes before analysts revise earnings estimates.

KEY POINT   An earnings estimate revision strategy works best when investors are focused on corporations' near-term earnings prospects. In periods in which stock price movement is being driven by other broad factors and investors seem to be ignoring earnings, the performance of an estimate revision strategy weakens.

Cyclical and Non-cyclical Stocks

A cyclical stock is a stock that tends to generate high earnings in periods of economic expansion, and tends to be hit very hard in periods of economic contraction. A standard cyclical stock would be an automobile company such as Ford or GM. When the economy is booming, people buy new cars. When we are in a recession, people try to keep the old car running for as long as they can.

A non-cyclical stock is a stock that produces earnings regardless of the economic environment. A good example would be a drug company like Merck. Good economic times or bad, people who need to have a prescription filled go ahead and fill them.

When the economy is actually in a recession, the stocks that receive upward earnings estimate revisions tend to be the non-cyclical stocks and stocks that are in a niche market that is shielded by the broad economic slowdown. During a recession, cyclical stocks for the most part tend to receive downward earnings estimate revisions.

However, when the economy is exiting a recession, investors will actually buy cyclical companies that are getting their earnings estimates cut. The reason for this is that cyclical companies are poised to benefit the greatest from an economic turnaround. Think of it this way: When the economy recovers, Ford benefits more than Merck.

Thus, it is not always the case that prices respond to earnings estimate revisions. But the majority of the time, if earnings estimates are revised upward, the price of the stock should immediately respond positively.

Using Earnings Estimate Revisions to Manage Your Portfolio

Focusing on revisions to analysts' earnings estimates is clearly the best use of analyst data.

Most importantly, a portfolio run using upward earnings estimate revisions outperformed the S&P 500 over the last fifteen years.

This is because of the two important facts previously mentioned, namely:

- Stocks that receive upward earnings estimate revisions are more likely to receive upward earnings estimate revisions in the future.

- Stocks that receive upward earnings estimate revisions are those that are in the process of actively being bought by institutional portfolio managers. There is usually a slight delay between the upward earnings estimate revisions and the price movement.

Because of these two facts, stocks that have been receiving upward earnings estimate revisions tend to outperform over the next ninety days.

You may want to use earnings estimate revisions to select stocks to buy as part of your investment strategy, or you may want to manage your entire portfolio using earning estimate revisions as the primary decision-making factor.

There are clear advantages to running a portfolio focused on revisions to analysts' earnings estimates.

With an estimate revision portfolio strategy, the only thing that matters is earnings. Specifically, by owning stocks that are receiving upward earnings estimate revisions you will own stocks whose earnings prospects are improving. Over time this focus on fundamentals will cause your portfolio to outperform.

By following an estimate-revision-driven strategy, wherever analysts are actively raising earnings estimates will determine which sectors and investment styles are over-weighted in your portfolio.

If technology companies are receiving the lion's share of upward earnings estimate revisions, tech companies are going to be over-weighted in your portfolio. Similarly, if retailers are receiving upward estimate revisions, retailers will be over-weighted. The same reasoning holds for style exposure. When analysts are raising earnings estimates on value stocks, an estimate-revision-driven portfolio will over-weight value; when analysts are raising earnings estimates on growth stocks, growth will be over-weighted.

Figure 5-10 shows the advantages of running a portfolio focused on revisions to analysts' earnings estimates. In this figure, a "Y" in a given year indicates when Portfolio #3 from Figure 5-9—which consisted of all those stocks that experienced an increase in their consensus earnings estimate over the past month—outperformed the S&P 500.

However, an estimate-revision-driven strategy is not without flaws. The biggest drawback of an estimate-revision-driven strategy is that stocks that have been receiving upward earnings estimate revisions often tend to be hit slightly harder than the broad market in periods of tremendous selling pressure, such as the 1987 crash and the 1998 Asian meltdown.

Figure 5-10 Portfolio #3 performance compared to S&P 500.

Year	Estimate Revision Portfolio #3 Outperformed the S&P 500
1988	Y
1989	Y
1990	N
1991	Y
1992	Y
1993	Y
1994	Y
1995	Y
1996	Y
1997	Y
1998	N
1999	Y
2000	Y
2001	Y
2002	Y

The explanation is straightforward.

A strategy based on buying stocks that are receiving upward earnings estimate revisions depends on institutional investors becoming more attracted to a stock when analysts raise their earnings estimates. During market sell-offs, institutional investors are generally not reacting to earnings estimate revisions, but are instead selling based on changing investor sentiment and even fear. Investors are, for the most part, selling across the board.

In these periods of broad-based selling, large-cap stocks tend to hold up better then stocks that are receiving upward earnings estimate revisions.

Figure 5-11 tells the whole story.

Figure 5-11 Ten worst months for the S&P 500 and how a portfolio that contains stocks that have been receiving upward earnings estimate revisions performed.

	Month	Rebalanced Monthly	S&P 500
1	Oct-87	−26.1	−21.5
2	Aug-98	−19.3	−14.5
3	Sep-02	−7.9	−10.9
4	Feb-01	−9.2	−9.1
5	Aug-90	−10.9	−9.0
6	Nov-87	−5.0	−8.2
7	Sep-01	−13.7	−8.1
8	Nov-00	−14.8	−7.9
9	Jul-02	−12.5	−7.8
10	Jun-02	−6.0	−7.1
Average		**−12.5**	**−10.4**

Summary

- You want to buy stocks for which the consensus earnings estimate for the current fiscal year has increased by more than 3% over the past thirty days.

- The greater the percentage change in the consensus earnings estimate over the last thirty days, the stronger the "buy" signal.

- You also want to buy stocks where the most recent analysts' earnings estimates are coming in above the consensus—these are stocks whose earnings estimate histograms have the Os to the right of the Xs.

- Try to buy stocks that are growing earnings by organic top-line revenue growth, and avoid stocks whose earnings estimates have increased due to accounting changes.

- Avoid stocks that are projected by analysts to lose money on a per-share basis in the coming and next fiscal years.

- If the consensus earnings estimate of a stock that you purchased falls, you should sell the stock.

- A portfolio focused on revisions to analysts' earnings estimates will substantially outperform the market over time, but not automatically every month. The key is to not abandon the estimate-revision discipline in tumultuous times or because of poor relative return in a given month.

Endnotes

[1] CC should always be positive, especially if following step one. If MAC is negative, the denominator should be the absolute value of MAC. For example, if MAC is −0.30, you should use +0.30 in the denominator.

[2] SunTrust Robinson Humphrey, September 25, 2002, Research Report, "AZO: Impressive Quarter, Impressive Story."

[3] Morgan Stanley, September 25, 2002, Research Report, "Analysis of Sales/Earnings, Autozone, Inc."

Chapter Six

The Earnings Surprise

What's ahead in this chapter?

■ What Exactly Is an Earnings Surprise?

■ Why Do Some Earnings Surprises Surprise More than Others?

■ Three Questions to Answer When a Company Reports Earnings in Order to Determine What the Price Response Will Be

■ Five Games Companies Play with Their Earnings Reports—and What You Can Do about Them

What Exactly Is an Earnings Surprise?

IN THE PREVIOUS TWO CHAPTERS, I examined how you can use revisions to analysts' earnings estimates to invest profitably. In this chapter, the focus turns toward another use of analysts' earnings estimates: the "earnings surprise."

"Earnings surprise" is a term coined by Zacks in 1982. It may sound exotic, but the idea basically boils down to a measure of how well a company is performing against Wall Street analysts' expectations. Essentially, earnings surprises are the means by which investors determine whether a company had a good or a bad quarter—a financial report card, if you will.

When a company reports earnings that are better than the quarterly consensus earnings estimate, it is called a positive earnings surprise, and when a company reports earnings that are worse or lower than the quarterly consensus earnings estimate, it is a negative surprise.

For the most part, if a company delivers earnings better than what analysts expected, investors rush to buy. The company's stock is "blessed by the market." The surprise has been a good one.

If, however, a company reports earnings less than what analysts expected, the company's stock is taken out to the wood-shed and unceremoniously shot for surprising in a negative way.

Why Does this Happen?

Practically all stocks that are publicly traded are required by law to issue a financial report to shareholders at the end of each and every fiscal quarter. This report is called a 10-Q.

Unlike newspaper stories, magazine articles, interviews with cable journalists, rumors, message board postings, and all the other baloney you may hear from stockbrokers of all types concerning "hot stocks to buy," the 10-Q, along with a company's annual report, is required by the SEC to be accurate.

If the reports are inaccurate, or if the reports contain fraudulent or misleading statements, the men in black at the SEC are likely to get involved. Fines and potentially jail time for a company's officers are possible.

The recent SEC regulations that require the corporate executives of America's largest companies to sign documents testifying to the veracity of their 10-Qs illustrates how important these documents are to the market. Although many individual investors rarely look at a 10-Q, if they are fraudulent—as was the case with WorldCom and Enron—the market can not properly function.

Before the actual 10-Q is issued, most companies send out a press release that contains the major points within the 10-Q, including what the company earned on a per-share basis.

Sometimes, the press release also includes statements regarding what the company expects to earn in the coming quarter or perhaps even in the coming fiscal year. These press releases are also required by law to be accurate.

It is when the press release is distributed that a company effectively "announces its earnings." The press release provides the "actual earnings" Zacks uses to calculate the earnings surprise.

Then, all hell breaks loose.

News That Moves Markets

Why do earnings reports cause such a stir?

The answer is "greed"—in the nicest sense of the word.

Investors intensely analyze the corporate earnings announcement with an eye toward answering the simple question: Will the company's stock price move up or down based on the information contained in the report?

Well, naturally, if the information is good, the stock's price should move up, and if the information is bad, the company's stock's price should move down.

The next logical question is: How do you determine if the information is good or bad?

That, too, is pretty straightforward. If IBM's earnings report leads you to believe that IBM is going to be earning more in the future than investors had previously expected, this is good news and IBM's stock price should rise. Conversely, if earnings are going to be less than expected, this is bad news and IBM's stock price should fall.

That makes perfect sense, but there is a problem: How do you know how much a company should earn?

The answer is, of course, you can't.

Well, suppose you really wanted to. You would go to the people who truly determine the price of a stock, the institutional investors. But this is impossible to do because the expectations of institutional investors are private and not available to the public.

Besides, in theory, investors' expectations are already built into a stock's price. IBM's stock price has either been going up, in anticipation of higher future earnings (remember the discussion of Mr. Hooper and the Qwik-E-Mart), or it's been declining because investors expect lower earnings.

So the question remains: If IBM earned $1.50 per share this quarter, how do you determine whether this is better or worse than what investors expected?

Measuring Investors' Earnings Expectations: The Story of Zacks and the Quarterly Consensus Earnings Estimate

Prior to Zacks' existence, investors used historical earnings to determine what a company was expected to earn in the future. Most investors prior to the early 1980s examined what a company had earned historically and how those earnings had grown over time; from that data a forecast of future earnings was calculated, and this was called trend-line analysis. As a result, academics coined the term standardized unexpected earnings (SUE), which essentially compared what a company actually reported as earnings to what was predicted through trend-line analysis. Huge variations in SUE values were common, mainly because trend-line expectations were often inaccurate.

When Zacks first started in 1980, we realized almost immediately that the SUE was not an accurate way of measuring whether reported earnings met investors' expectations.

In order to effectively evaluate quarterly earnings reports, we needed a way to figure out what investors expected a stock to earn. The breakthrough that led to the development of the quarterly earnings surprise was the realization that the quarterly consensus earnings estimate that Zacks created was a better proxy for investors' earnings expectations than trend-line analysis.

The key to solving the problem was the analyst data that we were already collecting. While individual and institutional investors' earnings expectations can not be easily measured, analysts' earnings expectations can.

And it turned out that the analysts' expectations served as a terrific surrogate for the market's expectations as a whole.

Once we know what the market expects, it is easy to discover when it is surprised.

KEY POINT   The quarterly consensus earnings estimate serves as a proxy for investors' earnings expectations. When a company reports earnings better than the consensus earnings estimate, it is considered a positive earnings surprise, because the company reported earnings better than what investors expected.

Looking at the Earnings Surprise in More Detail

So what is this earnings surprise about? And why is it important?

The quantitative value of the earnings surprise is calculated in the following way:

$$\frac{(\text{actual earnings} - \text{analysts' expectations})}{(\text{absolute value of analysts' expectations})}$$

Thus, if the quarterly consensus earnings estimate is $1.00, and the company actually reports earnings of $1.20, it is a ($1.20 – $1.00)/$1.00 or 20% upward earnings surprise. If analysts expect a loss of $0.25 a share and earnings come in at a loss of $0.30, then the earnings surprise is (–0.30 – (–0.25))/0.25, or a negative earnings surprise of 20%.

The magnitude of the surprise is as important as whether the surprise is positive or negative. A negative surprise is a big red mark against a company and the larger the magnitude, generally the larger the impact on a stock's price.

A company which analysts expect to earn $0.50 per share that reports a positive earnings surprise of $0.05 per share—that is, it reported earnings of $0.55, instead of the expected $0.50—can see its stock price increase far greater than that nickel a share. In fact, it is not uncommon for a $30 growth stock to see its price rise by $5 or even $10 on a better-than-expected earnings report.

Why Do Companies' Stock Prices React So Strongly to Earnings Surprises?

An earnings surprise is essentially a signal about what future earnings per share (EPS) are going to look like. If a company's earnings report leads market participants to believe the company is going to earn more on a per-share basis in future quarters than previously expected, the company's stock price should rise. If, however, the earnings report leads people to believe that the company is going to earn less than expected in the months ahead, then the company's stock price should fall.

The reason that stock prices react so dramatically to earnings reports that are above analysts' expectations is clear: When a company beats analysts' expectations, it effectively signals that earnings are going to be higher than expected not only in the current quarter, but also in future quarters. The converse also holds true: When a company misses earnings estimates, it effectively signals that earnings are likely to be lower than expected not only in the current quarter, but also in future quarters.

It is not the extra $0.05 per share that gets investors excited about an earnings surprise. Rather, it is what the extra $0.05 says about the future earnings prospects of a company that excites investors and gets a stock moving.

KEY POINT   What an earnings surprise signals about a company's future earnings prospects determines whether the earnings surprise will cause a stock's price to fall or rise.

Why Do Some Earnings Surprises Surprise More than Others?

Let's look at an example to see how all this plays out in practice.

Way back in January of 2000, Motorola (MOT) reported earnings of $0.82 per share, beating analysts' expectations by a penny and registering a 1.23% positive earnings surprise.

But Motorola's stock promptly sold off, falling $2.50 per share to $48.

The behavior of Motorola is slightly uncommon but not unheard of, and the incident demonstrates the need to ask three fundamental questions whenever a company reports earnings better than expectations.

KEY POINT   For the most part, stocks that report positive earnings surprises trade up on the news, but this is not always the case. Sometimes, it is possible for a stock to weaken on a positive earnings surprise.

Three Questions to Answer When a Company Reports Earnings in Order to Determine What the Price Response Will Be

Question One: What Is the Quality of the Earnings?

You need to determine whether a company beat the consensus earnings estimate through top-line revenue growth or through cost savings and/or acquisitions.

Earnings surprises due to revenue growth tend to elicit the strongest price response in the market. That is, if analysts expect a company to record quarterly sales of $1 billion, and it reports sales of $1.1 billion, which signifies a corresponding 10% Sales Surprise™, the effect on the stock price will almost always be dramatic and positive. This is especially true for growth stocks, since the majority of a growth company's value comes from earnings that are supposed to materialize several years in the future, following rapid sales growth.

In evaluating the quality of a company's reported earnings it is also important to determine exactly where the earnings derive from. Are the earnings due to continuing sales of core products, or do they stem from an ancillary business, like venture capital investments?

The stock of a company that beats earnings expectations by cutting costs will often not react as strongly to a positive earnings surprise as a company that beats expectations due to revenue growth.

Revenue growth is more sustainable over time than cost cutting. Think of earnings gains from cost-cutting like squeezing a water-drenched rag. After several quarters of squeezing, the rag is dry. Earnings surprises that are accomplished through revenue growth are therefore of a higher quality.

Question Two: What Is the Company's View of the Future?

An important question that an earnings report answers for investors is what the future earnings prospects look like for a company. Stock prices are always determined by what earnings are expected to materialize in the future.

If a company reported relatively good earnings for the past three months or even the past three quarters, but indicated that earnings will be unexpectedly weak for several quarters ahead, the company's stock price will fall.

Lots of companies employ a tactic of trying to lessen the impact of expected poor earnings in the future by bundling a negative earnings guidance announcement with a positive earnings report. In such cases, the stock almost always trades down, regardless of the positive earnings surprise.

You should realize that in these instances, the forward guidance always trumps the reported earnings.

It is important to remember that the market is ultimately forward-looking. It doesn't care about historical earnings. That's why when a company reports that earnings for the past quarter were good, but that the future earnings prospects do not look great, the market ignores the good earnings report and the stock almost always falls.

Question Three: Does the Earnings Report Represent New Information?

Try to determine whether the market "expected" a positive earnings surprise or if word of the positive earnings leaked out. Either or both will lessen the impact of a positive earnings surprise.

Whether the market expected a positive earnings surprise mostly has to do with the earnings of other companies in the same industry. If comparable companies have reported stellar earnings, the market is likely also expecting a positive earnings surprise for the company in question.

On the other hand, if the company's reported earnings move contrary to the industry trend—either up or down—the stock price response will be even more dramatic.

For instance, up until March of 2000 most investment banks and brokerages were recording their best earnings ever, so it was expected that a brokerage firm reporting earnings would report a positive surprise. If a brokerage firm were to report earnings at expectations for the quarter ending March of 2000, the brokerage firm's stock would quickly sell off.

Additionally, as I will show you in the next chapter, the market sometimes comes to expect that a company that has a history of beating analysts' expectations will continue to beat analysts' expectations in the future. In such instances, the company may report good earnings, yet the company's stock price may not respond. The reason is that the market expected the company to beat expectations. Such companies often tend to trade at very high valuation levels and can even prove to be somewhat dangerous, as the company must continue to beat earnings expectations simply for the company's stock prices to stay around current levels.

It is also important to realize that earnings information is often leaked to the market. This is illegal but not as uncommon as you might think. The leakage is very hard to prove, and sometimes the fact that a company is going to miss analysts' expectations can be conveyed simply by a roll of the eyes of management to investors. Although it is hard to prove, you should be aware that when information is leaked to the market, the price response to an earnings surprise is significantly lessened.

For this reason, if a stock has run up significantly in price prior to an earnings report, it may indicate that good news has leaked and the stock's price response to any positive earnings surprise will be somewhat muted.

So, What Happened to Motorola?

This brings us back to Motorola. The reason Motorola's stock price fell on a good earnings report most likely had to do with the fact that earlier in the month Intel reported stellar earnings, and the market expected Motorola to report stellar earnings as well. In fact, the day Intel reported their earnings, Motorola's price shot up almost 9.4% to $51. The move was not because Intel's and Motorola's business lines are so similar—rather, the Intel report was taken as a sign that the economy was strong and that tech spending was fairly strong as well. Essentially, Intel served as a tech bellwether and because of Intel, the market was already pricing in a great earnings report from Motorola, even though the companies are in very different businesses.

But a positive earnings surprise of 1.23% is not considered that great, and as a result, the stock sold off.

Additionally, although Motorola management indicated it was comfortable with a sales growth rate of 12% to 13%, concerns about gross margins and component shortages for wireless phones worried investors. Thus, Motorola hinted that going forward, things were not looking entirely rosy.

Therefore, Motorola's price was hit because the reported earnings did not live up to the enhanced expectations created by Intel's strong report, and because of investors' worries about what would happen in the future.

Five Games Companies Play with Their Earnings Reports—and What You Can Do about Them

Game One: Firms Guide Analysts' Earnings Estimates Low in Order to Beat Expectations

When you hear talk on a cable finance show or read in *The Wall Street Journal* about a company meeting or beating expectations, the discussion always refers to the consensus earnings estimate.

As I have noted, a public company's stock is usually punished if it misses earnings expectations without warning the market first. And even if the company does warn, things aren't much prettier. Over the years, companies have learned that the key to avoiding a slaughter is to simply beat analysts' expectations every quarter. One way to do this is to execute well—to sell more couches, semiconductors, or software packages, or win more accounts while keeping a handle on costs. But that is hard to do, and Wall Street remains unrelenting—continually demanding that a company report earnings better than analysts' expectations quarter after quarter.

As a result of the pressure from Wall Street to beat analysts' earnings expectations, many firms have started to play a game. The game is simply to always keep analysts' expectations low.

In other words, the key from the company's perspective is to underpromise and over-deliver. Not just for one quarter, but all the time.

Companies have been doing this for years. One tactic they employ is to first warn the market about potential problems, causing analysts to lower their expectations, and then report earnings that are better than analysts' lowered earnings estimates, estimates that were lowered in light of the warning.

When the company reports earnings, at first glance it looks as if the company has produced a positive earnings surprise. But a little digging reveals that the positive surprise occurred only because analysts drastically lowered their earnings estimates after the warning.

The practice of keeping analysts' earnings estimates low in order to report a positive earnings surprise has become very common over the past few years.

The best way to realize how prevalent this practice has become is to examine Figure 6-1. Figure 6-1 shows the percentage of earnings surprises that have been positive over the last twelve years. Notice that the percentage of positive earnings surprises has climbed dramatically and remains relatively high even in the face of a deteriorating economic environment.

There are two possible explanations for the rising number of positive earnings surprises. Companies are either truly generating earnings stronger than investors' expectations, which is unlikely given the performance of the S&P 500 over the past several years, or companies are doing a much better job of managing analysts' expectations.

One way to determine whether a company is guiding earnings expectations lower is to note if the company has reported a string of positive earnings surprises while the stock's price has continued to generally drift downward.

Figure 6-1 Percentage of companies reporting positive earnings surprises (1990 to 2002).

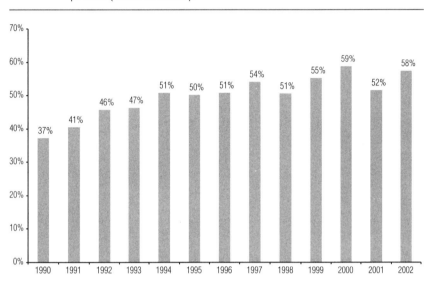

What do you do if a company is playing this game?

Very simply, you should discount the fact that the company beat the lower analysts' expectations, and as a rule stay away from such companies. There is little benefit to buying a stock that beats analysts' earnings expectations by simply keeping analysts' expectations continually low.

KEY POINT   When investigating a positive earnings surprise, always try to determine whether the positive earnings surprise followed on the heels of an earnings warning. In such cases, the firm is likely managing analysts' expectations in order to report a positive surprise and the positive surprise should be discounted.

Game Two: Firms Make Extensive Use of Legal Book-Cooking through Non-recurring Charges

Corporate America sometimes plays a game with investors that's just about as bad as those three-card monty games you can sometimes find on the subway or city street. But in this case, the game goes by the highbrow name of a "non-recurring" charge.

As noted previously, companies want to report earnings that exceed analysts' expectations because if they do, their share price usually rises.

The game revolves around the way analysts issue their earnings estimates. In preparing them, analysts traditionally estimate earnings per share (EPS) from continuing operations and try to exclude extraordinary and one-time items such as merger-related expenses, legal settlements, and even layoff expenses. Excluding non-recurring items has always struck me as the right approach.

Here's why.

Imagine you won the lottery and wanted to buy the local grocery store. Like any good investor, you'd ask to see the store's books. After a quick examination, you realize that because of an explosion at the nearby electricity plant, the grocery store had to write off all the milk and dairy products it had recently purchased because they spoiled during the power outage that followed the explosion.

In determining how much you would pay for the grocery store, you would probably adjust the grocery store's earnings in order to determine the profit that you would have realized if the milk had not gone rancid.

But it would not make sense to substantially decrease the value you were willing to pay for the grocery store due to the loss from the rancid milk, because the electrical problems were likely a one-time occurrence. If you buy the store, you do not expect the local electricity plant to explode on a regular basis.

Over the years companies have come to realize that analysts, and even investors to some extent, will discount or ignore poor earnings if they can be disguised as due to one-time, or non-recurring, charges.

What does this mean?

Effectively, companies who would otherwise report weak results can camouflage those weak results by attributing them to one-time charges.

By recording a non-recurring charge, the earnings reported from continuing operations will be artificially boosted higher.

Here's an example of how this game plays out.

Say a company is expected to earn $0.10 per share this quarter. A couple of days before issuing the press release detailing earnings, the CFO runs into the CEO's office and announces that it looks like earnings are actually going to come in at $0.09 per share and the company is going to miss analysts' expectations.

Instead of reporting a negative earnings surprise and watching the share price tank, the CFO proposes reporting earnings of $0.11 per share, while simultaneously announcing a one time non-recurring expense of $0.02.

The net result? The company beats expectations.

Nothing illegal is done. All that happens is that certain expenses are classified as non-recurring as opposed to continuing, and as a result—lo and behold—the company exceeds expectations.

It's a neat trick, and one that more and more companies are using in an effort not to disappoint Wall Street. For the quarter ending 12/01, slightly over 35% of the 1,000 largest companies reported non-recurring charges, while for the same quarter ending 12/97, the percentage was around 17%. Figure 6-2 shows the number of companies out of the 1,000 largest companies that reported a non-recurring charge in at least one quarter of the indicated fiscal year.

And if you dig deeper, what you find is that there are certain companies—large, well-known, respected companies—that report non-recurring charges almost every quarter.

Figure 6-2 Number of the 1,000 largest companies by market capitalization that reported a non-recurring charge for the given quarter.

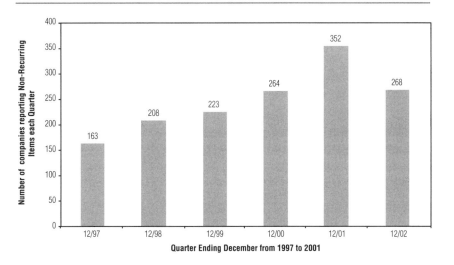

Figure 6-3 provides a sample list of these serial offenders. What is interesting is that many of them are technology companies—the reason is simply that for tech companies, beating analysts expectations is of utmost importance because the value of a technology company's shares is largely dependent upon future earnings expectations.

In fact, over the past two years, 28 of the 1,000 largest firms reported non-recurring charges in every quarter; 29 companies took non-recurring charges in seven of the previous eight quarters; and 34 took them in six.

Non-recurring items are by no means trivial. Of the 28 companies reporting non-recurring charges in each of the past eight quarters, 15 posted charges equal to at least 4% of their revenue. And in some cases, it was even higher—the net result of non-recurring charges is that earnings from continuing operations are inflated and the company has a greater chance of meeting analysts' expectations and reporting a positive earnings surprise.

What do you do about it? Have a cynical attitude toward one-time expenses. Whenever you find a large one-time charge that a company has some discretion over—such as an inventory write-down (something we will talk about in a second)—as opposed to a mandated payment—such as a lawsuit settlement, which is dictated by a judge—a red flag should go up.

Also, companies that continually report non-recurring charges should be viewed with an extremely critical eye.

KEY POINT   Because analysts and investors tend to focus heavily on earnings from continuing operations, companies often try to disguise poor quarters by reporting non-recurring charges that effectively hide an earnings miss. Any company that meets or exceeds the consensus earnings estimate and at the same time reports a non-recurring charge should be treated as if it missed earnings expectations, regardless of the market's reaction to the earnings announcement.

Figure 6-3 For the 20 reported quarters from 6/97 to 3/02, the number of quarters in which the company reported a non-recurring expense.

Company	Ticker	
Cardinal Health	CAH	19
Bea Systems Inc	BEAS	18
Bmc Software	BMC	18
Cisco Systems	CSCO	17
Motorola Inc	MOT	17
Kroger Co	KR	17
Celestica Inc	CLS	17
Cadence Design	CDN	17
Omnicare Inc	OCR	17
Yahoo! Inc	YHOO	16
Lincoln Natl-In	LNC	16
Nortel Networks	NT	16
Network Assoc	NET	16
Verizon Comm	VZ	15
Chevrontexaco	CVX	15
Pharmacia Corp	PHA	15
Texas Instrs	TXN	15
Qualcomm Inc	QCOM	15
Hca Inc	HCA	15
Waste Mgmt-New	WMI	15
Newell Rubbermd	NWL	15
Williams Cos	WMB	15
Tmp Worldwide	TMPW	15
Compuware Corp	CPWR	15

Game Three: Firms Make Use of Cookie-Jar Accounting

Over the years, one of the tricks CFOs have resorted to in order to boost EPS by a couple of pennies is to take an inventory write-down or other impairment charge.

The CFO then uses the write-down to set up a cookie jar of earnings that can be dipped into for future quarters.

This accounting gimmick has no real effect on the firm's business, but if the game is played correctly, even professional investors can be duped.

It works this way: Let's say there is a fictitious large company that sells television sets called BigTvCo. BigTvCo announces that because of the lack of demand for high-definition television sets, BigTvCo will take a $1 billion-plus write-down. The problem is that because the high-definition TVs are not selling and because the technology used in creating the TVs is changing so rapidly, the television components BigTvCo uses to create the sets are effectively worthless.

This write-down essentially means BigTvCo is telling the market that management bought now worthless television component parts that have no use in making a product.

To go back to our grocery store example, BigTvCo, according to the accounting rules, is effectively telling the market that the milk in BigTvCo's store is rancid due to a once-in-a-blue-moon problem.

The write-down is considered an extraordinary item, and analysts don't include the loss in earnings estimates or in the valuation models they use to price BigTvCo's stock.

What a Surprise!

However, a couple months down the road, BigTvCo indicates that its inventory is not totally worthless after all and that a few high-definition TVs have been sold. How does it let us know? It sells the inventory that it had labeled, in essence, as spoiled milk.

BigTvCo realizes a huge accounting profit on these high-definition television sets that it sells, since the accounting cost of obtaining the television component parts was significantly reduced by the earlier write-down, and it looks like a good corporate citizen to boot. By writing down that inventory, BigTvCo appeared to be extremely conservative in its accounting. But the reality is that it wrote down the inventory so it could boost EPS in the future.

Now here comes the real kicker. Because of the way the accounting rules work, the souped-up profits recognized on sales that are associated with reduced-cost inventory are considered operating or core earnings and are thus included in analysts' earnings estimates, effectively boosting the earnings BigTvCo reports for the quarter. As a result, BigTvCo is guaranteed to add a couple cents to reported earnings next quarter.

Not only is BigTvCo not penalized for realizing a one-time loss, it is rewarded by beating analyst estimates (resulting in a higher share price).

In reality, however, the quality of BigTvCo's earnings may be lacking.

KEY POINT   Beware of write-downs that are used to stock a cookie jar so that a firm can effectively beat analysts' earnings expectations in the future.

The way to determine whether a corporation is playing this game is to read the earnings release and company's quarterly statements, as opposed to just reacting to price changes at the time earnings are reported. You should be wary of large impairment charges and extraordinary nonrecurring charges.

Game Four: Firms Engage in Timing Games with Earnings

In the last couple of years, companies have started to spread good earnings over several reporting periods—in an attempt to beat earnings expectations on a continuing basis—while at the same time taking bad earnings and compressing them into one single period, to get the terrible news out of the way.

This is mostly done by changing when the company recognizes sales and expenses.

Here's an example of how this game is played. If it looks like a quarter is going to be bad, the CFO will record sales occurring near the end of the quarter in the next quarter. The CFO simply gets the sales manager to sign a few large contracts that arrive near the end of the quarter a couple of weeks later than he would have normally, and presto, sales and earnings are shifted to the future; as a result, earnings will be reported higher in the next quarter.

By engaging in such behavior, the company will miss the consensus earnings estimate in the current quarter—which was going to be lousy anyway—but will exceed the consensus in the coming quarters.

Essentially, by pushing the bad earnings information into one quarter, the company is attempting to lessen the pain of missing expectations and guarantee that the company will meet analysts' future earnings estimates.

Think of it in these terms: If you have bad news to deliver, do you want to give it all at once, or let it dribble out a little bit quarter after quarter?

You do not need a degree in psychology to realize that if you want to minimize the blow of bad news, it pays to bunch it all together.

It does a company very little good to miss earnings by a penny or two in each of the next four quarters. A company that knows it is likely to miss earnings expectations by one penny each quarter in the coming year is much better off missing expectations by $0.04 in the coming quarter, coaxing analysts to lower expectations for future quarters, and then consistently beating expectations for the next three.

What do you do about this kind of gamesmanship? First off, you should be wary of any company that beats analysts' expectations following a poor quarter. On the other hand, the bundling of bad news into one quarter has become so prevalent that if a company misses earnings by just $0.01, it may be an indication that the company's CFO is not experienced in timing earnings. This could be a good thing in that the company's earnings are less managed, that is, the company is not manipulating when it records sales and earnings. The income statement is clean.

But it also means that the CFO may lack the ability to spin Wall Street effectively. Therefore, companies that miss earnings by a penny should be seen as companies in which management is a little green, which is not the best thing in the world, because on Wall Street perception often becomes reality.

KEY POINT   Some degree of earnings gamesmanship on the part of a CFO ensures that bad news is minimized when reported. As a result, if a large company misses earnings estimates by a penny, it may indicate that the CFO is not effectively managing Wall Street analysts.

Game Five: Firms Beat Expectations through Serial Acquisitions

Some acquisitions are good for shareholders. However, you must be careful of serial acquirers, as a company's management can easily boost earnings simply by using their stock to acquire other companies that are trading at lower P/E levels.

The serial acquisition game is easy to understand. There are two rules that a company plays by in making serial acquisitions. The first rule is to find an investment banker at a firm that has an analyst who is well respected by the market. The second rule is to buy companies that trade at P/E ratios that are lower than the company's own P/E ratio.

Whenever a company buys a company trading at a lower P/E, the result is that the EPS of the acquiring company will go up. (Or in banker-speak, "The acquisition is accretive to earnings.") If you buy enough lower-P/E companies, you can really grow your earnings per share dramatically and continually beat analyst expectations.

The bankers who make big bucks by advising on the acquisition put pressure on the security analyst who works at their firm to go out into the marketplace and start to spin interesting yarns in order to support the acquiring company's share price.

The analyst will call up a money manager and mention how the industry is ripe for consolidation. Apparently some technological change or a financing advantage has created an economy of scale whereby larger companies can be more profitable than smaller companies. The reason analysts so heavily support such companies when they are growing is that a company that grows primarily through acquisitions is like a goose that lays golden eggs for an investment bank. Just think of the fees.

But these growth-by-acquisition stories always end the same way, with the big bad company that is doing the acquisitions either buying a company that explodes or running out of companies to acquire. In both cases the net result is more substantially reduced earnings growth than the market anticipated, and thus a substantially reduced stock price.

The real question in evaluating an acquisition is not whether the acquisition will be accretive to earnings, that is, whether the acquisition increases the acquiring company's earnings per share, but rather whether the acquiring company paid too much for the acquisition. Most of the time, acquiring companies overpay, and this is another reason you should be wary of a company that grows by acquisitions.

KEY POINT   Companies that beat analysts' expectations primarily through serial acquisitions are generally doomed to eventually collapse—you can make money on the way up, but make sure you are not holding the bag on the way down.

Summary

- Most of the time, a positive earnings surprise means a company's stock price will rise, while a negative earnings surprise means a company's stock price will fall. The larger the earnings surprise, the bigger the change in price.

- The reaction to all earnings news, however, is not equal. Company "A" can report an earnings surprise of 10% and watch its stock increase 20% in a matter of moments. Company "B" can report exactly the same earnings surprise at exactly the same moment and its stock can fall.

- Not all earnings are created equal. Knowing how investors and analysts view earnings, companies have taken to playing games to manipulate those earnings and the expectations about them.

- With a bit of work, you can parse the game-playing and figure out both real earnings and real expectations.

- When a company reports earnings, always check to make sure that the quality of earnings is high—that is, when the earnings gains are attributable to top-line revenue growth and not due to accounting changes.

- If comparable companies reported positive surprises, if information was leaked to the market, or if the company has a long history of reporting positive earnings surprises, the effect of a positive earnings surprise will be significantly lessened.

## Chapter Seven

Using the Earnings Surprise in Your Investment Process

What's ahead in this chapter?

- How to Use Earnings Surprises to Make Money
- Predicting an Earnings Surprise—The "Cockroach Effect"
- Four Methods for Predicting an Earnings Surprise

THIS CHAPTER IS ALL ABOUT HOW YOU CAN EFFECTIVELY use earnings surprises to make money. There really are two ways to make use of an earnings surprise: You can react to the earnings surprise, or better yet, you can predict the earnings surprise.

The first half of this chapter provides you with a three-step checklist that enables you to determine which earnings surprises you should react to. By going through the checklist you should be able to determine whether you should buy a stock that reports a positive earnings surprise. The second half of the chapter introduces the concept of the cockroach effect and some methods several hedge funds use to try to effectively predict earnings surprises.

If you are fairly risk-averse, you should focus on responding to an earnings surprise, while if you are willing to bear a higher level of risk in anticipation of higher returns, it pays to try to predict earnings surprises.

How to Use Earnings Surprises to Make Money

Step One: Determine the True Extent of the Surprise

The best way to quickly determine the extent of an earnings surprise is to compare reported earnings to the earnings estimate histogram that we talked about in Chapter Five.

In order for an earnings report to truly be considered positive, you want to see that the company beat both of the following:

- The consensus earnings estimate

- The most recent analyst earnings estimates, represented by the Os in the earnings estimate histogram

Let's look at an example in Figure 7-1.

In this case, Goodyear Tire (GT) is expected to report earnings for the 9/02 quarter on 10/30/02. If Goodyear reports earnings of $0.08, although this would represent a negative surprise relative to the full consensus, it would be a positive surprise relative to the most recent earnings estimates.

Thus, if Goodyear reported earnings at $0.08, four cents worse than the consensus earnings estimate, because the earnings are better than the most recent analysts' earnings estimates, the result is that the negative surprise will likely not cause Goodyear's stock to sell off that much.

Figure 7-1

```
     09/02 QTR:     GOODYEAR TIRE

     EXP REPT DATE: 10/30/02



       0                    X
     0 0     X              X
     !-----!-----!-----!-----!
     0.05  0.10  0.15  0.20  0.25

       MEAN      0.12 ( 6)
     MOST ACC    0.06 ( 3)
```

Generally, you want to ask the following questions of the earnings press release in order to determine the extent of the earnings surprise:

1. Were the reported earnings better than the quarterly consensus earnings estimate?
2. Were the reported earnings better than the most recent analyst earnings estimates (found on the histogram)?
3. Were there extraordinary items that helped boost earnings?
4. Did the company warn for future quarters?
5. Did the company warn prior to announcing earnings?
6. Was the earnings surprise expected by the market?

You only want to buy stocks for which the answers to questions 1 and 2 are "yes," and the answers to 3 through 6 are "no." Only companies that answer the questions this way are reporting "true" or "clean" earnings surprises.

Obviously, as you go through the checklist, question 6 is the hardest to determine, but there is a short-cut. The market is generally very good at evaluating earnings surprises, and an excellent way for a novice investor to determine whether the earnings report is positive or not is to look at the market's immediate reaction.

If the market responds negatively, and the answers to questions 1 and 2 arc "yes," while the answers to 3 through 5 are "no," chances are the surprise was expected by the market.

It usually makes sense to invest in companies reporting positive earnings surprises on some weakness—that is, after the stock drops in price a bit after the initial run up. If the stock in the next couple of weeks trades below the price it was at before it reported good earnings—due to general market weakness—it usually is a good idea to buy the stock. Buying stocks that exceed earnings expectations is, as we shall see, quite a reasonable strategy.

KEY POINT   In order for an earnings report to be considered a true positive surprise, reported earnings should exceed the consensus earnings estimate as well as the most recent earnings estimates. Additionally, there should be no extraordinary items, no warning about future quarters, and no warning prior to reporting.

Step Two: Determine the Quality of the Earnings Surprise and Examine the Sales Numbers

A Tale of Two Companies

For the third quarter of 2000, two companies reported earnings on the same day. On Tuesday October 10, Abbott Labs (ABT) said it earned $0.42 per share at 8:16 a.m., while Motorola Inc. (MOT) reported earnings of $0.26 per share after the markets closed.

Both companies reported third-quarter earnings exactly in line with analysts' estimates.

Yet Motorola's stock price fell from a little above $26 on the day of the announcement to close at the end of the week at $22-and-change, while Abbott's shares took off from slightly under $48 a share to end the week at $50.25.

The obvious question is why, if both companies met analysts' expectations, did Motorola falter and Abbott Labs pole-vault over its previous 52-week high?

The answer is not that the market had lost its senses, but rather that the disparity was caused by a new metric called a Sales Surprise™.

As mentioned previously, a positive earnings surprise is good news, while a negative earnings surprise is bad news. Positive earnings surprise, you buy; negative earnings surprise, you sell. This is the picture in broad strokes.

But investors often ask a very pertinent follow-up question: How do you measure the quality of the earnings reported? It is here that the Sales Surprise™ comes in.

Quality of Earnings

In order to determine the quality of earnings reported, you should first determine whether the company indicated anything about future earnings. For instance, in our example, Motorola pointed out that fourth-quarter earnings were going to be weak. A big part of the reason for the weakness was attributed to "slower than anticipated growth in semiconductors and cell phones."

At the time, just about all that Motorola produced was semiconductors and cell phones, so the announcement was akin to having the Chicago Bears say they expected to win the Super Bowl, but their passing and running games were weak, their defense was porous, and their special teams were lousy. This less-than-stellar forecast explains:

- Part of the reason for Motorola's sell-off

- Why you always want to pay attention to what a company says it is expecting in the way of upcoming financial results

With the issue of future guidance resolved, you should next study the company's reported sales numbers in order to determine the quality of the earnings.

As indicated previously, earnings growth can come from two primary sources: Either a company can have higher sales, or a company can cut the amount of money it costs to make those sales.

Earnings growth driven by growing sales is far more relevant and important than earnings growth driven by cost savings. The reason is simple: You can only cut costs so much.

KEY POINT   There is a limited amount of earnings growth that can be squeezed out of a company from controlling costs, and most of this has already been fully accomplished by large-cap companies. That's why, in looking at the quality of earnings, it is best to focus on the firm's revenues.

Essentially, earnings growth attributable to cost-cutting is not sustainable over the long haul. At some point, all the possible cost cutting has been done and there is nothing left. For this reason, when the quarterly numbers are announced, it is very important to look at how sales came in relative to analyst expectations.

Our Motorola/Abbott comparison can serve as a case in point. In addition to making earnings estimates, the analysts who follow Motorola and Abbot also make sales estimates. Zacks calculates a sales consensus estimate from these individual analyst estimates and according to the Zacks Sales Consensus, the fifteen analysts following Abbott Labs expected the company to report sales of $3.3 billion for the quarter, and that's exactly what Abbott turned in.

Given both the slumping state of the market back then, and the fact that every media outlet was screaming about slowing revenue growth nationwide, reporting revenues in line with analysts' expectations was good news and to some extent unexpected by investors. Meeting sales expectations when every other large-cap stock was reporting slowing revenue growth propelled Abbott to its 52-week high.

A Sales Surprise™ also helps explain what happened with Motorola. The company reported third-quarter revenues of $9.4 billion. That is a huge number, but the twenty analysts following the company expected sales of $10 billion. Motorola missed the sales consensus estimate by 6%. And a sales shortfall of $600 million is not chicken feed.

That negative Sales Surprise™ contributed to Motorola's decline because it indicated to the market that quality was lacking in Motorola's earnings. That is, the market concluded that Motorola met its earnings number by cutting costs, not by enlarging its core business through greater sales.

Combining the Sales Surprise™ with the Earnings Surprise

Immediately following an earnings report, you need to determine as quickly as possible whether the earnings are of high quality. The easiest way to do this is to use Figure 7–2.

Essentially, a Sales Surprise™ telegraphs the quality of the earnings reported, but you should still rely on the earnings surprise to tell you when to sell.

Figure 7-2 Assessing the quality of earnings.

The reason is simple: Without growing earnings, it does not matter how fast sales are growing.

For this reason, stocks you are thinking about buying should not only exceed earnings estimates, but should exceed sales estimates as well.

Why? In part because it is harder for a company to fudge sales numbers. Chief financial officers who fudge sales numbers are more likely to be arrested. Earnings are easier to manipulate, and any competent CFO can usually find an extra penny a share by performing some of the accounting tricks detailed in the last chapter. As a result, there are substantially more companies that report negative Sales Surprises™ than report negative earnings surprises, since Sales Surprises™ are tougher to concoct.

For this reason, the Sales Surprise™, when used in conjunction with the earnings surprise, can provide a more accurate prediction of how the market will react to an earnings report.

KEY POINT   The market reacts most strongly to earnings reports in which both earnings and sales are reported higher than analysts' expectations. You want to be buying stocks which have reported a positive Sales Surprise™ as well as a positive earnings surprise.

Step Three: React

It is 8:00 a.m. The market has yet to open and all of a sudden a story comes in over Bloomberg and the AP wire that Procter & Gamble is reporting earnings greater than analysts' expectations.

You read the report, and run through the questions in step one.

1. P&G beat the quarterly consensus earnings estimate.

2. Earnings also exceeded the Os on the histogram.

3. No extraordinary or non-recurring items were reported.

4. No warning was issued about future quarters; in fact, the opposite occurred: P&G indicated they are expecting to exceed analyst expectations for the next few quarters.

5. There was no prior earnings warning.

6. Surprise was definitely not expected by the market, considering how skittish the stock had been prior to announcing earnings.

Everything looks good. To double-check, you examine the sales numbers which, in fact, were also above what analysts were expecting.

The question is, do you buy the stock on the news, gobbling up as many shares as you can when the market opens?

The answer is no.

What you find if you study the market's immediate price response to earnings surprises is that once "clean" earnings surprises are reported, a stock's price reacts immediately. In this instance, if you put your buy order in "on the open," you will get your shares, but the price will not be anywhere close to where P&G closed the night before. Basically, P&G will "gap open"—which means that the price shares exchange hands at will not be close to the closing price the night before.

Basically, quickly responding to earnings surprises is such a widely followed strategy by both hedge funds and traders that the days in which you could profit by quickly reacting to an earnings surprise are long since gone. In fact, stocks in many cases tend to initially overreact to an earnings surprise. The stock goes up very quickly, and usually gives back some of those gains over the next few days.

So what should you do?

When using earnings surprises, what is important is not necessarily the immediate reaction period. Rather, what you want to focus on is the movement of the stock over the next couple of months following the positive earnings surprise.

What many investors do not realize is that stocks that report positive earnings surprises tend to exhibit strength not just on the day of the earnings surprise, but also over the next one to three months.

Although it does not make much sense to buy a stock immediately following a positive earnings announcement in an attempt to beat other investors to the punch—especially if the earnings announcement is reported on Bloomberg television or CNBC, and the stock is widely followed—it does make sense to wait a few days and buy the stock on any weakness, with the anticipation of holding the stock for a couple of months.

KEY POINT Companies that report positive earnings surprises tend to outperform over the next one to three months, in addition to the day that earnings are actually reported. Similarly, companies that report negative earnings surprises tend to decrease in value over the next one to three months.

This increase in a stock's price following a positive earnings surprise—and decline after a negative one—is referred to as "post-earnings announcement drift."

"Post-earnings announcement drift" is quite a mouthful, but basically it means that stocks that report positive earnings surprises tend to exhibit strength at least until their next earnings report.

The reason for this is simple and goes back to the institutional investors.

When P&G comes out and reports better than expected clean earnings, the hedge funds and day traders immediately go bananas, but the stock also becomes more attractive to many large, institutional players, such as mutual and pension funds that control large amounts of money.

These institutional players do not react immediately, although the institutional players are reacting quicker than they have historically. Instead, they may do a little more research and buy P&G a bit later on, maybe even a month or two later when the institutional manager is looking for a consumer staples stock.

The net result is that a positive earnings surprise makes an institutional investor more likely to eventually buy the stock, which results in a gradually increasing stock price over the next few months. Initially, though, stocks reporting positive earnings surprises have a tendency to overreact.

KEY POINT It is a good idea to buy stocks that report earnings better than analysts' expectations—not on the news but rather a few days after the news—and to hold those stocks for a three-month period, selling prior to next quarter's earnings report.

Figure 7-3 shows the annualized return differential between stocks of companies that reported positive earnings surprises and the stocks of companies that reported negative earnings surprises. The portfolios measured are rebalanced monthly based on the last reported earnings surprise.

This chart shows that stocks that report positive earnings surprises tend to outperform, while stocks that report negative earnings surprises tend to under-perform. A portfolio consisting of stocks whose last reported earnings surprise is greater than 1% generated an annualized return of 16.7% over the past twelve years, while over the same time period the S&P 500 rose at an annualized rate of 11.0%.

Figure 7-3 Annualized returns of stocks reporting earnings surprises (November 1990 to September 2002).*

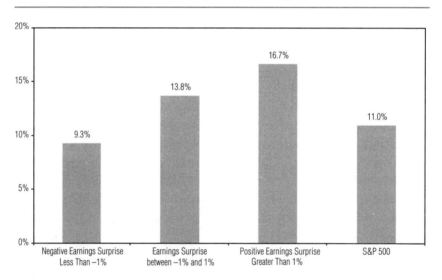

*Over the period, an equal-weighted universe of the stocks included in the study appreciated at an annualized rate of 13.7% per year, slightly higher than the S&P 500.

Predicting the Earnings Surprise—The "Cockroach Effect"

In addition to the post-earnings surprise drift, there is another good reason to buy the stocks of companies that are reporting positive earnings surprises: Companies that have historically reported positive earnings surprises are more likely to report positive earnings surprises in the future. This phenomenon is colorfully called the "Cockroach Effect."

The cockroach effect is mainly an empirically observed phenomenon. It refers to the fact that earnings surprises are in many ways like cockroaches: Once you have seen one, more are likely to follow.

Unlike the herding of analysts that we discussed previously, there really is no behavioral explanation for why the cockroach effect occurs.

I do have a theory though. Basically, when a company undergoes fundamental changes that cause its earnings to either increase or decrease, these changes occur incrementally over time. Like Rome, Microsoft was not built in a quarter. Rather, earnings improvements gradually evolve over time and are not the result of a punctuated event.

Microsoft serves as an excellent example. When the company initially sold its MS-DOS® operating system, it was not clear that everyone, and I mean everyone, would ultimately have to buy it. But ultimately, MS-DOS® proved to be far more indispensable than the hardware it ran on.

Still, the demand for Microsoft was not apparent to the market through Microsoft's quarterly financial statements at any one point in time. It became apparent only over many, many quarters, as Microsoft continued to exceed analyst expectations in the course of its evolution as a company.

Whatever the reason, the net result of this cockroach effect is that companies that have had a history of positive earnings surprises are more likely to report positive earnings surprises in the future. Similarly, companies that have had a history of negative earnings surprises are more likely to disappoint the market going forward.

Figure 7-4 demonstrates the cockroach effect and shows that over a given time period a company is far more likely to report a positive earnings surprise if the company has a history of reporting positive earnings surprises.

KEY POINT   Earnings surprises are a lot like cockroaches. When you find one, more are sure to follow. For this reason, a company that has historically reported earnings surprises in the past has a greater chance of reporting earnings surprises in the future.

Figure 7-4 Cockroach effect (June 1991 to September 2002).

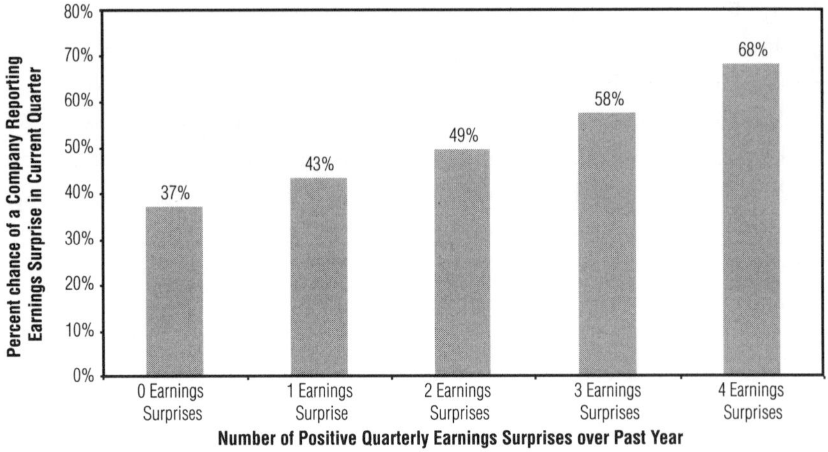

This, however, is only half of the story. Although companies that have been receiving positive earnings surprises are more likely to report a positive earnings surprise in the future, the market fully begins to anticipate this fact. Thus, when a company with a long history of generating positive earning surprises generates another positive earnings surprise, the price response is often not as substantial as it has been historically, mainly because the market has come to anticipate a positive earnings surprise.

The price response to an earnings surprise is greatest for companies that do not have a history of generating positive earnings surprises simply because in these instances, a positive earnings surprise is more of an unexpected event.

KEY POINT   Any investor trying to predict earnings surprises should be aware that although he or she stands a better chance of predicting a positive earnings surprise based upon a string of historical positive earnings surprises, the price response is likely to be more muted because a positive earning surprise is, in fact, more likely to be expected from companies that have a history of reporting positive earnings surprises.

Four Methods for Predicting an Earnings Surprise

The key to using earnings surprises effectively is to predict the surprise rather than to react to it. You want to buy stocks *prior* to the announcement of positive earnings surprises, and sell them *before* negative earnings surprises are announced.

There are four methods—actively employed by hedge funds—that you can use to try to predict which stocks are likely to report earnings better (or worse) than expectations.

Applying these techniques requires a bit of common sense. And correctly predicting an earnings surprise does not necessarily mean prices will respond as anticipated. As we have discussed throughout, a stock's price response to an earnings surprise is totally dependent on expectations built into the price prior to the earnings announcement.

Find the Most Accurate Analysts

The easiest way to predict what a company will earn is to go with the analysts who have the best crystal ball.

At Zacks, we measure the accuracy of brokerage analysts based on two characteristics: How well their recommendations fared, and how accurate the analyst has been in predicting quarterly and yearly earnings.

The key piece of information to look at is where the most accurate analysts are coming in relative to the consensus. If the analysts with the best track records predict earnings a penny or two above the consensus, look for a positive surprise. Similarly, if the most accurate analysts predict earnings a penny or two below the consensus, look for a negative earnings surprise.

Let me stop here to underscore the obvious. Just because these analysts have been the most accurate in the past is no guarantee that they will be the most accurate going forward. Nevertheless, surprises predicted by this methodology often result in identifying stocks that tend to respond strongly to earnings surprises.

The Most Recent Estimates Method

In this method, instead of looking for the most accurate analysts, you look at the most recent earnings estimates.

By its very nature, the consensus estimate contains individual earnings estimates that may be somewhat old, since it is possible that some of the estimates making up the average were made over two months ago.

Thus, by looking at where the most recent estimates are coming in, *relative to the standard consensus,* a determination can be made as to whether earnings are going to come in above or below expectations.

Here's the easiest way to do it. Look at where the 30-day consensus earnings estimate is coming in relative to the standard consensus earnings estimate. If the 30-day consensus earnings estimate is higher than the standard consensus earnings estimate, it means there is a chance for a positive earnings surprise. Are the most recent estimates coming in lower? Then a negative earnings surprise is more likely.

This methodology is more effective at predicting surprises, but the surprises often deliver less of a punch, because the positive surprises that materialize with this methodology often do not result in price movement as dramatic as the "most accurate analyst" methodology.

KEY POINT   You can also use the earnings estimate histogram to determine where the most recent analysts' earnings estimates are coming in relative to the consensus. If a week or two before earnings are reported, the Os are to the right of the Xs, it is an indication that a positive earnings surprise is likely.

Whisper in My Ear

This method, which has been used since the 1970s to predict earnings surprises, is extraordinarily simple, but can be extremely misleading.

For the last twenty years or so, traders have been trying to predict earnings surprises by examining price movements just prior to when earnings are going to be reported. Generally, as I have mentioned, there is some leakage of information prior to an earnings report. This leakage is not caused by investors having inside information; rather, it is attributable to whispers and rumors originating from suppliers, competitors, analysts, portfolio managers and low-level employees. All this buzzing finds its way into the stock's price.

Very simply, if a company's stock exhibits strength prior to an earnings report, it may be an indication the stock is going to beat expectations, while if the stock is weak prior to an earnings report it could be an indication that the company may report a negative earnings surprise.

According to this theory, you look for these price movements and hop on the bandwagon.

The key, of course, is to differentiate the information from the noise contained in all that buzzing. And with all the media attention devoted today to the financial markets, there is an awful lot of noise. Because of this noise, I would not recommend that investors use price movements prior to an earnings announcement in order to predict the earnings surprise. The methodology is simply too widely used at this point, and more often than not results in bad calls.

Safety in Numbers

I have saved the best for last. The fourth and final method an investor can use to predict an earnings surprise is to look for agreement among estimate revisions. That is, if all the analysts following a stock raise their earnings estimates, even if it is only by a penny, prior to an earnings announcement, it is one of the strongest indications that a company may, in fact, beat expectations.

The reason is fairly simple and has to do with the behavior of analysts that we examined earlier. As we saw, analysts, like all professionals, tend to be conservative and risk-averse. Once an analyst has committed to a certain EPS estimate, he is reluctant to revise it because he does not want to go back to his clients and say that his initial estimate was wrong.

That's why there is safety in numbers. If an analyst is wrong along with everyone else, he has a defense for a bad estimate. For this reason, analysts, as we have seen, tend to herd together like cattle when it comes time to make their estimates of future earnings. As a result, when all the analysts following a certain stock revise earnings estimates upward prior to an earnings announcement, it is a clear indication that earnings prospects are improving and a positive earnings surprise is likely.

KEY POINT If several analysts revise their earnings estimates upward shortly prior to an earnings announcement, it is a good signal that the company will beat analysts' expectations. Similarly, if several analysts revise their earnings estimates downward prior to the company announcing earnings, it is a sign that the company may be in store for a negative earnings surprise.

Those are the four techniques, and as I said, I like the last one the best.

When would you apply the fourth technique, or any of the other three?

During the month following the end of the fiscal quarter—which, for most companies on a December year-end, would mean January, April, July, and October. These are when the majority of companies report quarterly earnings, so these are the times when it is useful to try to predict earnings surprises.

Summary

- Companies that report positive earnings surprises tend to outperform over the next three months; this is called post-earnings announcement drift.

- Generally, the companies exhibiting the greatest strength following a positive earnings announcement are companies whose earnings exceeded the most recent analysts' earnings estimates.

- When playing the post-earnings announcement drift, you should give preference to companies that, in addition to reporting a positive earnings surprise, also reported a positive Sales Surprise™.

- You should avoid companies that reported a positive earnings surprise due to non-recurring expenses.

- You should also avoid companies that lowered earnings guidance prior to or concurrent with a good earnings report.

- Stocks sometimes overreact to a positive earnings surprise, and as a result, you should not try to be the first investor to react to an earnings announcement.

- Companies that have reported positive earnings surprises in the past are more likely to report positive earnings surprises in the future; this is called the cockroach effect.

- In addition to the cockroach effect, there are four good ways to predict an earnings surprise: examining where the most accurate analysts have issued their earnings estimates; seeing where the most recent earnings estimates are coming in relative to the consensus; looking for pre-earnings announcement price movement; and, most importantly, focusing on multiple revisions to analysts' earnings estimates prior to a company reporting its earnings.

- If immediately prior to a company announcing earnings, multiple analysts cut their earnings estimates on a stock you are holding, beware—you may be in store for a negative earnings surprise.

## Chapter Eight

It All Comes Together— The Zacks Rank: The Key to Successful Investing

What's ahead in this chapter:

- What Is the Zacks Rank?
- How Good is the Zacks Rank at Picking Stocks?
- Questions about the Zacks Rank
- The Zacks Rank in Action: What Causes Stocks to Rise
- Can the Zacks Rank Help You Pick Winners?

What Is the Zacks Rank?

IF YOU WANT TO AVOID THE WORK AND EFFORT of tracking earnings estimate revisions and earnings surprises yourself, the Zacks Rank provides a very useful means of simplifying the information flow. Essentially, the Zacks Rank condenses the analyst-related data on a given stock down into a single actionable piece of advice. The Zacks Rank saves you from having to track, record, and analyze the data yourself and serves as your indicator as to which stocks will be going up and down in price over the next three months.

The Zacks Rank incorporates much of the information we have discussed in the previous chapters and distills the data down to a simple, understandable recommendation that you can use to determine whether to buy, sell, or hold a stock.

Unlike the recommendations that are available from Wall Street analysts through brokerage firms, the Zacks Rank is unbiased and it works in both up and down markets.

As I will show in the next couple of chapters, the Zacks Rank is one of the most statistically effective ways of determining how a stock will perform over the next one to three months.

KEY POINT The Zacks Rank works by effectively predicting future earnings estimate revisions and by identifying those stocks that have recently received upward earnings estimate revisions and reported positive earnings surprises. In both cases, the ranking identifies stocks that institutional investors are likely to be buying in the immediate future.

Where the Ranking Comes From

The Zacks Rank is a proprietary, quantitative model that has worked for the past twenty years. Although I am not going to tell you exactly how the Zacks Rank is constructed, from the previous chapters you might correctly guess that the Zacks Rank focuses on the factors that I have noted have the greatest impact on future stock price performance: revisions to analysts' earnings estimates and earnings surprises.

In general, broad strokes, the Zacks Rank is based on the following four factors:

- **Agreement**
  The extent to which all brokerage analysts are revising their EPS estimates in the same direction. The more analysts who are revising upward, the higher the ranking.

- **Magnitude**
  The size of recent changes in the consensus estimates for the current fiscal year and the next one. (This is very similar to the percentage change in the consensus earnings estimate for the coming year.) Example: An earnings estimate revision that causes the consensus estimate to increase by 6% is a more powerful signal than an earnings estimate revision that causes a 2% rise in the consensus.

- **Upside**

  The deviation between the most accurate earnings estimates issued by the analysts with the best track record and the consensus earnings estimate. There is no benefit for the analyst to put out a substantially higher earnings estimate unless the analyst knows something special. This measure of potential upside is an excellent early indicator of a potential earnings surprise.

- **Surprise**

  The more often a company has posted a positive surprise in the recent past, the more likely it will continue to do so. (Similarly, companies posting negative earnings surprises often continue to do so.)

How the Zacks Rank Is Created

Every night a team of professionals at Zacks recalculates these four factors for the universe of 4,300 stocks covered by the Zacks Rank. These four measures are combined into a composite score, which is then used to assign a ranking to the stock. The Zacks Rank is, at its core, a statistical summary of the key information contained in the 30,000 most recent brokerage research reports produced by the 3,000 investment analysts employed by over 250 U.S. and Canadian brokerage firms.

Each day we record 6,000 new earnings estimate revisions and changes in brokerage firm recommendations. All this information is incorporated into the Zacks Rank.

The Zacks #1 Ranked stocks are available from the Zacks.com website, updated on a weekly basis free of charge. You simply go to the Zacks.com home page, click on the portfolio tab second from the left on the top of the page, and then click on the link labeled Zacks #1 Ranked list.

The Zacks #1 Ranked stocks are also updated on a daily basis from zacksadvisor.com and Appendix I provides you with a free one-month subscription to this premium website.

KEY POINT   Analysts are collectively paid well over $1 billion a year to create research reports and the Zacks Rank is your best way of extracting unbiased and useful information from those reports.

Ultimately, stocks are classified into five groups: 1, 2, 3, 4, and 5 (1 being the most desirable and 5 being the least desirable). Each ranking corresponds to a specific recommendation, as shown in Figure 8-1.

Figure 8-1 Zacks Rank recommendations.

Zacks Rank	Recommendation
1	Strong Buy
2	Buy
3	Hold
4	Sell
5	Strong Sell

The Zacks Rank Is Unbiased

As I discussed earlier, Wall Street research analysts tend to be far more likely to issue a buy or over-weight recommendation than a sell or under-weight recommendation.

Even with some of the reforms being implemented to try to separate the investment banking division from the research department at brokerage firms, the bias in Wall Street recommendations will likely persist.

The Zacks Rank is, as you may have guessed, a quantitative ranking algorithm. For this reason, there are just as many stocks that bear a recommendation of "Strong Buy" as a recommendation of "Strong Sell." Thus, the Zacks Rank provides *unbiased* advice.

Figure 8-2 shows just how unbiased the Zacks Rank is: There are an equal number of "Strong Buys" and "Strong Sells."

As you will note, the universe of stocks takes on a "bell-shaped" distribution when divided by the Zacks Rank. This means there are a lot of companies with a neutral rank but relatively few companies with a 1 (Strong Buy) or a 5 (Strong Sell) ranking.

Therefore, the Zacks #1 Ranked stocks are truly the "cream of the crop," since they represent the top 5% of all stocks that are covered by at least one analyst and are expected to be experiencing the strongest earnings estimate revisions in the future.

Figure 8-2 Distribution of Zacks Rank recommendations.

Zacks Rank	Percent of Universe	# of Companies As of July 15, 2002
1	5%	217
2	15%	647
3	60%	2,588
4	15%	631
5	5%	215
Total Stocks Covered:		4,298

How Good Is the Zacks Rank at Picking Stocks?

Since its inception in 1980, the Zacks Rank has proven to be a very reliable indicator for predicting future movements in stock prices over the next one to three months.

How reliable has it been?

From 1980 through September 2002, an equal-weighted portfolio of Zacks #1 Ranked stocks generated an average annual return of 31.8% versus 12.6% for the S&P 500 over the same time period.

The yearly returns of the Zacks Rank are given below. The returns of the Zacks Rank are not generated by a back-test. The Zacks #1 Ranked portfolio return is based upon the actual stock rankings published by Zacks on a monthly basis over the past twenty years.

The distinction is very important. It is relatively easy to generate a back-test that indicates excellent historical returns but does not do well in the future. In this case, however, we are dealing with actual results.

Figure 8-3a shows the yearly returns of the Zacks Rank without adjusting for transaction costs over the past twenty years.

Let me break down the numbers in the table. Performance statistics for the Zacks #1 Ranked stocks represent the annual compounded returns of a sequence of single-month performance statistics for a series of portfolios consisting of all of the Zacks #1 Ranked stocks.

At the end of each month, the entire universe of stocks is reevaluated. Stocks which no longer deserve a #1 ranking are eliminated from the

Figure 8-3a Zacks #1 Ranked returns.

Period	Zacks Rank #1 Stocks % Return	Benchmark S&P 500 % Return	Zacks Rank #5 Stocks % Return
2002 [a]	−5.90%	−28.16%	−27.44%
2001	18.67%	−11.88%	24.74%
2000	16.24%	−9.10%	−5.73%
1999	48.75%	21.03%	16.18%
1998	21.88%	28.57%	−15.08%
1997	45.75%	33.25%	3.72%
1996	45.44%	22.36%	10.10%
1995	53.84%	36.31%	10.82%
1994	15.58%	0.59%	−11.85%
1993	44.62%	10.07%	8.18%
1992	43.20%	7.51%	16.81%
1991	81.91%	30.40%	34.91%
1990	−1.14%	−3.10%	−33.85%
1989	45.19%	31.67%	−5.38%
1988	43.16%	16.24%	18.79%
1987	7.47%	5.07%	−22.62%
1986	30.00%	18.60%	−6.80%
1985	49.00%	31.00%	5.00%
1984	0.60%	6.30%	−10.70%
1983	48.30%	22.60%	19.20%
1982	42.30%	21.60%	1.70%
1981	14.10%	−5.30%	N/A [b]
1980	55.00%	32.40%	N/A [b]

[a] Returns for 2002 are through September of 2002.

[b] Zacks #5 Ranking was not created until 1982.

Fig 8-3b Annualized return of Zacks #1 Ranked stocks vs. S&P 500 (January 1980 through September 2002).

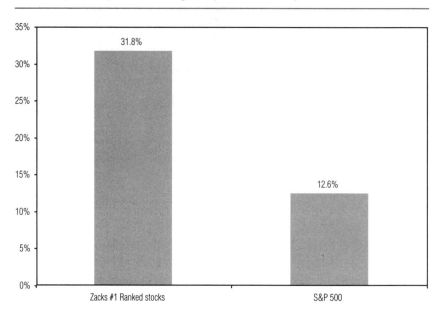

portfolio, stocks having a #1 ranking are added to the portfolio, and the portfolio is rebalanced to assign an equal weighting to the dollar-value for each #1-ranked stock. This new portfolio is held for an entire month, and then the process is repeated. (The same thing is done, by the way, for the portfolios that have rankings of 2, 3, 4, and 5.) Each single month's performance represents the average percentage return at the end of the month (including dividends, but excluding all transaction costs.)

Note that the portfolios used to generate the preceding return include all stocks having a Zacks Rank of 1, and thus include stocks followed by only one analyst, and also may include Canadian stocks which are traded only on Canadian exchanges. Note also that the preceding returns are compounded monthly, based on a portfolio's performance, and reconstituted and rebalanced on a monthly basis.

Finally, the basis of the Zacks Rank—the assumption that the most powerful driver of stock prices is the revisions to analysts' earnings estimates—is backed by an extensive amount of academic research.

KEY POINT   By focusing on revisions to analysts' earnings estimates and earnings surprises, the Zacks Rank has generated annualized returns of 32% per year over the past twenty years. The results are clear: You should buy stocks that have a Zacks Rank of 1 and avoid or sell stocks that have a Zacks Rank of 5.

Questions about the Zacks Rank

Time after time, clients and investors ask the same two questions about the Zacks Rank. Let me answer them here.

Why does the Zacks Rank change so quickly? One day a stock is rated as #1 and the next it could be #2, or even lower. How can a stock go from being a "strong buy" to being a "neutral" in the course of only one day and on very little news?

Answer: The Zacks Rank is a very "sensitive" indicator that is updated daily. As you have already seen, only 5% of the stocks in the full universe of 4,300 stocks can be ranked a #1 Zacks stock at any time. That is pretty stiff competition for those premier slots. That's why if a Zacks #1 Ranked company experiences any negative changes in their earnings estimates or earnings surprises—or any other companies experience stronger upward earnings estimate revisions—a #1-rated stock can quickly fall in rank.

As a result, I suggest that *short-term* investors strictly adhere to the process of buying Zacks #1 Ranked stocks, and sell positions when the rank falls to 2 or below. On the other hand, *longer-term investors* should use a more flexible approach. I suggest longer-term investors buy or add to existing positions in stocks ranked #1 and #2 and reduce holdings of stocks ranked #4 and #5.

KEY POINT   The Zacks Rank is a *short-term indicator* of potential excess market returns and must be used in that context. The Zacks Rank predicts stock price movement over the next one to three months.

I view the ability of the Zacks Rank to change dramatically over time as more of a benefit than a hindrance. Unlike a broker's recommendation, the Zacks Rank is not influenced at all by what the historical Zacks Rank for a company has been. The quantitative algorithm that creates the Zacks Rank has no emotions. As a result, you never have the problem that you run into with analysts in which an analyst is afraid of changing a recommendation suddenly for fear of losing credibility among investors.

Instead, the Zacks Rank deals totally with what is going on now, and with what is anticipated to occur in the future. This effectively ensures that the Zacks Rank is completely unbiased. Additionally, the Zacks Rank is never influenced by any of the conflicts of interest that plague research analysts—the Zacks Rank does not alter its recommendation based upon political factors such as the presence of investment banking revenue.

KEY POINT   The Zacks Rank is unbiased—it does not suffer from the conflicts of interest that we see with analysts' recommendations.

What value does the Zacks Rank have for a long-term investor?

Answer: The Zacks Rank is a fabulous indicator of a stock's performance relative to the market over the next one to three months.

However, as Zacks has tracked the performance of the Zacks #1 Ranked stocks over the last twenty years, we have discovered that many companies experience extended cycles of positive earnings momentum that lead to multiple consecutive quarters with a high Zacks Rank. Therefore, one could effectively use the Zacks Rank to uncover profitable long-term holdings as well as short-term trading opportunities.

But I make no claims for the performance of a Zacks #1 Ranked stock over periods longer than three months.

The Zacks Rank in Action: What Causes Stocks to Rise

This is where the rubber meets the road. So far I have discussed all the elements that comprise the Zacks Rank, but now I will put the pieces together to show how the Zacks Rank can alert you that a stock's price may be about to rise.

To illustrate this process I will use an imaginary company, XYZ Corporation.

Step One: Brokerage Analysts Start to Upwardly Revise Earnings Estimates for XYZ Corporation

Let's say analysts at major brokerage firms raised their earnings estimates on XYZ Corporation. Maybe they saw something in a quarterly earnings report. Or maybe the notion came from meetings with management. Regardless, when the analysts sensed that things at XYZ were going better than expected, they started to increase their earnings estimates for subsequent quarters.

This information is immediately sent to their clients (such as money managers) and to the appropriate folks at Zacks who are responsible for analyzing the data and adjusting it to exclude extraordinary items.

Step Two: Daily Updating of the Zacks Rank— Your Personal Signal

Every night the four factors that make up the Zacks Rank (Agreement, Magnitude, Upside, and Surprise) are calculated and the whole universe of stocks is reclassified into their appropriate rankings. Given the upward surge in EPS estimates for XYZ, it now becomes a Zacks #1 Ranked stock.

Step Three: Institutional Money Starts Flowing into the Stock

As I have indicated, large institutional investors (mutual funds, pension plans, money managers, etc.) have the greatest buying power to influence a stock's price. And as I have also talked about before, most of these institutional investors employ valuation models that use earnings estimates as a prime component. Thus, when they receive the new research from the analysts that indicates that XYZ's EPS estimate is going up, their projected value for XYZ will also rise, making the stock seem cheap at its current price.

So now these institutional investors suddenly want to purchase more of XYZ. However, since they have so much money to spend and don't want to run the price up by themselves, by buying huge amounts of XYZ all at once, they end up accumulating shares over the coming weeks and months. Buying Zacks #1 Ranked stocks gives the individual investor plenty of time to sneak in ahead of the slower-moving institutions and reap the rewards of a share price that will be going up in the future due to increased institutional buying.

Step Four: Momentum & Technical Analysis—Investors Jump on the Bandwagon

There is a vast legion of investors who employ charting and other quantitative models that look for trends like a rising share price and the increase in daily trading activity to spot winning stocks.

In general, these investors believe that a stock on the rise will continue its ascent over the short term. Therefore, given the impetus in the stock price and volume from the institutional investors in Step Three, these momentum and technical analysis investors may jump on board XYZ (at least for the short term) and drive the price even further.

Step Five: Earnings Surprise

Nothing catapults a stock faster than posting a strong earnings surprise. And when you buy a Zacks #1 Ranked stock you dramatically increase the chance of owning companies that will do just that.

That is because three of the four factors used in the Zacks Rank (Upside, Surprise, and Agreement) look for stocks with the strongest potential to announce a positive earnings surprise. So, in the case of XYZ Corporation's stock, you would certainly profit if they announced a stellar earnings report. Thus, by buying Zacks #1 Ranked stocks you have a better chance of owning a stock that is likely to report a positive earnings surprise.

KEY POINT   Zacks #1 Ranked stocks are more likely to report a positive earnings surprise. Conversely, Zacks #5 Ranked stocks are more likely to report a negative earnings surprise. Examining the Zacks Rank prior to a company reporting its earnings is an excellent way of predicting an earnings surprise.

Step Six: Rinse and Repeat

If XYZ Corporation indeed posted an upside earnings surprise and gave solid guidance for the future, then it is very likely that this positive cycle will start all over again at Step One.

Summing Up

In many cases the Zacks Rank is the earliest possible signal you will receive about the future potential of a stock. Please note that this chain of events also plays out—but to the detriment of the share price and your portfolio—when the Zacks Rank falls to a 4 or 5. So you should use any Zacks Rank of 4 or 5 as a negative signal to sell or lower your exposure to a company.

WorldCom: A Cautionary Tale

Let's take a look at how the Zacks Rank can help you avoid and sell losing positions.

Figure 8-4 is the historical Zacks Rank for WorldCom (WCOM) from June 30th, 2000, when WCOM was trading at $45.88, to June 22nd, 2002, when WCOM was going for just over one buck, along with the recommendations you would have received from various brokerage firms if you had accounts there.

That every major brokerage firm was recommending WCOM as a buy or a hold almost until the very end should not surprise you. WCOM had a voracious appetite for acquisitions which generated hundreds of millions of dollars in investment banking fees. Analysts, as we have seen, are extremely reluctant to bite the hand that feeds them.

KEY POINT   However, at the same time the brokerage firms were actively recommending WCOM, the Zacks Rank was providing the exact opposite advice.

Again, if you focus on the earnings estimate revisions, you can extract an unbiased recommendation from the Wall Street analysts.

Figure 8-4 The sad but not surprising story of WorldCom.

Date	Price	Zacks Rank	Meaning of Zacks Rank	Analyst Recommendations					
				# Str. Buys	# Buys	# Hlds	# Sells	# Str Sells	Total #
06/30/00	$45.88	4	Sell	17	6	0	0	0	23
07/07/00	$47.00	4	Sell	17	6	0	0	0	23
07/14/00	$49.19	4	Sell	17	7	0	0	0	24
07/21/00	$45.13	4	Sell	16	8	0	0	0	24
07/28/00	$36.56	4	Sell	15	8	1	0	0	24
08/04/00	$37.63	4	Sell	14	8	1	0	0	23
08/11/00	$33.69	4	Sell	14	8	1	0	0	23
08/18/00	$34.56	4	Sell	16	7	1	0	0	24
08/25/00	$36.06	4	Sell	16	7	1	0	0	24
09/01/00	$36.94	4	Sell	18	6	1	0	0	25
09/08/00	$29.94	5	Strong Sell	15	10	1	0	0	26
09/15/00	$29.44	5	Strong Sell	15	10	1	0	0	26
09/22/00	$26.50	5	Strong Sell	15	10	1	0	0	26
09/29/00	$30.38	5	Strong Sell	15	10	1	0	0	26
10/06/00	$25.19	4	Sell	14	10	1	0	0	25
10/13/00	$24.31	4	Sell	14	10	1	0	0	25
10/20/00	$25.69	5	Strong Sell	15	9	1	0	0	25
10/27/00	$22.06	5	Strong Sell	15	7	2	0	0	24
11/03/00	$18.00	5	Strong Sell	13	1	10	0	0	24
11/10/00	$15.50	5	Strong Sell	12	1	10	0	0	23
11/17/00	$15.75	5	Strong Sell	12	1	10	0	0	23
11/24/00	$15.81	5	Strong Sell	12	1	10	0	0	23
12/01/00	$16.00	5	Strong Sell	11	2	11	0	0	24
12/08/00	$15.19	5	Strong Sell	11	3	11	0	0	25
12/15/00	$17.44	5	Strong Sell	11	3	11	0	0	25
12/22/00	$13.88	5	Strong Sell	11	4	10	0	0	25
12/29/00	$14.06	5	Strong Sell	11	4	10	0	0	25

| Date | Price | Zacks Rank | Meaning of Zacks Rank | Analyst Recommendations | | | | | |
				# Str. Buys	# Buys	# Hlds	# Sells	# Str Sells	Total #
01/05/01	$18.44	5	Strong Sell	10	4	10	0	0	24
01/12/01	$21.75	5	Strong Sell	9	4	10	0	0	23
01/19/01	$22.00	5	Strong Sell	9	4	10	0	0	23
01/26/01	$21.31	5	Strong Sell	9	3	11	0	0	23
02/02/01	$20.06	4	Sell	9	3	11	0	0	23
02/09/01	$19.00	4	Sell	9	4	11	0	0	24
02/16/01	$15.81	4	Sell	9	4	11	0	0	24
02/23/01	$16.50	4	Sell	9	4	11	0	0	24
03/02/01	$16.19	3	Neutral	9	3	12	0	0	24
03/09/01	$16.94	3	Neutral	9	4	12	0	0	25
03/16/01	$17.44	3	Neutral	9	4	12	0	0	25
03/23/01	$16.88	3	Neutral	9	4	12	0	0	25
03/30/01	$18.69	3	Neutral	9	5	12	0	0	26
04/06/01	$18.38	3	Neutral	9	5	12	0	0	26
04/13/01	$19.68	3	Neutral	9	5	12	0	0	26
04/20/01	$19.04	3	Neutral	9	5	12	0	0	26
04/27/01	$18.71	3	Neutral	9	4	13	0	0	26
05/04/01	$18.60	3	Neutral	8	4	12	0	0	24
05/11/01	$17.62	3	Neutral	8	4	11	0	0	23
05/18/01	$17.70	3	Neutral	8	4	11	0	0	23
05/25/01	$18.15	3	Neutral	7	3	12	0	0	22
06/01/01	$18.07	3	Neutral	7	3	12	0	0	22
06/08/01	$17.85	4	Sell	7	3	12	0	0	22
06/15/01	$15.80	4	Sell	7	3	13	0	0	23
06/22/01	$14.29	4	Sell	7	4	13	0	0	24
06/29/01	$14.20	3	Neutral	7	4	13	0	0	24
07/06/01	$13.84	4	Sell	7	4	13	0	0	24
07/13/01	$14.50	5	Strong Sell	7	4	15	0	0	26

Figure 8-4 (*cont.*)

Date	Price	Zacks Rank	Meaning of Zacks Rank	Analyst Recommendations					
				# Str. Buys	# Buys	# Hlds	# Sells	# Str Sells	Total #
07/20/01	$13.83	5	Strong Sell	7	4	15	0	0	26
07/27/01	$15.21	5	Strong Sell	7	4	15	0	0	26
08/03/01	$14.27	4	Sell	6	4	15	0	0	25
08/10/01	$13.66	4	Sell	5	4	15	0	0	24
08/17/01	$13.54	4	Sell	5	4	15	0	0	24
08/24/01	$13.53	5	Strong Sell	5	4	15	0	0	24
08/31/01	$12.86	5	Strong Sell	5	4	15	0	0	24
09/07/01	$12.98	5	Strong Sell	6	3	15	0	0	24
09/14/01	$12.92	5	Strong Sell	6	3	15	0	0	24
09/21/01	$12.38	5	Strong Sell	6	3	15	0	0	24
09/28/01	$15.04	5	Strong Sell	8	2	14	0	0	24
10/05/01	$13.33	4	Sell	8	2	14	0	0	24
10/12/01	$13.88	3	Neutral	9	2	13	0	0	24
10/19/01	$13.17	3	Neutral	9	2	14	0	0	25
10/26/01	$13.38	3	Neutral	9	3	13	0	0	25
11/02/01	$13.48	3	Neutral	9	3	13	0	0	25
11/09/01	$13.99	3	Neutral	10	2	13	0	0	25
11/16/01	$14.48	3	Neutral	11	2	13	0	0	26
11/23/01	$14.47	3	Neutral	12	2	12	0	0	26
11/30/01	$14.54	4	Sell	13	2	11	0	0	26
12/07/01	$15.67	4	Sell	13	3	11	0	0	27
12/14/01	$14.75	4	Sell	13	4	11	0	0	28
12/21/01	$14.75	4	Sell	13	4	11	0	0	28
12/28/01	$14.43	4	Sell	13	4	11	0	0	28
01/04/02	$14.61	5	Strong Sell	12	5	11	0	0	28
01/11/02	$13.77	3	Neutral	12	6	10	0	0	28

Date	Price	Zacks Rank	Meaning of Zacks Rank	Analyst Recommendations					
				# Str. Buys	# Buys	# Hlds	# Sells	# Str Sells	Total #
01/18/02	$12.78	3	Neutral	12	6	9	0	0	27
01/25/02	$12.22	3	Neutral	12	6	10	0	0	28
02/01/02	$9.61	3	Neutral	12	6	10	0	0	28
02/08/02	$8.18	3	Neutral	10	10	8	0	0	28
02/15/02	$6.73	3	Neutral	10	10	8	0	0	28
02/22/02	$7.09	3	Neutral	10	10	8	0	0	28
03/01/02	$7.99	3	Neutral	10	10	8	0	0	28
03/08/02	$9.19	3	Neutral	10	9	10	0	0	29
03/15/02	$7.40	3	Neutral	9	8	12	0	0	29
03/22/02	$6.98	3	Neutral	8	8	12	0	0	28
03/29/02	$6.74	3	Neutral	8	7	13	0	0	28
04/05/02	$6.26	3	Neutral	7	7	14	0	0	28
04/12/02	$5.01	3	Neutral	7	5	16	0	1	29
04/19/02	$5.95	3	Neutral	7	5	16	0	1	29
04/26/02	$3.27	3	Neutral	4	6	14	1	4	29
05/03/02	$1.79	4	Sell	3	6	13	1	5	28
05/10/02	$1.58	3	Neutral	3	6	13	1	5	28
05/17/02	$1.35	3	Neutral	3	5	12	1	6	27
05/24/02	$1.76	3	Neutral	3	4	12	1	6	26
05/31/02	$1.66	4	Sell	3	4	12	1	7	27
06/07/02	$1.69	4	Sell	3	4	12	1	7	27
06/14/02	$1.60	4	Sell	3	4	12	1	7	27
06/21/02	$1.22	3	Neutral	3	4	11	1	8	27

- "Price" is the closing price of WCOM on the given day.
- "Zacks Rank" is Zacks' independent ranking of the stock based on the four factors detailed previously.
- "Analyst Recommendations" are the buy/hold/sell recommendations issued by brokerage firms.

The first sell recommendation by a brokerage firm on WCOM did not surface until the week ending April 12, 2002. At that point WCOM had fallen in value from $45.88 to $5.01.

On the other hand, the Zacks Rank indicated a sell recommendation on WCOM at $45.88 all the way back in June of 2000. By comparison, every single analyst at any one of twenty-three brokerage firms in the country was, as of June 2000, telling investors that WCOM was a "buy" or "strong-buy."

From the WorldCom example it is clear that the Zacks Rank can help you avoid stocks that are hyped by Wall Street analysts but that will be going down in price because earnings estimates are being cut.

Can the Zacks Rank Help You Pick Winners?

The answer is yes. Let's look at the stock Ryland Homes (RYL). At the beginning of September 2000 Ryland was trading at a split-adjusted price of $12.06 per share. At this point in time the Zacks Rank indicated a "Strong Buy" while none of the four analysts following the stock had issued a "Strong Buy."

Ryland appreciated roughly 265% over the next two years to $44 a share in August 2002. For most of that time, the Zacks Rank had Ryland homes as a "Strong Buy" or "Buy."

KEY POINT   As these two examples show, and obviously not all stocks work this well, it makes far more sense to focus on revisions to analysts' earnings estimates and earnings surprises than to focus on analysts' recommendations. It is far better to follow the Zacks Rank than the biased buy/hold/sell recommendations from Wall Street analysts.

Summary

- It is possible to synthesize everything we have talked about in the previous chapters into a numerical rating. This numerical rating is the Zacks Rank.

- The Zacks Rank is an unbiased ranking system—there are as many stocks that receive a rank of 1 (Strong Buy) as receive a rank of 5 (Strong Sell).

- The Zacks Rank works by effectively predicting earnings estimate revisions and earnings surprises. There are four components to the Zacks Rank: Agreement, Magnitude, Upside, and Surprise.

- Stocks that receive a Zacks Rank of 1 tend to outperform over the next one to three months, while stocks that receive a Zacks Rank of 5 tend to under-perform over the next one to three months.

- Zacks #1 Ranked stocks are more likely than average to report a positive earnings surprise, while Zacks #5 Ranked stocks are more likely than average to report a negative earnings surprise.

- Not only can the Zacks Rank help you spot stocks likely to plummet in the near future, as we saw with the WCOM example, the Zacks Rank can get you into stocks that are likely to rise in the immediate future.

- The Zacks Rank works—An equal-weighted portfolio of Zacks #1 Ranked stocks that is rebalanced on a monthly basis has generated annualized returns of 32% per year gross of transaction costs over the past twenty years.

Chapter Nine

Effectively Implementing the Zacks Rank

What's ahead in this chapter?

- The Zacks Rank Works No Matter What Kind of Investor You Are
- Limitations of the Zacks Rank
- Implementing the Zacks Rank—Six Steps

The Zacks Rank Works No Matter What Kind of Investor You Are

THIS CHAPTER FOCUSES ON HOW YOU CAN effectively implement an investment process driven by the Zacks Rank. There are many different schools of investing, yet the Zacks Rank has been proven effective for most of them due to its reliance on two of the most important investment criteria: revisions to analysts' earnings estimates and earnings surprises.

The first half of this chapter illustrates how the different schools of investing make use of the Zacks Rank. After a brief discussion of some of the limitations of the Zacks Rank, the second half of the chapter focuses on effectively implementing the Zacks Rank through a series of six steps. Of all the strategies detailed in this book, focusing on the Zacks Rank will generate the best returns.

Let's begin with a description of how the major classes of investors utilize the Zacks Rank.

Value Investors

Value investors look for stocks selling at prices below their "fair value" and have the patience to wait for other investors to see the same inherent value that they do. Many value investors rely on earnings-driven valuation measures like P/E (price/earnings multiple) or PEG ratio (P/E divided by growth rate) to figure out the fair value of a stock.

Several value investors also use such tools as a dividend discount model—which is a means to calculate the current value of all the potential dividends a company will pay to shareholders. Another tool used by many investors is a valuation based on private enterprise value, which is essentially the price an investor would be willing to pay to own a company in its entirety. Another common valuation metric is a multiple of free cash flow.

Value investors face two obstacles. The biggest is estimating the fair value of a stock; many times the fair value is truly in the eye of the beholder. The second big obstacle is that the annualized return of a value investor may be sapped over time while the investor waits for a catalyst to cause his value stocks to rise.

When you buy a stock because you believe it is fundamentally undervalued, you are making a bet that the market is incorrectly undervaluing a security, and that at some point in the future the market will eventually realize the security is undervalued Once it does, people will rush in and bid the stock up and you will make a profit.

But something has to happen to cause the market to come around to your point of view.

Sometimes the event is as simple as an earnings surprise. This is where the Zacks Rank can be useful to value investors. The ranking helps them predict which companies will beat analysts' earnings estimates, and a positive earnings surprise often serves as the catalysts value investors are looking for.

Remember that every night Zacks ranks thousands of stocks to find those that have experienced the largest and most frequent earnings estimates revisions. When the Zacks Rank signals a "Strong Buy" (1) or a "Buy" (2), it means that earnings estimates are being raised higher for a firm. Most likely, institutional investors will begin to be attracted to these stocks, given the new information, and they will run up their price.

The Zacks Rank serves as a timeliness rating for a value investor. Basically, among those stocks that a value investor may consider undervalued, the Zacks Rank indicates which ones institutional investors will likely be buying in the near future (i.e., those stocks whose Zacks Rank is rising.)

KEY POINT   In essence, the Zacks Rank helps a value investor identify which value stocks are likely to experience a price catalyst in the near future in the form of a positive earnings surprise. Combining the Zacks #1 Ranked list with a value screen is an excellent strategy for a value investor to employ.

Value investors may want to take this one step further and look at the Zacks #1 Ranked stock list for stocks also trading at an attractive PEG or P/E ratio. Rarely is a stock considered a value stock if its PEG ratio or P/E ratio is high.

Combining the #1 Zacks Rank with a low P/E or PEG ratio often makes for a winning combination.

Long-term Investors

Long-term investors like to "buy and hold" the stocks of sound companies over an extended period of time, usually at least a year. Buy and hold investors seek companies of value and virtue, firms they believe will consistently report solid earnings that will push the share price higher year after year. Long-term investors do not worry as much about short-term volatility in a stock's price. Rather, long-term investors are more concerned with buying quality companies at good prices for the long haul.

The key ingredients for a long-term investor are good fundamentals such as earnings growth, strong management/leadership, excellent products, and a sustainable competitive advantage.

What is the most tangible proof that a company is worth holding for the long-term?

The answer is earnings—or more specifically, earnings growth over time. This is because a company that has strong management, excellent products, a sustainable competitive advantage, and all the other good things that I have mentioned should grow earnings quarter after quarter.

Additionally, companies that for a structural reason tend to have a moat around their businesses that prevents competitors from moving in are also favorites of long-term investors.

An important question is, how do you determine which companies possess such a moat and thus which companies are worth holding for the long term?

One of the best means of determining whether a company possesses such a moat is to examine its earnings. Companies that have sustainable competitive advantages and thus big moats around their businesses should receive greater upward earnings estimate revisions than other companies and should grow earnings quarter after quarter at a greater rate than Wall Street anticipates.

Now, remember that earnings estimate revisions are the cornerstone of the Zacks Rank. Generally, positive earnings estimate revisions signal that a company's fundamentals are moving in the right direction, and it is a candidate for long-term ownership.

However, not all of the Zacks #1 Ranked companies are appropriate for holding long-term. In fact, in some months I have looked at the Zacks #1 Ranked list of companies and found quite a few that I would not want to hold for longer than three months because they seem to be far too speculative.

As a long-term investor, though, you must always remember that the Zacks #1 Ranked stocks are expected to outperform the market over the next one to three months as opposed to the next several years.

Therefore, for the long-term investor the Zacks Rank should be used more as a timing factor, helping you to select among stocks that are potential long-term plays. In other words, as a long-term investor you should use the Zacks Rank to select among stocks that you would consider holding for the long term regardless of the recent earnings estimate revisions.

Note that large-cap companies are usually best suited for long-term ownership, since they generate a steadier and more stable flow of earnings. So a long-term investor may want to broaden his or her focus to stocks ranked #1 and #2 with market capitalization levels above $10 billion.

Additionally, the Zacks Rank should be monitored for deciding when it is time to sell a long-term holding. Generally, a Zacks Rank of 4 (Sell) or 5 (Strong Sell) indicates a stock is going to be weak over the next three months and is an indication that it might be time to sell or to take profits in a long-term holding.

Growth Investors

Growth investors are generally more aggressive in nature than value investors and long-term investors. Growth investors look for companies that will increase their earnings dramatically in the immediate future, something that should propel their stock price higher.

Growth stocks usually come with a bit more risk, since high earnings growth (generally considered to be above 20% a year) is extremely hard to sustain over the long haul. When the high growth dissipates, a growth stock often shrivels up like a balloon that has had its air let out. For this reason, a tremendous amount of care must be taken not to hold growth stocks for too long.

Can the Zacks Rank help growth investors? Yes, because once again we find a group of investors who are focused on earnings. By combining Zacks #1 Ranked companies with historical growth data, you can uncover a group of stocks that have exhibited good historical earnings growth and which are also predicted to grow earnings in the future.

The most important part is that the Zacks Rank will alert a growth investor at the earliest possible stage that future earnings prospects for the firm are looking brighter, which generally leads to higher share prices, especially among stocks that are valued primarily on their growth prospects.

And just as helpful, the Zacks Rank will let you know the first sign of expected earnings weakness so you can sell your position as early as possible to avoid unnecessary losses.

Many large growth-driven hedge funds actively use the Zacks Rank or a similar strategy in their investment process.

Momentum and Technical Analysis Investors

These folks are generally interested in turning short-term profits based on the general direction/momentum of a stock and changes in its daily trading volume. The newspaper *Investors Business Daily* (*IBD*) and charting software providers are the biggest "torch-bearers" for this movement.

The Zacks Rank is a great fundamental companion for investors who rely on technical analysis and momentum because it tips momentum investors off early as to which stocks are likely to pick up price momentum—in one direction or another—very soon.

Essentially, we are talking about "cause and effect." The cause of a momentum stock's initial move is first indicated by the Zacks Rank, identifying stocks that are receiving positive earnings estimate revisions. This upward shift in earnings estimates prompts more and more investors to become interested in the company, with the effect being that the shares in the company start off a bull run. This initial move in price results in an increase in volume that also attracts new momentum players.

However, if you were just to rely exclusively on technical analysis, then your chart would not show a buy signal until the rally had already started.

In many cases, using the Zacks Rank, you will be able to get in right at the outset of the major move of momentum stocks.

KEY POINT Momentum and technical analysis investors should concentrate on stocks with a Zacks Rank of 1. More specifically, by buying those stocks most recently added to the Zacks #1 Ranked list you have the best chance of getting yourself into a momentum stock at the beginning of a price run.

Limitations of the Zacks Rank

While the Zacks Rank is an incredibly powerful investment tool, it is by no means foolproof, and it is not a panacea.

Following are the main limitations of the Zacks Rank. If you do not take these potential shortfalls into account, then you may make poor investment decisions, and that is the last thing I want to see happen. So, be sure to understand this section fully before you attempt to use the Zacks Rank to enhance your investment returns.

Performance Relative to the Market

The most powerful force affecting any individual stock is the movement of the overall market. For example, it is very difficult for a stock to rise in the face of a bear market. We saw countless cases of that during the market downdraft in 2000–2002.

Since the movement of the overall stock market is key, it is best to think of the Zacks Rank as an indication of a stock's relative performance to the overall market. For example, if the market is tumbling down, then a Zacks #1 Ranked stock will most likely be down, but not as much as the market overall. And when the overall market is up, then a Zacks #5 Ranked stock may very well be up, but not to the same degree as the average stock.

The Zacks Rank is a Short-Term Indicator

With over twenty years of data behind us, it is clear that the effects of earnings estimate revisions last for one to three months. This makes sense when you consider that every three months a company will provide a new round of actual earnings that wipes the slate clean on any previous announcements.

Yet I have found that many long-term investors get caught up with wanting to own just #1-ranked stocks. Unfortunately, investing for the long term and investing only in #1-ranked stocks are not 100% compatible.

Remember that only the top 5% of companies receiving positive earnings estimate revisions will be ranked #1 by Zacks. There is pretty stiff competition for those slots, and a company can be on today and be off tomorrow if another company receives stronger earnings estimate revisions.

However, the company that slipped out of the #1-ranked position may still be an excellent investment. So, long-term investors should be comfortable with ownership of shares that have a Zacks Rank ranging from 1 to 3. Long-term investors that employ the Zacks Rank use slippages to 4 or 5 to trim or completely sell their long-term position in the stock.

KEY POINT   Keep in mind that only 5% of all stocks covered receive a Zacks Rank of 1. Therefore, long-term investors should also seek to own stocks with a Zacks Rank of 1 or 2, and in some cases 3.

Blind to Everything But Four Measures

There are only four measures used to calculate the Zacks Rank. Three of the four—agreement, magnitude, and upside—look at analyst earnings estimate revisions. The fourth measure considers the size and direction of the most recent earnings surprises.

You will note there is no accommodation for other fundamental metrics such as P/E, book value, Return on Equity, Return on Assets, debt ratios, growth rates, and so forth. Nor does the ranking consider technical attributes such as recent changes in price or volume.

So, in reality the Zacks Rank acts as an initial filter that provides a raw list of potentially successful investment candidates. With these raw lists you can do additional screening according to your own investment criteria.

Market Cap

The larger the company, the more analysts are likely to cover the stock. The more analysts covering a stock, the tougher it is for the stock to score big on any of the four measures of the Zacks Rank.

As a result, the list of Zacks #1 Ranked stocks will be over-represented by small to mid-cap stocks. That is why a large-cap stock with a Zacks Rank of 2 is actually a very good ranking and may still provide excellent upside potential relative to the overall market. (Remember to keep a diversified portfolio that includes a mix of stocks by both market cap and industry.)

Too Many Speculative Stocks—Necessary to Stay Diversified

Speculative stocks, such as those issued by new technology firms, have the hardest earnings to predict. That's because small companies are often dependent on one product or one technological niche and do not have the history or stability of an earnings stream like Coca-Cola (KO).

KEY POINT   Your desire to blindly invest in #1-rated stocks should never out-weigh your need for diversification. You never want to be severely over-weighted in any one sector or industry.

If business conditions are right for a speculative company, the company can receive incredible earnings estimate revisions that lead to an exceptionally high scoring in the Zacks Rank.

As a result, those who strictly adhere to buying stocks with a Zacks Rank of 1 may end up having a disproportionate number of small growth companies in new and emerging industries. The reason is that companies in emerging industries tend to have greater potential for strong earnings growth.

At times that may be of benefit, such as when the NASDAQ is soaring. Speculative stocks that were receiving upward earnings estimate revisions but then report poor earnings tend to see their Zacks Rank quickly fall to a 4 (Sell) or a 5 (Strong Sell). Thus, following the Zacks Rank will provide you with exposure to speculative stocks when the speculative stocks' earnings prospects are improving and get you out of them when their earnings prospects sour. Despite this, there is still the need to keep a diversified portfolio and ensure that you do not have too much exposure to speculative stocks.

Turnover of the Zacks Rank

It is important to remember that because only 5% of the companies are given a Zacks Rank of 1 that it is relatively hard to remain a Zacks #1 Ranked stock. Of the stocks that have a Zacks #1 Ranking at the beginning of the month, only 44% will have that ranking by the end of the month.

Over a 15-year period, the transition of Zacks #1 Ranked stocks over a month's time period is given in Figure 9-1.

As you can see, roughly 3% of Zacks #1 Ranked stocks will have a Zacks Rank of 4 (Sell) or 5 (Strong Sell) by the end of the month.

Figure 9-1 Rank of Zacks #1 Ranked stocks one month later (average from 7/87–9/02).

44.17%	Zacks Rank #1
28.16%	Zacks Rank #2
24.76%	Zacks Rank #3
1.94%	Zacks Rank #4
0.97%	Zacks Rank #5

KEY POINT   Figure 9-1 indicates that of the Zacks #1 Ranked companies that you bought at the beginning of the month, on average, roughly half of them will not have a Zacks Rank of 1 by the end of the month.

If you only sell stocks in your portfolio when their Zacks Rank falls to a 4 or 5, the turnover of your portfolio will be significantly reduced from a strategy that sells a stock whenever the Zacks Rank falls below 1. Returns will be lower, but transaction costs will drop dramatically.

This trade-off between returns and transaction costs brings us to the six-step methodology detailed below. This six-step methodology is a means of implementing the Zacks Rank at a discount brokerage firm.

Implementing the Zacks Rank—Six Steps

The six steps involved in implementing the Zacks Rank using quarterly rebalancing are detailed here. The biggest obstacle that you will face is keeping turnover low to minimize commission expenses.

Because of the high turnover, for all practical purposes, the methodology detailed here must be carried out at a discount brokerage firm or in a folio trading platform. At a discount brokerage firm, the minimum investment necessary to implement the six-step process described here is $25,000.

To use a full-service broker that charges over $30 per trade is not efficient unless you can negotiate a flat-asset based fee for unlimited trading. In order to qualify for a flat-asset based fee with unlimited trading at a brokerage firm, an account usually must be at least $500,000 in value.

If your account size falls below the minimum account size, do not despair. You can still implement the steps detailed here to trade a few select stocks; however, you can not implement the strategy in your entire portfolio, as the transaction costs will be too high.

Step One: Determine the Number of Securities to hold

As a general rule of thumb, you should have at least $1,000 invested in every stock you own using this six-step method. This may seem high, but it is driven by a need to keep commissions low. If you stay focused on the Zacks Rank, rebalance quarterly, and hold $1,000 per position, commissions should be limited to about 2% per year.

Here's the reasoning behind this calculation. If you rebalance quarterly, for each $1,000 position you will make on average four trades per year, per position. Your average holding time for a position will be around six months. At a rock-bottom commission cost of around $5 per trade, this translates to $20 in commissions per year per $1,000 invested or around 2% per year in commissions. At $10 a trade, your commission costs will rise to 4% per year, which is far too high.

KEY POINT   For any investment strategy you employ, you should always actively strive to keep your total commission costs below 2% per year. It is very important to calculate what your annual commission costs will be before you begin to implement any strategy.

The table in Figure 9-2 makes this point explicitly. Figure 9-2 assumes a $5 per trade commission and quarterly turnover in which roughly 50% of the positions in the portfolio are replaced over a given quarter. Again this indicates an average holding period of six months for a stock. (If you pay $10 per trade you should double the values, and if you pay $15 a trade you should triple the values. Again, it is extremely important to keep commissions low.)

The percentages in Figure 9-2 represent the annual commission costs you will incur implementing the Zacks Rank with quarterly rebalancing. You should actively strive to hold the most number of stocks possible while keeping your total commission costs under 2%.

How the Portfolio Should Be Divided Up

Positions in your portfolio initially should be equal-weighted. This means you should try to keep an equal dollar amount in each stock that you own.

The general rule of thumb presented previously of $1,000 per position assumes that you have, at a bare minimum, twenty-five positions; this means you own at least twenty-five stocks. This minimum number of positions is necessary to maintain adequate diversification.

Figure 9-2 Cost in annual percentage terms due to commissions.

Size of Portfolio	Number of Positions					
	25 Stocks	50 stocks	75 Stocks	100 Stocks	125 Stocks	150 Stocks
$ 5,000	10.00%	20.00%	30.00%	40.00%	50.00%	60.00%
$ 10,000	5.00%	10.00%	15.00%	20.00%	25.00%	30.00%
$ 25,000	2.00%	4.00%	6.00%	8.00%	10.00%	12.00%
$ 50,000	1.00%	2.00%	3.00%	4.00%	5.00%	6.00%
$ 75,000	0.67%	1.33%	2.00%	2.67%	3.33%	4.00%
$ 100,000	0.50%	1.00%	1.50%	2.00%	2.50%	3.00%
$ 150,000	0.33%	0.67%	1.00%	1.33%	1.67%	2.00%
$ 300,000	0.17%	0.33%	0.50%	0.67%	0.83%	1.00%
$ 450,000	0.11%	0.22%	0.33%	0.44%	0.56%	0.67%
$ 600,000	0.08%	0.17%	0.25%	0.33%	0.42%	0.50%
$ 750,000	0.07%	0.13%	0.20%	0.27%	0.33%	0.40%
$ 900,000	0.06%	0.11%	0.17%	0.22%	0.28%	0.33%
$ 1,050,000	0.05%	0.10%	0.14%	0.19%	0.24%	0.29%
$ 1,200,000	0.04%	0.08%	0.13%	0.17%	0.21%	0.25%
$ 1,350,000	0.04%	0.07%	0.11%	0.15%	0.19%	0.22%
$ 1,500,000	0.03%	0.07%	0.10%	0.13%	0.17%	0.20%

If you do not have $25,000 to invest, you can still make use of the Zacks Rank by buying several Zacks #1 Ranked stocks and holding them for a quarter, as detailed in the following section.

Step Two: Set Sector Targets

It is not enough merely to have twenty-five or more positions in your portfolio. You must also have adequate sector diversification. I am far more concerned that your positions be adequately diversified across sectors than I am about diversification across capitalization or across investment style, such as growth versus value.

The best way to determine sector exposure is to use the Zacks #1 Ranked portfolio as a guide. By dividing the number of Zacks #1 Ranked stocks in each of the sixteen economic sectors by the total number of Zacks #1 Ranked stocks, you can determine the target percentage sector exposure.

Figure 9-3 shows the sector exposure of the Zacks #1 Ranked stocks in the full universe as of August 4th, 2002. The target sector exposure is very time-sensitive and changes as the Zacks #1 Ranked portfolio changes. As a result, you should check the current sector exposure online before setting your target weightings.

Figure 9-3 Sector exposure of Zacks #1 Ranked stocks as of mid-year 2002.

Sector Name	# of Stocks
Consumer Staples	15
Consumer Discretionary	6
Retail / Wholesale	14
Medical	21
Autos / Tires / Trucks	8
Basic Materials	11
Industrial Products	6
Construction	12
Multi-Sector Conglomerates	2
Computer & Technology	24
Aerospace	1
Oils / Energy	10
Finance	29
Utilities	1
Transportation	8
Business Services	5
All Sectors	173

Essentially, determining the target sector exposure is a two-step process. First, you should take the number of Zacks #1 Ranked stocks in each of the sixteen economic sectors from the Zacks.com website and the total number of Zacks #1 Ranked stocks in order to calculate the target sector exposure in percentage terms.

So, as an example, in Figure 9-3, there are 21 Zacks #1 Ranked stocks in the medical sector and 173 Zacks #1 Ranked stocks overall. From this data, it is possible to calculate that the target medical exposure is 21/173 or 12.1%.

The next step is to multiply this target sector exposure by the number of stocks you should hold in your portfolio. This means that if your target portfolio size is fifty stocks, roughly six of those stocks should be in the medical sector.

The net result of these two steps is that you should determine a target number of positions in each sector. Each of these positions should be equal-weighted and roughly $1,000 in size.

The next step is the most important one: determining exactly which stocks to buy and when to buy them.

Step Three: Determine Which Stocks to Buy

After you have determined the targeted number of positions to hold in each sector, you want to figure out which of the Zacks #1 Ranked stocks in each sector you should hold in your portfolio. The following selection guidelines are a means of trying to select the very best stocks from among all stocks that have a Zacks Rank of 1. The reasoning behind these additional selection criteria is contained throughout the book.

When selecting among the Zacks #1 Ranked stocks you should give preference to the following:

- *Recent additions to the Zacks #1 Ranked portfolio.* Stocks that have recently become Zacks #1 Ranked stocks most likely have the freshest earnings estimate revisions, and thus you can benefit the most from the institutional delay in reacting to the positive earnings estimate revisions.

- *Stocks that are receiving upward earnings estimate revisions due to organic top-line growth.* Top-line revenue growth means improving fundamentals, whereas earnings estimate revisions due to cost savings are not sustainable over time. You want to be careful to avoid earnings estimate revisions due to accounting changes. A good way to determine whether a stock's earnings estimate revisions are the result of top-line revenue growth is to actually look at an analyst's research report.

- *Zacks #1 Ranked stocks that have recently reported positive earnings surprises.* Again, look for companies that beat earnings expectations by posting strong revenue growth. Essentially, you want to take advantage of the post-earnings announcement drift—the tendency of stocks that report earnings in excess of expectations to exhibit strength over the next one to three months.

- *Zacks #1 Ranked stocks that have recently raised earnings guidance.* If a company recently raised earnings guidance it is a very strong indication that analysts will be raising earnings estimates in the future.

- *Zacks #1 Ranked stocks that are trading at reasonable valuation levels based on the forward P/E calculated on the coming year's consensus earnings estimate.* As we shall see later in the book, excess returns can be achieved over time by buying stocks that are trading at low P/E levels. Also, as I illustrate a little later on, you should actively avoid any stock that is trading at a forward P/E level above 65.

- *Zacks #1 Ranked stocks that have recently received recommendation upgrades.* We will see that stocks that receive recommendation upgrades tend to outperform over the next month. You should use this knowledge to your advantage by leaning toward companies that have recently received recommendation upgrades.

- *Zacks #1 Ranked stocks that have experienced some degree of insider buying or have recently issued a share buy-back.* Both of these are strongly positive signals that usually occur prior to a strengthening share price.

- *Zacks #1 Ranked stocks that pay a dividend and Zacks #1 Ranked stocks that have recently increased their dividend payments.* An increased dividend payment signals that management believes their company's cash flow situation has permanently improved, whereas insider buying indicates that management believes that the stock represents a compelling value.

KEY POINT   You want to buy Zacks #1 Ranked stocks that are reasonably valued and have

- recently been added to the Zacks #1 Ranked list
- been growing earnings organically
- recently received analyst recommendation upgrades
- recently reported good earnings or raised guidance
- recently increased their dividend payment
- experienced some degree of insider buying or issued share buy-backs

---

By the same token, you should try to lean away from Zacks #1 Ranked stocks that exhibit the following characteristics:

- *Are experiencing extensive insider selling.* It is never a good sign when the rats are leaving the ship.

- *Have recently been downgraded by brokerage firms.* The analyst, for all his faults, does not downgrade stocks lightly; as we saw, stocks receiving downward recommendation changes tend to underperform over the next month.

- *Have lowered their dividend payments in the past.* Lowering a dividend payment is a good sign of lower cash flow levels in the future.

- *Are trading at high valuation levels based on P/E.* Again, avoid companies with forward P/E ratios above 65.

- *Have high projected earnings growth rates.* As we shall see later on in the book, when analysts collectively believe that a company's long-term growth prospects are explosive, chances are the market has overpaid for the stock.

- *Have not historically responded to positive earnings surprises.* When a stock does not respond to a positive earnings surprise, it is a clear signal that upward revisions to analysts' earnings estimates are already reflected in the stock's price.

- *Beat analysts' earnings estimates through non-recurring items.* Definitely a no-no. Non-recurring items are essentially a firm's way of engaging in legal book-cooking; you do not need to get involved with them.

KEY POINT   You should always keep an eye out for a stock's valuation. If a Zacks #1 Ranked stock is trading at a rich valuation—a forward P/E level above 65—and you have any intention of holding the position longer than three months, you should think twice before buying.

Step Four: Determine When to Buy

Whether you are looking at moving averages, Treasury yields, dividend discount models, hemlines, sunspots, or market sentiment surveys, market timing has proven to be a loser's game.

The absolute best market-timing model anyone has ever developed is very simple: Remain invested at all times. Ignore the pain, ignore the emotion, and realize that no one can time the market and that statistically the U.S. stock market has trended upward over time.

It is important to remember that the majority of the market's gains for an entire year occur during a scant few days. If you happen to miss those key days by not being invested, you will wind up underperforming over time.

Thus if you are sitting on the sidelines worried about a further sell-off in the market, my suggestion is that instead of worrying you should dollar-cost-average into the market.

Dollar-cost-averaging means that you take a portion of your money and put it to work in the market on a regular basis, and then stay invested through the good and bad times over an extended period of time. Over the long run, the next five to ten years, this strategy will prove to be better than trying to time the market.

Once you have decided to be invested, you should dollar-cost-average into the market, that is, put the same amount of money into the market at regular intervals. For example, once you decide to be invested, I would recommend investing roughly one-sixth of the total dollar amount you want to invest every couple of weeks over the next several months. Note that dollar-cost averaging is simply a way for you to deal psychologically with the volatility of the market; there's nothing inherently magical about it.

After you are invested in the market, decide how much you want to invest and stick to this dollar-cost-averaging strategy regardless of how the market performs while you are dollar-cost-averaging into it. Once fully invested, it is absolutely paramount that you stay invested through the good and bad times.

Over the long run, being fully invested in stocks that are actively receiving upward earnings estimate revisions will generate greater returns than trying to determine the exact best point in time to become invested.

Step Five: Decide When to Sell Your Entire Position in a Stock

You should monitor the Zacks Rank of the stocks in your portfolio on a regular basis. If you choose not to monitor the Zacks Rank, you should absolutely monitor all earnings estimate revisions to your portfolio.

If the Zacks Rank drops to a 4 or 5 at any time, or if there are substantial negative earnings estimate revisions, you should sell the stock immediately.

Otherwise, try to hold the stock for at least three months. If after three months the Zacks Rank of the stock is a three or lower, you should definitely sell.

If the Zacks Rank falls to a three prior to the three-month-evaluation, it is a judgment call as to whether to sell. Generally, I would only sell if the fall in the Zacks Rank to 3 was precipitated by a poor earnings report or poor earnings guidance issued by the company.

KEY POINT   Whenever possible, try to hold a stock for at least three months after purchasing it. If you make too much of a habit of selling stocks prior to the quarterly rebalancing period due to a falling Zacks Rank, your commission costs will increase. Remember, a Zacks Rank of 3 (Neutral) simply implies the stock will be a market performer over the next one to three months.

Additionally, if a company reports earnings below expectations, or warns about future earnings, the stock should be sold—do not wait for analysts to lower their earnings estimates.

Any news story—such as a poor monthly sales numbers for a retailer—that leads you to believe analysts will be lowering their earnings estimates in the future should also result in your selling the stock.

Finally, if any stock you own falls more than 35% relative to the performance of the S&P 500, sell. This sell signal is easy to calculate. Simply take the return on the stock since it was bought, and subtract the return off the S&P 500. If the value is less than 35%, the stock should be sold.

This stop-loss technique becomes less important the more diversified your portfolio, because the more stocks you own, the less the under-performance of an individual stock can seriously hurt you. But this technique should be strictly adhered to if you are holding fewer than fifty stocks in your portfolio.

Step Six: Determine When to Partially Sell a Position and When to Rebalance

Two activities should result in your partially selling a position.

Generally, any substantial insider selling or analyst recommendation downgrades should cause you to partially sell a position. The degree of your selling depends on the situation, but for the most part it should be limited to selling 25% of the position.

I generally do not recommend adding to a losing position under any circumstance. The strategy of "doubling-down" by adding money to a losing position in order to lower your average cost generally does not work with Zacks #1 Ranked stocks.

The Zacks Rank is not a long-term stock selection model, and stocks with a #1 Rank are expected to outperform the market over the near term. If a Zacks #1 Ranked stock falls in value after being bought, the stock does not become more attractive, it becomes substantially less attractive.

This is because when a Zacks #1 Ranked stock underperforms the market it means that the market is not responding to the upward earnings estimate revisions. In such cases, even if you successfully predict future earnings estimate revisions for the stock, the market may continue to ignore the estimate revisions. In such instances, you do not want to add to a position.

Similarly, if a stock is performing well, you should let the stock ride without adding or reducing exposure until the quarterly rebalancing period. Profit-taking should be limited to the quarterly rebalancing period.

Rebalance Quarterly

Every quarter you should do a little pruning of your portfolio in a quarterly rebalancing. The quarterly rebalancing entails changing your portfolio weightings so that the weighting of every position is again equal-weighted.

This is the only time I would add to a losing position. If after three months a losing position is still a Zacks #1 Ranked stock, it makes some sense to increase the losing position to an equal weighting.

Summary

- The Zacks Rank can be used effectively by different types of investors, but there are some limitations.

- Combining the Zacks #1 Ranked list with a value screen is an excellent strategy for a value investor to employ.

- Roughly half of the stocks that have a Zacks Rank of 1 at the beginning of the month will not have a Zacks Rank of 1 by the end of the month.

- Because of this high degree of turnover individuals should implement the Zacks Rank through the following six steps.

  - Step One: Make sure to hold enough positions in order to keep commission costs below 2% annually.

  - Step Two: Set sector exposure to match the sector exposure of the Zacks #1 Ranked portfolio.

  - Step Three: You want to buy Zacks #1 Ranked stocks that are reasonably valued and have
    - recently been added to the Zacks #1 Ranked list
    - been growing earnings organically
    - recently received analyst recommendation upgrades
    - recently reported good earnings or raised guidance
    - recently increased their dividend payment
    - experienced some degree of insider buying, or issued share buy-backs

- Step Four: Instead of trying to time the market, decide how much you want to be invested in the market and dollar-cost average into the market over a period of time.

- Step Five: Sell a stock if after three months the Zacks Rank falls to 3 or below. Sell a stock prior to three months if the Zacks Rank falls to 4 or 5 or if a stock announces a negative earnings surprise, or lowers earnings guidance.

- Step Six: Rebalance positions at the end of three months.

## Chapter Ten

How to Effectively Use Analysts' Recommendations

What's ahead in this chapter?

- The Consensus Recommendation Score
- How to Use the Consensus Recommendation Score to Adjust for Analyst Bias
- Does Comparing Consensus Recommendation Scores across Stocks Help You Pick Winners?
- Why Did the Stocks Most Highly Recommended by Analysts Perform So Poorly Recently?
- Piggybacking—A Strategy that Works in Up and Down Markets
- Returns Due to Piggybacking

AT THIS POINT, AFTER SEEING HOW TO EFFECTIVELY USE earnings estimates and earnings surprises, you likely have the following practical and appropriate question regarding analysts' recommendations:

> So analysts boil down their research report into one directed piece of advice that tells you whether to buy, hold, or sell a stock. And with these recommendations, analysts almost never issue sell recommendations and the recommendations often do not reflect what an analyst actually thinks about a stock because of the big, bad investment bankers. But is there any way I can use analysts' recommendations to my advantage to make money?

The answer is yes, and this chapter is about how you should and should not use analyst recommendations. If correctly interpreted, analyst recommendations can be extremely helpful in selecting from among stocks that are receiving upward earnings estimate revisions and reporting positive earnings surprises.

But, you have to use analyst recommendations in a rather non-obvious way. In fact, if you use analyst recommendations in the conventional manner, you may end up enriching large institutional players.

It is important, in any case, that you understand how to adjust analysts' recommendations for the scarcity of sell or negative recommendations.

Once this is accomplished, you want to focus on buying stocks for which analysts have recently upgraded their recommendations and selling stocks for which analysts have recently downgraded their recommendations. This strategy is called "piggybacking" because you are investing on the coattails of analysts' recommendations, and I will explain how to implement this strategy in this chapter.

Before you can implement a piggybacking strategy, though, it is necessary to examine a statistic called the consensus recommendation score.

The Consensus Recommendation Score

When we began tracking analyst recommendations at Zacks roughly fifteen years ago, we quickly realized that analysts are horribly biased. Rather than distribute biased data, we decided to try to correct the bias. The result is a simple statistic that is called the consensus recommendation score.

The consensus recommendation score is a number that represents the average of all the recommendations issued by the analysts following a certain stock. This score can be found throughout the Internet on any one of hundreds of web pages displaying the distribution of analyst recommendations. The consensus recommendation score may sound sophisticated but it is really quite simple.

Think of it this way: You've been told to go to a university where grade inflation is rampant and hire the hardest-working students. Looking through the student transcripts, you become discouraged as it appears that everyone receives marks of a B+. Thus, students who have B+ grades are in reality not exceptional students, but just average. Instead of qualitatively examining the grades of the students, you need a more robust methodology.

The key is a student's grade point average. Whether there is grade inflation—whether the average grade at the university is a B+ or a C— does not change the fact that those students with the highest grade point averages should be more studious than those students with the lowest grade point averages. As long as all grades are inflated roughly equally, the grade point average should help you to identify the truly diligent students.

This is essentially what we did with analyst recommendations. We calculated a grade point average for each and every stock based on the outstanding recommendations issued by analysts. We called this grade point average of stocks a consensus recommendation score. By ranking stocks according to the consensus recommendation score, you have a rough methodology of de-biasing the recommendations issued by analysts.

Remember that each brokerage firm has its own set of recommendations that the firm's analysts can issue. The first step to creating the consensus recommendation score entails translating each and every brokerage firm's unique recommendation scheme to a standard 1–5 rating classification.

The next step is to assign values to the translated recommendation, as is done in Figure 10-1.

Figure 10-1 Consensus recommendation score values.

Recommendation	Value
Strong Buy	1
Buy	2
Hold	3
Sell	4
Strong Sell	5

Calculate the consensus recommendation score by adding up the total number of points derived from each analyst's most recent recommendation and then dividing by the total number of recommendations.

For example, Figure 10-2 contains the most recent recommendations for IBM, as of August 2002.

Figure 10-2 Current broker recommendations for IBM.

Current Broker Recommendations		Average Recommendation	
Strong Buy	6	(Buy) 1.00–5.00 (Sell)	
Buy	3	This Week	2.21
Hold	10	Last Week	2.30
Sell	0	Change	
Strong Sell	0		
Covering Brokers	19		

IBM has nineteen analysts issuing recommendations. Six analysts issued a "Strong Buy" recommendation, three issued a "Buy" recommendation, and ten issued a "Hold" recommendation. The consensus recommendation score is then calculated as 2.21. [1]

As we have seen, the consensus recommendation score is essentially a number that ranges from 1 to 5. A consensus recommendation score is like a golf score; a lower value represents a more bullish signal for a stock. The advantage of the consensus recommendation score is that it enables you to quantitatively rank stocks against one another and thus to some extent eliminate the bias in the analyst recommendations.

Even though analysts tend to be far too optimistic and not issue enough negative recommendations, ranking stocks according to the consensus recommendation score enables you to determine which stocks analysts are the most and least enthusiastic about.

KEY POINT   What makes the consensus recommendation score useful is that it counteracts analysts' two forms of bias—their reluctance to issue sell recommendations and their influence by investment banks. Ranking stocks by their consensus recommendation score allows you to determine which stocks analysts are the most enthused over.

This method of calculating a consensus recommendation score was invented by Zacks and very quickly adopted by other firms distributing analyst data—and the consensus recommendation score methodology is now an accepted industry standard.

What Is the Difference between the Consensus Recommendation Score and the Zacks Rank?

The consensus recommendation score is displayed for free on hundreds of websites. Like the Zacks Rank, the consensus recommendation score is shown in a range between 1 and 5. However, the consensus recommendation score will generally be displayed with decimal places (e.g., 1.52) whereas the Zacks Rank is displayed only in whole numbers (1, 2, 3, etc.).

However, their differences go far beyond these cosmetic issues.

In essence, the consensus recommendation score is based on brokerage firm stock recommendations, while the Zacks Rank, on the other hand, is based purely on earnings fundamentals. Additionally, the Zacks Rank has proven to be a much more powerful signal and works in both up and down markets.

How to Use the Consensus Recommendation Score to Adjust for Analyst Bias

"Hello, it's Jim, your broker over here at EF Stanley."

"Hey Jim, what's up? Is there something wrong with my portfolio?"

"Not at all, but I think it is a good time to buy IBM."

"Well, I don't know, Jim; I never did like IBM."

"I understand what you are saying, but of the nineteen analysts with outstanding recommendations on IBM, six are 'Strong Buys,' three are 'Buys,' and ten are 'Holds.' Almost half of the analysts following IBM have a 'Buy' recommendation on it—any way you look at it, IBM is a winner."

"Aw right then, put me down for 300 shares, but buy them on some weakness...."

KEY POINT   Do not mistakenly assume that because nine of the nineteen analysts following IBM have a buy recommendation that this is a bullish signal. Looking at the most recent recommendations for a given stock is not helpful.

The fact that of the nineteen recommendations outstanding on IBM, six are "Strong Buys," three are "Buys," and ten are "Holds" is a meaningless statistic in isolation. It is like answering 70% of the questions correctly on a test. The percent of questions you answered correctly means nothing unless examined in comparison with how the other people in the class performed.

In order to use analyst recommendations effectively, you must compare the distribution of recommendations across stocks in the same sector, rather than simply looking at the most recent recommendations on just one stock. The consensus recommendation score makes this possible.

The consensus recommendation score enables you to create a ranking of stocks across a given sector, effectively adjusting for the fact that analysts rarely issue sell recommendations. The reason is simple: In any ranking, there will be a stock ranked first and a stock ranked last.

Instead of looking at the distribution of recommendations on IBM in isolation, you should compare the consensus recommendation score for IBM relative to stocks like Cisco (CSCO), Hewlett Packard (HPQ), Microsoft (MSFT), Sun Microsystems (SUNW), Electronic Data Systems (EDS), and perhaps other large-cap hardware and/or IT consulting companies. By comparing the consensus recommendation score across similar types of stocks, you will be better able to draw a conclusion as to whether the existing analyst recommendations for IBM are in fact bullish or bearish.

In this case, Figure 10-3 shows the consensus recommendation scores for the stocks mentioned above.

Figure 10-3 Comparative consensus recommendation scores.

	Consensus Recommendation Score	Rank
MSFT	1.7	1
CSCO	1.9	2
HPQ	2.1	3
IBM	**2.2**	**4**
EDS	2.4	5
SUNW	2.5	6

In this instance, analysts' recommendations for IBM are actually slightly worse than average relative to analysts' recommendations for other, similar types of stocks. The consensus recommendation score indicates that analysts, on average, are less bullish on IBM than they are on Microsoft, Cisco, and to some extent Hewlett Packard.

However, analysts are more bullish on IBM than they are on EDS and Sun Microsystems. It is important to realize that even though roughly half of the analysts following IBM's stock recommend the stock as a "buy," the recommendations taken in aggregate are not bullish when compared to the recommendations analysts are issuing on other, similar stocks.

A reasonable question is whether it is fair to compare consensus recommendation scores for companies with different numbers of analysts following the stock. For instance, imagine there are two companies, one with three analysts covering it and the other company with twenty analysts covering it.

There is a greater chance that all three analysts will issue strong buy recommendations than there is for all twenty analysts to issue strong buy recommendations.

As a result, you should try to compare consensus recommendation scores across stocks with relatively the same number of analysts issuing recommendations. In the example above, all the stocks compared to IBM have approximately the same number of analysts issuing recommendations.

KEY POINT   When you compare consensus recommendation scores across stocks, try to ensure that the stocks being compared are in the same sector, if not industry, and have the same number of analysts following them.

Does Comparing Consensus Recommendation Scores Across Stocks Help You Pick Winners?

In order to answer this question you must examine how you would have fared if over the past ten years you used the consensus recommendation score to directly manage two portfolios.

The 3,300 largest companies serve as the universe of companies that the following two portfolios are constructed from:

- *"Loved by the Analysts."* A portfolio consisting of those stocks that were the most highly recommended by analysts, as determined by the consensus recommendation score.

- *"Spurned by the Analysts."* A portfolio consisting of those stocks that were the least highly recommended by analysts, as determined by the consensus recommendation score.

These two portfolios are rebalanced on a monthly basis based on the consensus recommendation scores calculated from analyst recommendations that were available at the time of the rebalance.

At the end of each month from April 1992 to September 2002, the "Loved by the Analysts" portfolio contains those 330 stocks that have the most positive consensus recommendation scores, while the "Spurned by the Analysts" portfolio consists of those 330 stocks that have the worst consensus recommendation scores.

An equal dollar amount is invested into each position in both of these two portfolios and the positions are held for an entire month.

At the end of the month, the process is repeated.

Ignoring transaction costs, the strategy would have generated the annualized returns shown in Figure 10-4.

Figure 10-4 Annualized returns (April 1992 to March 2000).

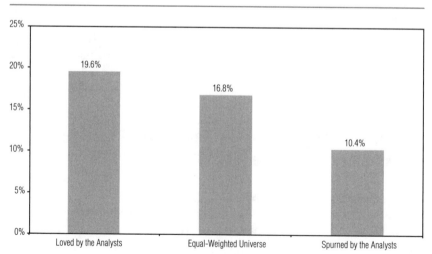

The conclusion from this study is that for most of the 1990s, buying shares in companies that were the most highly recommended by analysts would have made you money. As you can see, the portfolio of stocks that were the most highly recommended was up an average of 19.6% per year, far outdistancing not only the portfolio of the least-recommended stocks but also slightly exceeding the return you would have received from an equal-weighted index consisting of all stocks you could have potentially bought.

Thus, over the eight-year period from April of 1992 to March of 2000, you could have beaten the market by simply buying those stocks that were the most highly recommended by analysts.

Armed with this knowledge, you become very excited. You mortgage your house, and beginning in March of 2000 you start implementing this strategy with a vengeance. Sure, the NASDAQ just crashed, but you are empowered by the market-beating returns of buying those stocks that were "loved by the analysts" over the past eight years. What happens over the next two years?

It isn't pretty.

Just look at Figure 10-5 below.

As you can see, by buying those stocks that are loved by the analysts, you will lose, on an annualized basis, 22.5% of your money over the next two-and-a-half years. In total, this amounts to losing 47.1% of

Figure 10-5 Annualized returns (April 2000 to March 2002).

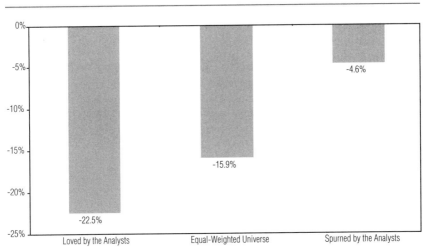

your assets over the next two-and-a-half years due to compounding. To add insult to injury, the way you could have substantially lessened your losses was to buy those stocks that actually had the worst consensus recommendation scores, those stocks that were the least recommended by analysts.

Indeed, if you combine both periods—the eight years when the strategy of buying those stocks most highly recommended by analysts worked, and the two-and-a-half when the strategy's performance gave new meaning to the word "dreadful"—what you find is that analysts do not seem to have much ability at all to select stocks.

Over the ten-and-a-half years from April 1992 to September 2002, those stocks that were the most highly recommended by analysts rose, on average, 7.8% per year, while those stocks that bore the worst analyst recommendations rose at an annualized rate of 6.6% per year. Both portfolios under-performed the equal-weighted index, which rose at an annualized rate of 8.0% over the same ten-and-a-half-year period.

Given these results, you might conclude that buying stocks that are the most highly recommended by analysts is not a viable strategy.

That is one possible explanation, but this overlooks the fact that those stocks most highly recommended by analysts performed relatively well from 1992 to 2000.

The real explanation gets to the heart of whether you can use analysts' recommendations to make money.

Why Did the Stocks Most Highly Recommended by Analysts Perform So Poorly Recently?

If you dig a little deeper, what you find is that the reason for the perverse performance over the past two-and-a-half years of stocks that are highly recommended by analysts is that the stocks that are highly recommended by analysts tend to outperform the market when the market rises, but also tend to under-perform the market when the market falls.

It is not that analysts are lousy stockpickers all the time—rather, it is that analysts are lousy stockpickers when the market goes down. Analysts, for what it is worth, collectively remain decent stockpickers when the market is trending upwards.

This has as much to do with the behavior of investors as it does with the stock-picking ability of analysts. When the market is trending upwards, investors actively buy those stocks that analysts are the most enthused over, but when the overall market is falling, investors actively sell the same stocks.

KEY POINT   Analysts are poor stockpickers when the market falls. As a result, in periods when the market goes up, stocks that are highly recommended by analysts tend to outperform, while in periods when the market goes down, stocks that are highly recommended by analysts tend to under-perform.

How do we know this is true? The answer lies in examining the performance of the portfolio of stocks that are "loved by analysts" in up and down markets, not just over the past two-and-a-half years from April 2000 to September 2002, but also over the eight-year period from 1992 to 2000. What you should look for is whether the "Loved by Analysts" portfolio performs differently in up and down markets over the two periods.

Figure 10-6 shows the percentage of months in which the portfolio consisting of the stocks that are "loved by analysts" outperformed the equal-weighted index from January 1992 to March 2000.

And Figure 10-7 shows the percentage of months from April 2000 to September 2002 in which the "Loved by the Analysts" portfolio outperformed the equal-weighted index.

In total, from January 1992 to March of 2000, in 72.7% of the months when the market went up, the portfolio of stocks that were "loved by the analysts" (those stocks that were the most highly recommended by analysts) outperformed the equal-weighted index.

However, over the same time period, in only 26.7% of the months when the market fell did those stocks that were the most highly recommended by analysts outperform the equal-weighted index.

The statistics look surprisingly similar for the period between April 2000 and September 2002. From 1992 to 2000 when the market went down, stocks that were "loved by the analysts" outperformed the benchmark 26.7% of the time, while from 2000 to 2002 the percentage rose slightly to 27.8%.

Figure 10-6 Percent of the months when the "Loved by the Analysts" portfolio outperformed the equal-weighted benchmark (April 1992 to March 2000).

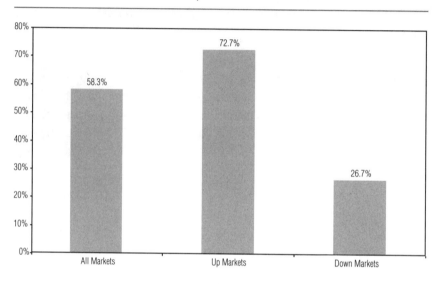

Figure 10-7 Percent of the months when the "Loved by the Analysts" portfolio outperformed the equal-weighted benchmark (April 2000 to September 2002).

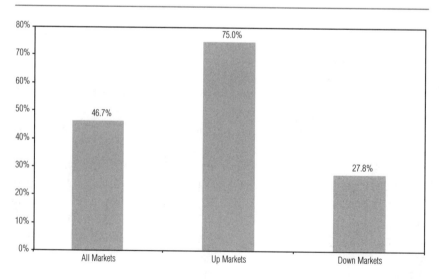

Essentially, the stocks that are the most highly recommended by analysts never do well when the market goes down—it is simply that over the last couple of years there have been significantly more down months than there were from 1992 to 2000.

The reason stocks that are highly recommended by analysts have performed so poorly recently has little to do with the rising conflict of interest between banking and research, or the reluctance of analysts to issue sell recommendations.

Rather, over the past twelve years, when the market goes south those stocks that have been the most highly recommended or promoted by analysts are the ones that sell off the quickest and the furthest.

This could be because analysts tend to recommend stocks that are poised for "action"—stocks that will make good returns if the market goes up, but stocks that also are hit the hardest when the market turns.

Thus, whether you should use the consensus recommendation score to select among stocks depends on your outlook on the market. In a bull market, it makes sense to buy those stocks with the best consensus recommendation scores (closest to a value of one); however, in a bear market it makes much more sense to buy stocks that have the worst consensus recommendation scores (closest to a value of five).

KEY POINT   In a bull market, it makes sense to buy those stocks that are the most highly recommended by analysts; but in a bear market, the opposite strategy—buying those stocks that are least recommended by analysts—performs better.

Piggybacking—A Strategy that Works in Up and Down Markets

The best way to use the consensus recommendation score is not to compare the consensus recommendation score across stocks, but rather to compare the consensus recommendation score over time. You want to buy stocks whose consensus recommendation score is improving over time. This strategy is called "piggybacking"—essentially, you are getting a free ride on the fervor that the analyst creates with the change in his recommendation.

In order to effectively piggyback, it is not the consensus recommendation score that you must analyze; rather, it is the change in the consensus recommendation score over time.

This piggybacking strategy is the most effective use of analyst recommendations that I have uncovered. Basically, the strategy entails buying stocks based on degree of change to the consensus recommendation score over the past month.

Although the stocks that are the most highly recommended by analysts do not outperform the market if the market goes down, those stocks that received the greatest degree of recommendation upgrades by analysts over the past month do tend to outperform over the next month regardless of whether the market moves up or down.

The data clearly shows that the best way to use analyst recommendations is to buy stocks whose consensus recommendation scores have improved the most over the past thirty days, and hold those stocks for a very brief period, one to three months, before selling.

KEY POINT   Piggybacking is the best use of analysts' recommendations. This strategy entails buying stocks whose consensus recommendation score has improved the most during the past thirty days.

How exactly do you put this strategy to work? It's a three-step plan.

Step One: Calculate the Change in the Consensus Recommendation Score over the Past Month

Calculate the change in the consensus recommendation score over the past month. The historical consensus recommendation score is readily available through almost any Internet site that tracks analysts' recommendations.

Figure 10-8 contains the consensus recommendation score summary for the Apollo Group (APOL), a private education provider, taken from the Microsoft Money website (moneycentral.msn.com).

In order to calculate the change in the consensus recommendation score, take the current score and subtract from it the consensus recommendation score from the previous month. In Figure 10-8, the consensus recommendation score is labeled as the "Mean Rec." row.

Figure 10-8 Apollo Group, Inc. (APOL)—analyst ratings.

Recommendations	Current	1 Month Ago	2 Months Ago	3 Months Ago
Strong Buy	5	3	3	3
Moderate Buy	8	9	9	9
Hold	2	3	3	3
Moderate Sell	0	0	0	0
Strong Sell	0	0	0	0
Mean Rec.	1.80	2.00	2.00	2.00

Remember, the best possible consensus recommendation score a stock could have is 1.0, which would indicate all brokerage firms are ranking the stock a "Strong Buy," and the lower the consensus recommendation score the better. As a result, you want the difference between the current consensus recommendation score and the consensus recommendation score from one month ago to be negative, and the more negative the difference the better.

For instance, in the example shown in Figure 10-8, Apollo (APOL) has a current consensus recommendation score of 1.8 and last month had a consensus recommendation score of 2.0. Thus, the calculation of the change in the consensus recommendation score would look like this:

1.8 (this month's score) − 2.0 (last month's score) = −0.20.

So, the change in the consensus recommendation score over the past month is −0.20.

Step Two: Determine whether the Change Signals a "Buy"

Once you have calculated the change in the consensus recommendation score over the past month, the next step is to determine whether the change in the consensus recommendation score is large enough to signal a "Buy" for the stock.

Based on my analysis, you generally want the change in the consensus recommendation score over the past month to place a stock in the top 10% or decile of all stocks covered by two or more analysts.

To determine whether the upward recommendations are strong enough to make a stock a buy candidate, see what the cut-off or break-point is in order to be included in the top 10% of all stocks covered by analysts.

KEY POINT   To be a buy candidate, you want the change in the consensus rec-ommendation score over the past month to put a stock in the top 10% of all stocks covered by analysts. You need to determine the cut-off or breakpoint to be included in this top 10%.

Figure 10-9 shows what the breakpoint has historically been in order for a stock to be in the top 10% of all stocks covered by two or more ana-lysts. In order to be a buy signal, you want the change in the consensus recommendation score to be more negative than the current breakpoint.

If the change in the consensus recommendation score over the past month is less than or equal to the most recent breakpoint (in this case, −0.12), the stock can be considered a buy candidate.

Figure 10-9 Top decile based on change in consensus recommendation over one month.

Year	Value
1991	− 0.17
1992	− 0.17
1993	− 0.16
1994	− 0.15
1995	− 0.15
1996	− 0.15
1997	− 0.16
1998	− 0.14
1999	− 0.14
2000	− 0.13
2001	− 0.11
2002	− 0.12

In Figure 10-8, the change in the consensus recommendation score for APOL over the past month is −0.20, which is more negative than the break point of −0.12, so APOL is a buy candidate. In this case you would be piggybacking on one analyst who raised his recommendation from a "Buy" to a "Strong Buy" and another analyst who raised his recommendation to a "Strong Buy" from a "Hold."

The piggybacking strategy contends that as a result of these recommendation changes, APOL stock will exhibit strength over the next month.

Step Three: Determine When to Sell

In one month's time, recalculate the change in the stock's consensus recommendation score. Because the piggybacking strategy focuses on the change to the consensus recommendation score over the past month, it is unlikely that a stock in the top decile at the beginning of the month will remain in the top decile at the end of the month. In 2002, for example, roughly 30% of the stocks for which analysts had issued recommendations had their consensus recommendation scores improve over the past month.

In order to limit turnover, I suggest that you sell a stock if after one month there are no additional upward recommendation changes. This means that a stock should be held only as long as the consensus recommendation score improves (becomes lower) over the last month.

KEY POINT   After one month, recalculate the change in the stock's recommendation score, and sell if there are no additional upward recommendation changes.

If you follow this sell condition—selling a stock if the consensus recommendation score does not improve over the past month—the holding period for piggybacking will average slightly higher than one month.

This would be considered extremely high turnover, so in order to implement the piggybacking strategy it is absolutely necessary to make certain that you keep transaction costs low.

The best means for an individual to keep transaction costs down is through a fractional share trading program, as is now offered by

FolioFN, E★Trade, or Fidelity. Do not even try to implement a piggy-backing strategy at a full-service brokerage firm, as the transaction costs will eat you alive.

Very few investors implement an investment strategy totally based on piggybacking. Instead, most hedge funds and traders use the piggy-backing strategy to help select among potential stock picks. The piggy-backing strategy indicates that preference should be given to stocks that have recently received substantial recommendation upgrades from analysts—such stocks are likely to exhibit greater than normal strength over the next couple of months.

Caveats to Piggybacking Strategy

It is important to keep in mind that although "piggybacking" does work, it is not as effective as focusing on revisions to analysts' earnings estimates. The two main problems that I have with a piggybacking strategy is that the turnover is extraordinarily high and you are not buying on fundamentals, such as earnings, but are rather buying on "hype." With piggybacking you are effectively expecting that the upward recommendations by analysts will create enough of a "buzz" about a stock that it will continue to exhibit above normal buying over the next month.

Although, as I have said, it is very hard to read an analyst report and absolutely ignore the recommendations, for the most part that is exactly what you should do. Again, instead of reacting to the recom-mendations on the top of a research report, it is far more useful to focus on changes to the analysts' earnings estimates. If you do want to use analyst recommendations, it is important to piggyback and to not buy the stocks that are the most highly recommended by analysts. Instead, buy the stocks whose consensus recommendation score has improved the most over the past month.

Returns Due to Piggybacking

Let's look at the returns that you can generate by using the piggyback-ing strategy of focusing on changes to the consensus recommendation score due to analyst recommendation upgrades.

At the end of each and every month from January 1992 to March 2002, select from the 3,300 largest companies the 330 stocks for which analysts have upgraded their recommendations to the greatest degree and the 330 stocks for which analysts have downgraded their recommendations to the greatest degree. Then put an equal dollar amount into every stock in each of these two portfolios and hold the portfolio for the entire month.

At the end of every month, sell everything and go back to the drawing board, using any new recommendations issued by analysts during the month to totally re-balance the portfolios.

This strategy will have a huge monthly turnover and you would wind up turning over your entire portfolio almost nine times every year. For this reason, you really should use piggybacking to select a few stocks to own over the short term. Due to the high turnover, it is not a desirable strategy to employ on a full portfolio.

KEY POINT   Because of high turnover, use piggybacking only on a few stocks to own, not a full portfolio.

The returns of the two portfolios are given in Figure 10-10 for the period from April 1992 to March 2000.

As you can see in Figure 10-10, focusing on recommendation changes generated returns in excess of the Equal-Weighted Index over the bull market from 1992 to 2000. Additionally, the piggybacking strategy of focusing on changes in analyst recommendations also worked in the recent bear market, as shown in Figure 10-11.

By focusing on the changes to analysts' recommendations, rather than the recommendations themselves, you are able to generate positive returns over both bull and bear markets. Over the full ten-and-a-half years from April 1992 to September 2002, those stocks that experienced the greatest degree of analyst recommendation upgrades rose, on average, 16.1% annually, while those stocks that have received the greatest degree of recommendation downgrades fell 1.5% per year on average.

As you can see, those stocks that have received the greatest degree of analyst recommendation upgrades over the previous month tend to outperform over the next month, while those stocks that have received the greatest degree of analyst recommendation downgrades tend to under-perform over the next month.

Figure 10-10 Annualized returns due to piggybacking strategy (April 1992 to March 2000).

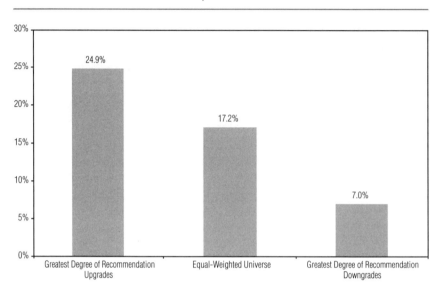

Figure 10-11 Annualized returns due to piggybacking strategy (April 2002 to September 2002).

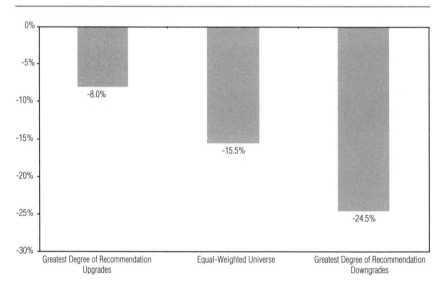

There are three very important points to realize:

- Turnover is extremely high. The stocks that receive the greatest degree of analyst recommendation upgrades over the previous month almost never receive the greatest degree of analyst recommendation upgrades over the coming month.

- Stocks that receive the greatest degree of analyst recommendation upgrades are stocks that were not highly regarded by analysts to begin with. Similarly, stocks that receive the greatest degree of analyst recommendation downgrades over the previous month were likely highly recommended by analysts to begin with.

- The returns listed in Figures 10-10 and 10-11 do not take into account transaction costs and market impact. You have to pay close attention to (the potentially crushing) transaction costs to implement this strategy in its entirety, but if you are looking to just purchase one or two stocks and are looking to pick the stocks based on analyst recommendations, it makes sense to focus on stocks that have recently received several analyst recommendation upgrades.

Summary

- The consensus recommendation score is an effective means of adjusting the recommendations issued by analysts to address the fact that analysts rarely issue sell recommendations. By ranking stocks according to their consensus recommendation score, you can determine which stocks analysts are truly positive about.

- Buying those stocks that are the most highly recommended by analysts according to the consensus recommendation score is a strategy that works well when the market is going up. However, when the market trades down, those stocks that are the most highly recommended by analysts tend to perform horribly. In fact, over the last bear market those stocks most highly recommended by analysts actually fell 47%.

- A far more effective way to use the consensus recommendation score is to piggyback on changes to analysts' recommendations over time.

- Stocks that analysts have recently raised their recommendations on—and thus have a more positive consensus recommendation score than one month ago—tend to outperform over the next month.

Endnotes

[1] For those who like arithmetic, the consensus recommendation score is $(6 \times 1) + (3 \times 2) + (10 \times 3) + (0 \times 4) + (0 \times 5)$ (Total number of points from assorted recommendations) = 42 then 42/19 (total number of analysts issuing recommendations) = 2.21.

## Chapter Eleven

Analyst Neglect and Long-Term Earnings Growth Estimates

What's ahead in this chapter?

■ Neglect
■ Analysts and Their Long-term Earnings Growth Estimates

IN THE PAST COUPLE OF CHAPTERS, we looked at how you can use the Zacks Rank, changes to analysts' recommendations, revisions to analysts' earnings estimates, and the earnings surprises calculated from the quarterly consensus earnings estimate.

Of these four strategies, the two that work the best in getting you ahead of the market are focusing on revisions to analysts' earnings estimates and the Zacks Rank.

In this chapter and Chapter 12, I will introduce you to some additional ways to use analyst data to pick stocks.

These supplemental stock selection techniques can be used on a stand-alone basis or as a means of selecting among stocks that have a Zacks #1 Rank or have recently received upward earnings estimate revisions.

As we shall see in this chapter, it makes sense to give preference to stocks that are receiving increasing analyst coverage while avoiding stocks whose analyst coverage is decreasing and stocks that analysts project to exhibit a very high (above 30%) degree of earnings growth over the next three to five years.

Think of the stock selection techniques presented in this and the next couple of chapters as the dessert to the main course being served. The steak of the meal remains the Zacks Rank and its focus on owning stocks that are receiving upward earnings estimate revisions and reporting positive earnings surprises.

Neglect

Neglect usually refers to a stock that is not well-known to institutional money managers. A neglected stock goes beyond a stock that is not in vogue. A neglected stock is a stock that most professional money managers have never even heard of.

One of the best indicators that a stock is "neglected" is the number of analysts covering the stock. Generally, the more analysts following a company, the better known the stock will be to money managers. This makes sense, as stocks that have greater analyst coverage are more likely to be pitched to a money manager by an institutional salesman using an analyst's research reports.

What is important to realize is that sometimes the lower visibility of a neglected stock makes the stock a good buy—the reason is simply that not enough managers are aware the stock even exists to cause the stock's price to correctly reflect the true earnings potential of the company.

Why Are Certain Stocks Neglected by Analysts?

In many ways, analyst coverage is directly related to potential banking fees. For this reason, stocks in hot sectors often have greater analyst coverage than stocks in sectors that are out of favor or mature.

As Figure 11-1 shows, in the height of the technology boom in February 2000, there were more analysts covering Amazon.com and Yahoo than established blue-chip companies like IBM, Citigroup, or General Electric.

The reason for the analyst coverage listed in Figure 11-1 was simple. A good Internet analyst in the tech bubble could help generate huge underwriting fees, while an analyst well versed in Citigroup, IBM, or GE would likely not generate any extra banking revenue.

Figure 11-1 Comparison of analyst coverage.

Company	Ticker	# Analysts Covering Stock 02/25/00
Yahoo! Inc	YHOO	30
Amazon.Com Inc	AMZN	29
Intl Bus Mach	IBM	26
Citigroup Inc	C	23
Genl Electric	GE	19

Additionally, analyst coverage is driven by investor interest. At the turn of the century, in the height of tech mania, investors were far more interested in Yahoo than in GE. This was for the simple reason that Yahoo shares had been doubling in price and investors wanted in.

KEY POINT   For the most part, neglected stocks tend to be stocks that are less likely to generate investment banking revenue for brokerage firms and stocks that institutional investors, for various reasons, are not interested in.

I have also found that neglected stocks tend to be "outsiders." Sometimes neglected stocks are stocks that were not taken public through traditional means by a name-brand investment bank. Many times, the management of neglected firms lacks the relationships with Wall Street to help establish additional analyst coverage.

How Do Hedge Funds Profit from Neglect?

There is a relatively small cadre of money managers called "activist" portfolio managers. These activist managers seek to influence the companies whose stocks that they purchase. For instance, an activist manager might purchase a stock and then seek to encourage the company to buy back shares thus boosting the company's stock price.

There are a few activist managers playing the neglect game. These activist managers like to buy neglected stocks and then attempt to raise the neglected company's visibility by increasing the analyst coverage on the stocks through introducing the stock's management and the company to small regional investment banks.

It is a creative strategy, but it is harder to implement than it sounds. The problem lies with persuading a brokerage firm either to hire another analyst or to redirect an existing analyst to cover the stock in question.

It helps if the activist manager is already executing trades through the investment bank, and thus is essentially paying the investment bank a massive amount in commissions.

Still, actively increasing analyst coverage for relatively neglected stocks can be accomplished by relatively small portfolio managers. And what always happens is that as the analyst coverage increases, the price of the stock will rise as well. This is especially the case if the stock has a compelling story, or is fundamentally undervalued. The activist manager, who obviously bought the company's stock before introducing the company to the brokerage firm, clearly is the one who benefits from this strategy. Additionally, the activist portfolio manager often does not simply pick any old neglected stock to champion; rather, the manager extensively investigates the company. Thus stocks that are receiving increasing analyst coverage are often deemed to be undervalued and represent an opportunity to the investors pushing for the increased analyst coverage.

Does Increasing Analyst Coverage Yield Higher Returns?

Yes, you can generate very slight excess returns by buying stocks that are receiving increased analyst coverage as a result of these activist manager's efforts. The chart in Figure 11-2 shows that this is the case.

I divided the 3,300 largest publicly-held companies into three equal-weighted portfolios based on changes in analyst coverage over the past month. The portfolios are created and rebalanced monthly based on the change in analyst coverage over the previous month. The returns are annualized from October 1987 to September 2002 and displayed in Figure 11-2.

Figure 11-2 Annualized return based on change in analyst coverage (October 1987 to September 2002).

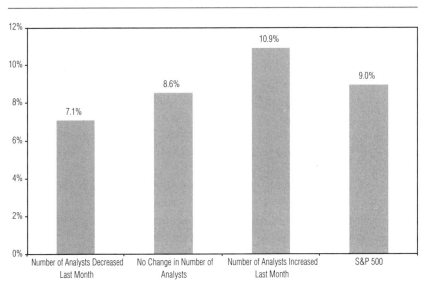

KEY POINT   On an annualized basis, stocks that increased their analyst coverage over the past month have generated slightly higher returns over the next three months relative to companies for which analysts did not increase their coverage.

Note that increasing coverage means that an analyst starts to write a research report on the stock. It does not necessarily mean that what the analyst writes will be positive.

However, most of the time when an analyst starts covering a stock, especially a stock not already widely followed by other analysts, the analyst almost always initiates coverage with a positive recommendation. The reason the analyst is writing a research report is that he is trying to bring an "undiscovered gem" to the attention of some of his portfolio manager clients. After all, what would be the point of issuing a research report on a company that no one else is covering if only to say, "Well, the stock is fully valued."

Similarly, decreasing analyst coverage is almost always a negative sign, and when analysts drop coverage on a stock it should send up a warning flag.

KEY POINT   The reason decreasing analyst coverage is such a negative signal goes back to the reluctance of analysts to issue sell recommendations. An analyst will often signal a sell recommendation by dropping coverage in order to avoid upsetting an investment banking relationship.

This may explain why companies for which analyst coverage is decreasing tend to under-perform—the decreasing analyst coverage is really a sign that investors should sell the stock.

How Can You Make Money from Analyst Neglect?

"So what?" you say.

Unless you are a hedge fund—or a private investor with tens of millions of dollars—you can not increase the analyst coverage of unknown companies. This is true.

But what you can do is participate in the free ride created by these hedge funds.

The results in Figure 11-2 occur from buying *after* analyst coverage increased, not *before*. So even though you can not obtain the insider returns the hedge fund makes, you can obtain a reasonable rate of excess return by buying companies for which analyst coverage has recently increased.

If you want to free-ride on the analyst coverage charted previously, the best metric to focus on is the change over the last month in the number of analysts covering the stock.

An easy way to determine the number of analysts covering a stock is to focus on the number of analysts issuing recommendations on a stock. If this number has increased over the past month it is a fairly bullish signal, if the number has decreased it is a bearish signal. It is usually bullish if the number of analysts issuing recommendations on a given stock has gone from zero to one or greater.

Where do you find information concerning the number of analysts covering a stock? It actually is very easy. The number of analysts issuing recommendations is widely available in almost any analyst summary on literally hundreds of websites (See Appendix III for four of the largest ones). Most of these summaries also show how the analyst coverage—the number of analysts issuing recommendations—has changed over time. Through examining how the total number of analysts covering a stock has changed over time you can easily determine whether analyst coverage is increasing or decreasing.

KEY POINT   Buying stocks for which analyst coverage is increasing works best when the company goes from having no analyst coverage to having some analyst coverage.

The stamp of approval of just one analyst is what provides many portfolio managers with the confidence they need to actually buy a certain stock.

Think of it this way: If you are a portfolio manager and buy Alcoa, there is no question as to whether Alcoa is a real company. If Alcoa falls in value, it can be chalked up to a bad decision. But, if you buy a company with a market cap of $60 million that no one has ever heard of, you need some assurance that the company is a real entity—even if you only put less than half a percent of your money in the company. The last thing as a portfolio manager that you want to be doing is trying to explain to your investors why you were duped by a sham $60 million company that no one has ever heard of.

The coverage by just one analyst provides that assurance. At the very least, an analyst from a reputable firm, before he or she starts coverage, will likely visit the company to make sure the company exists—that it has real revenue, with real employees.

Other suggestions for implementing the "neglect" strategy:

- Make 100% sure that the analyst initializing coverage works at a reputable firm. Lots of boiler rooms have names that are intended to sound like reputable firms. A classic example is A.S. Goldman which sounds a lot like Goldman Sachs. Zacks excludes these companies from our consensus calculations and the data we re–distribute. It is generally a good rule of thumb that if you have never heard of the brokerage firm, then you should not listen to the recommendation.

- Be careful if there is too large an initial spike when the analyst coverage is announced. If it seems like a stock went crazy on the announcement of analyst coverage, it could be a "pump and dump." This is a fraud in which a boiler room will tell you to buy the stock that it already owns and then when you start buying, it will dump its shares, pocketing the higher price you paid. You actually are looking for a more muted response to the establishment of analyst coverage.

- Also, be wary of a large spike in a firm's stock price prior to the announcement of coverage. This is a sure indication that the information was leaked. For your first couple of trades you should stick to stocks that already have at least one analyst covering them.

- Never buy a company solely because of increasing analyst coverage. The increase in analyst coverage should be used as a secondary screen.

- Avoid stocks under $5. If a stock is trading under $5 it may not be able to be bought by an institutional portfolio manager due to his firm's investment guidelines. (Investment firms are also unlikely to purchase stocks trading under $5 because they do not want to have to explain the position to clients.) Since the key to profiting from the "neglect" strategy is that institutional interest will be generated by the analyst coverage, buying a stock priced under $5 defeats the purpose of the strategy.

A Brief Warning about Avoiding Neglected Stocks with Poor Investor Relations Departments

When dealing with neglected stocks you should be careful about companies that have weak investor relations departments. Usually, large corporations have a special division devoted to interacting with investors. These investor relations departments also try to raise a company's profile by convincing more analysts to follow the company.

Analyst neglect may be the result of a weak investor relations department, or it could be attributed to structural issues in the market. For instance, technology firms generally have greater analyst coverage than comparably sized industrial companies.

KEY POINT   If a stock is neglected because of a poor investor relations department, it may be a signal of a management team that is unconcerned with their stock's price and the stock should be avoided.

However, as we have seen, there are instances in which good solid stocks just have not popped up on analysts' radar screens.

A good way for you to determine whether analyst neglect is due to a weak investor relations department is to send an e-mail to the investor relations department directly and ask for an explanation for a stock's weak analyst coverage. Strong investor relations departments will give a satisfactory response—a reasonable explanation for the poor coverage. No response after repeated attempts indicates the stock may be neglected for a good reason.

Analysts and Their Long-term Earnings Growth Estimates

Analysts, in addition to issuing EPS estimates for the upcoming fiscal quarters and the next two fiscal years, also make long-term earnings growth estimates. This is essentially an estimate of how fast the analyst expects a company to grow earnings on a per-year basis over the next five years.

The consensus long-term earnings growth estimate is similar to the consensus quarterly earnings estimate, in that it is the average of all the individual long-term earnings growth estimates issued by analysts.

KEY POINT   The consensus long-term earnings growth estimate is often used as an indication of whether or not a company's shares should be considered a "growth" or "value" stock.

Firms that have a high projected earnings growth rate as indicated by the consensus are considered "growth" companies and should trade at relatively higher valuation levels—usually signified by a higher P/E level.

However, it is not widely known whether it is profitable to invest in the stocks that analysts expect will exhibit the greatest rate of earnings growth over the next five years.

If companies that are projected to grow earnings at a high rate in the future tend to outperform the market as a whole, it would mean that the market tends to underprice growth.

If, however, companies that analysts expect will be growing earnings at a relatively fast rate tend to underperform, it would show that either the market on average pays too much for expected growth, or that actual growth almost never meets analysts' expectations.

So the question is: Do companies that analysts project to exhibit strong earnings growth live up to their potential?

The Returns from Buying Stocks with High Projected Long-term Earnings Growth Estimates

In Figure 11-3, we see the returns generated from five portfolios constructed from the 3,300 largest companies based on the consensus long-term earnings growth estimate. The portfolios are rebalanced monthly. Portfolio #1 contains stocks which analysts on the whole project to grow earnings at a low rate, while Portfolio #5 contains stocks which analysts on the whole project to grow earnings at a relatively high rate.

What we find in Figure 11-3 is that an equal-weighted portfolio consisting of those stocks that analysts projected to grow earnings at the fastest rate, has dramatically under-performed the S&P 500 over the past fifteen years.

It appears that the stocks which analysts collectively believe will exhibit the strongest earnings growth over the next five years tend to ultimately underperform the market and disappoint shareholders.

The consensus long-term earnings growth estimate is a tricky statistic and many investors assume that it is a good sign if analysts are projecting a very high earnings growth rate over the next five years.

This, however, is often not the case. Why?

Figure 11-3 Annualized return of portfolios based on consensus long-term earnings growth estimates (October 1987 to September 2002).

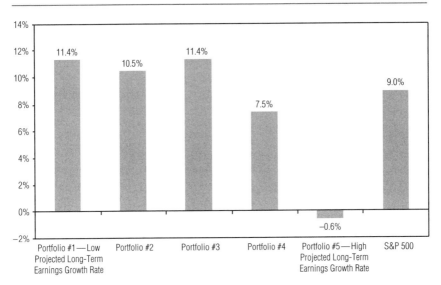

The explanation stems from an analyst's inability to see far into the future, and the market's tendency to overpay for a cheery consensus.

Essentially, a very high consensus long-term earnings growth estimate is a negative signal with regards to a stock's future price performance.

Here's why.

In buying companies that are receiving upward earnings estimate revisions, you are buying companies that analysts expect will be earning more *in the coming year* than what the analysts expected just a couple of months ago. You are effectively buying companies whose immediate earnings outlook is improving. This makes eminent sense, for as analysts raise their earnings estimates institutional investors are more likely to buy the stock, and upward earnings estimate revisions are a fairly good signal that earnings estimates will be raised in the future.

However, in buying stocks that have a high consensus long-term earnings growth estimate, you are buying companies based on analysts' long-term views regarding the company's future earnings prospects.

No one, not even the most capable analyst, knows what is going to happen with a company three, let alone five, years into the future.

As a result, when making their long-term earnings growth estimates, individual analysts tend to take their cues from other analysts and the market. This means that if an analyst believes a certain company has an extremely high long-term earnings growth rate, the market as a whole also thinks the long-term earnings prospects for the company are stellar.

The net result is that when you buy a company that is projected by analysts to exhibit high long-term earnings growth, you are essentially buying a company that both the analysts and the market believe is in a "hot" growth area.

The problem with these "hot" growth companies is two-fold:

- The high projected earnings growth often does not materialize.

- Companies that analysts collectively agree will generate extensive long-term earnings growth often trade at far too rich valuation levels.

Does the Earnings Growth Projected by Analysts Ever Materialize?

The table in Figure 11-4 shows data for the twenty-five companies that are currently in the S&P 500 which analysts expected to exhibit the greatest long-term earnings growth as of the beginning of 1998. The reason we are looking at these companies is that it enables us to then determine whether in fact the earnings growth projected by analysts materialized from 1998–2001.

The table enables you to compare the rate at which analysts expected these companies to be able to grow earnings annually in 1998 against the actual annual earnings growth rate realized by the companies from 1998 to 2002 (actual earnings growth is adjusted to exclude non-recurring items in order to be comparable to the same way that analysts estimate earnings growth).

For instance, in 1998, analysts in aggregate expected Cisco (CSCO) to be able to grow earnings per share at 31.3% per year over the next several years. In reality, over the next three years CSCO grew earnings at 12.2% annually—a far cry from what was expected.

Figure 11-4 Companies with greatest projected long-term earnings growth (1998).

Company	Ticker	Projected Annual EPS growth over the next 3-5 years 01/02/98	Actual Annual Growth Per Year 12/98 to 12/01	
Yahoo!	YHOO	59.17%	32.64%	Lower Than Expected
Veritas Softwre	VRTS	50.00%	61.18%	
Peoplesoft	PSFT	47.71%	0.57%	Lower Than Expected
AOL Time Warner	AOL	46.07%	Not Meaningful due to Acquisition	
Ciena	CIEN	45.71%	25.99%	Lower Than Expected
Tmp Worldwide	TMPW	44.00%	32.37%	Lower Than Expected
Siebel Systems	SEBL	44.00%	51.83%	
Citrix Sys	CTXS	42.00%	21.03%	Lower Than Expected
Vitesse Semicon	VTSS	40.50%	−25.60%	Lower Than Expected
Quintiles Trans	QTRN	38.65%	−30.88%	Lower Than Expected
Network Applian	NTAP	38.00%	65.97%	
Univision Comm	UVN	37.33%	22.17%	Lower Than Expected
Starbucks	SBUX	34.56%	27.87%	Lower Than Expected
Pmc-Sierra	PMCS	33.83%	−208.46%	Lower Than Expected

Figure 11-4 (*cont.*)

Company	Ticker	Projected Annual EPS growth over the next 3-5 years 01/02/98	Actual Annual Growth Per Year 12/98 to 12/01	
Mercury Interac	MERQ	33.00%	33.89%	
Qualcomm Inc	QCOM	32.33%	60.61%	
Concord Efs Inc	CEFT	31.75%	36.89%	
Clear Channel	CCU	31.29%	−307.31%	Lower Than Expected
Cisco Systems	CSCO	31.27%	12.24%	Lower Than Expected
Jabil Circuit	JBL	31.25%	17.50%	Lower Than Expected
Apollo Group	APOL	30.27%	32.15%	
Dell Computer	DELL	30.23%	37.95%	
Comverse Tech	CMVT	30.00%	39.63%	
Tellabs	TLAB	29.67%	−26.86%	Lower Than Expected
Adc Telecomm	ADCT	29.30%	−187.36%	Lower Than Expected
Average		37.68%	1.40%	60% Lower Than Expected

As you can see, in 60% of the cases, the consensus long-term earnings growth estimate proved to be far too optimistic.

Part of the explanation for why analysts can be so far off regarding the long-term growth prospects for a stock may be due to optimism on the part of analysts, and some of the problem may be a result of the tech bubble bursting in 2000, but remember that the 1998–2001 period contained periods of both expansion and contraction.

The message, though, is clear: If analysts collectively expect a stock to exhibit huge earnings growth in the future, odds are the stock is already richly priced and it is likely not a good investment.

KEY POINT   Stocks that have a very high consensus long-term earnings growth estimate should be avoided. When the analysts collectively believe a company is going to exhibit extensive earnings growth over the next three to five years, it is not a positive signal.

The reverse, however, does not appear to hold. That is, stocks that analysts expect to exhibit low earnings growth over the next five years do not necessarily make terrific investments.

The preceding analysis was instrumental in guiding us at Zacks to avoid many of the super-high growth technology stocks from 1998 to 2002, with excellent long-term results for the portfolios that we manage.

Essentially, you should be wary about buying a company that analysts expect to be growing earnings at huge rates per year over the next five years.

KEY POINT   Both analysts and the market tend to overestimate the long-term earnings potential of high-growth stocks. As a result, stocks that analysts project to grow earnings at over 30% per year for the next three to five years do not make good long-term investments.

How to Use Analysts' Long-term Earnings Growth Estimates to Avoid Losing Money

Be cautious of companies whose long-term projected earnings growth rate is greater than 30%. For the most part, you should not buy stocks that analysts expect to grow long-term earnings at greater than 30% per year. Such high growth rates are generally not sustainable, and you are setting yourself up for a fall—as stocks which analysts agree will grow earnings at greater than 30% per year are usually not cheap.

To give you some perspective, the companies that make up the S&P 500, in the aggregate, are projected to grow earnings at 8% to 12% per year over the next three to five years, and that level of growth seems optimistic especially given current macro-economic weakness.

Projected earnings growth rates above 30% per year are usually the result of undue optimism on the part of equity analysts. The market compounds the problem by overpaying for companies that are projected to grow earnings at a very high annual rate over time.

Additionally, high-projected-growth companies tend to provide excess volatility without comparable excess returns. Essentially, high-projected-growth companies tend to be significantly more volatile than on your average stock.

KEY POINT   Although you should avoid companies that are projected by analysts to exhibit extremely high projected earnings growth over the next five years, you should not necessarily buy the stocks of companies that are projected by analysts to exhibit low annual earnings growth over the next five years.

The performance data indicates that there appears to be very little benefit to buying stocks that exhibit a very low expected earnings growth rate.

The preceding results do not mean that growth investing does not work. It simply means that the long-term consensus growth estimate is not a good metric to use in selecting growth stocks.

Part of this may be attributable to the fact that the long-term growth estimate has a tendency to become stale over time. Analysts tend to maintain their long-term earnings growth estimates even in the face of negative earnings surprises and even in light of their own downward earnings estimate revisions for the fiscal year and the quarter. It is always better to focus on revisions to earnings estimates and earnings surprises than the long-term projected growth rate.

While it is not profitable to buy stocks with a high projected five-year growth rate, it does make sense to buy stocks whose long-term growth rate has increased over the last month, as Figure 11-5 shows.

Figure 11-5 Annualized return based on change in consensus long-term earnings growth estimates (October 1987 to September 2002).

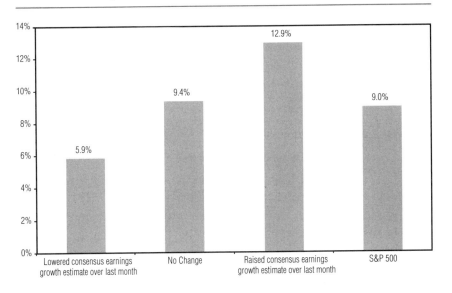

The take-away message is clear: The best way to use the long-term projected growth rate is to focus on those companies whose consensus long-term earnings growth rate has increased over the last month.

KEY POINT   As Figure 11-5 indicates, stocks that have had their long-term earnings growth estimates raised over the past month tend to out-perform over the next month. This is consistent with what we saw earlier when we discussed the importance of changes in the con-sensus earnings estimate over the short term.

There is another way to effectively use the consensus long-term earnings growth rate besides telling you which stocks to avoid: as part of the PEG ratio, which is the subject of the next chapter.

Summary

- There are additional strategies that can be employed using analyst data besides the big four of following the Zacks Rank, analyst recommendation changes, earning surprises and earnings estimate revisions. These additional strategies should be used in conjunction with what is beyond doubt the best use of analyst data, namely, focusing on owning stocks for which analysts are revising their earnings estimates upward.

- Neglect—you can generate slight excess returns by buying companies for which analyst coverage has recently increased.

- You can generate much higher returns if you actively increase analyst coverage on stocks that you own.

- An analyst will often signal a sell recommendation by dropping coverage in order to avoid upsetting an investment banking relationship.

- The stocks of companies that analysts collectively believe are going to exhibit extensive earnings growth over the next three to five years (greater than 30%) have historically not generated great returns.

- The market tends to over-pay for such companies and, to make matters worse, the earnings growth usually does not materialize.

- Stocks that have had their long-term earnings growth estimates raised over the past month tend to outperform over the next month.

## Chapter Twelve

Valuation, Earnings Uncertainty, and the Fed Model

What's ahead in this chapter?

- Valuation—PEG and P/E ratios
- Earnings Uncertainty
- The Fed Model and the Market

MOST OF THE STRATEGIES MENTIONED SO FAR have relatively short time horizons, limited to approximately one quarter. In this chapter, we will examine two more stock selection strategies that also make use of data produced by analysts but have longer time horizons.

Specifically, I will illustrate why it makes sense to give preference to stocks that are trading at low or attractive valuation levels, as well as stocks that exhibit a low degree of expected earnings uncertainty, while avoiding stocks that trade at rich valuation levels or exhibit a large degree of earnings uncertainty.

While examining valuation levels and focusing on earnings uncertainty are excellent strategies, they should be used to supplement the core strategy. Your focus should always remain on owning stocks that are likely to receive upward earnings estimate revisions and report positive earnings surprises in the immediate future.

Finally, we will take a look at an asset allocation model that makes use of analysts' earnings estimates called the Fed model. The Fed model is not a stock selection strategy per se, but is instead a means of determining what your exposure to the stock market should be.

Valuation—PEG and P/E Ratios

As we have seen throughout the book, earnings are the most important determinant of stock prices. The reason is simple. At the end of the day, after the hype is gone, after the investment bankers' spiel grows tired and the froth gives way to rational thought, a stock derives intrinsic value from the earnings of the company it represents.

For this reason, ratios that focus on earnings are often extraordinarily useful to value investors.

There are two widely used valuation ratios that should be of interest to you: the PEG Ratio and the P/E ratio.

The PEG of Value

The PEG ratio is an attempt to measure and uncover value.

As I mentioned briefly back in Chapter 2, the PEG ratio consists of a price-to-earnings ratio (the "PE" of the PEG) divided by analysts' long-run growth estimates (the "G" of the PEG).

Begin with the P/E Ratio: How Is It Calculated?

A P/E ratio is calculated by taking a company's current stock price and dividing it by the company's earnings per share (EPS) over a twelve-month period. The question is, of course, what twelve-month period do you use?

There are really only two choices. You can either use trailing twelve-month earnings (what the company has earned over the previous four quarters) or you can use the consensus earnings estimate for the coming fiscal year.[1]

Using the consensus earnings estimate is the preferred method for most professional money managers because it makes the P/E forward-looking—it calculates a P/E ratio based on what a company is *expected* to earn in the future rather than what a company has earned in the past.

There is some validity to the claim that projected consensus earnings are unknown so it is better to stick with what is already known, which would be trailing earnings. However, for the most part, investors acknowledge that a stock is valued based on what the stock is expected to earn in the future, not what the stock has earned in the past.

KEY POINT   The most appropriate P/E ratio to analyze is the forward-looking ratio, for the simple reason that a company's stock price should trade on future rather than historical earnings.

Where Can I Find Forward P/E Ratios?

You can find the forward P/E ratio for a stock in almost any online stock profile. You have to be a little careful to make sure the P/E ratio is truly forward-looking. Forward-looking P/E ratios are, for the most part, lower than backward-looking P/E ratios.

If you still are not sure, you can always calculate the forward P/E ratio by taking the stock's price and dividing by the coming fiscal year's consensus earnings estimate.

What Does the P/E Ratio Tell You?

A P/E ratio indicates how much the market is willing to pay today for one dollar's worth of future earnings. Essentially, a P/E ratio is an indication of how excited investors are about the growth prospects of a company.

A high P/E multiple indicates the market anticipates substantial earnings growth, while a low P/E multiple indicates the market anticipates low earnings growth.

KEY POINT   The important question to ask when buying a stock is not whether a stock's P/E is high or low, but rather whether the P/E is justified by the company's future growth prospects.

A value investor—an investor who looks to buy cheap stocks—does not just want low P/E stocks. Rather, the value investor wants stocks whose true earnings growth prospects are greater than what is reflected in the P/E ratio.

Adding the Long-term Growth Estimate to the Picture

The desire to find stocks whose earning growth prospects are greater than what is reflected in the P/E ratio brings us back to the long-term growth estimate. As we saw earlier, the long-term growth estimate represents what analysts believe a stock's earnings growth rate will be per year over the next five years, and as we have seen, it tends to be overly optimistic.

Generally, though, the higher the analysts' long-term growth estimates, the higher the P/E ratio should be.

If we take the P/E ratio and divide it by the earnings growth rate projected by analysts we derive the PEG ratio. The PEG ratio gives us a back-of-the-envelope idea of whether the P/E ratio is justified.

KEY POINT   A high PEG ratio indicates the market is significantly more enthused about the growth prospects of a company than are analysts, while a low PEG ratio indicates that analysts are more excited about the company's growth prospects than the market.

Essentially, the PEG ratio is a means to uncover value—and a low PEG ratio is one sign of value.

An Example of a PEG Ratio Calculation

In the table in Figure 12-1, the PEG ratio calculation is shown for five companies as of August 2002.

Figure 12-1 PEG ratios as of August 2002.

Company	Ticker	Current Price	Current Fiscal Yr Consensus Earnings Estimate	Projected P/E Ratio	Growth Rate	PEG Ratio
3m Co	MMM	$126.57	$5.25	24.10	11.00	2.19
Alcoa Inc	AA	$24.77	$1.26	19.72	13.57	1.45
Oracle Corp	ORCL	$10.39	$0.42	24.78	18.21	1.36
Coors Adolph B	RKY	$61.09	$4.53	13.49	11.38	1.19
Dole Food Co	DOL	$27.56	$2.66	10.37	11.00	0.94

For 3M Co. (MMM), the PEG ratio is relatively high. For Dole Food (DOL), the PEG ratio is relatively low.

This is to some extent expected as, for the most part, larger-cap companies have tended to have slightly higher PEG ratios. As you might guess, investors are willing to pay more for growth if the growth is coming from a more stable company.

For MMM, the relatively high PEG ratio tells you that the market is more enthused about the growth prospects than are analysts. MMM is trading at a P/E ratio of 24.10 based on the current year consensus earnings estimate—this P/E ratio is more than double what analysts believe MMM can grow earnings at on a per-share basis over the next five years.

With Dole Food (DOL), the opposite is the case. DOL's low PEG ratio indicates that the market is far less enthused about the growth prospects for the company than are the analysts. DOL is expected by analysts to grow EPS at 11% per year over the next three to five years, identical to the growth rate projected for MMM, but DOL trades at a P/E level that is almost half of what MMM trades at. In DOL's case, analysts are more enthused about DOL's potential growth than the market.

Thus, based on its PEG ratio, MMM would be considered somewhat expensive and DOL would be considered cheap. (As a means of reference, the PEG ratio for the S&P 500 is currently around 1.90.)

Having done the math and calculated the PEG ratio, the obvious question is, does it make sense to buy stocks that are trading at low relative PEG levels?

An important related question is, does it make sense to buy stocks that are trading at low P/E levels?

I'll take the second question first.

Does It Make Sense to Buy Stocks Trading at Low P/E Levels?

P/E ratios are better at telling you which stocks to avoid than which stocks to buy.

Look at Figure 12-2, which shows how poorly very high P/E stocks (stocks with a P/E level of 65 or higher, based on projected earnings) have performed on an annualized basis over the past fifteen years.[2]

Although the 65 P/E level was somewhat arbitrarily selected, the chart shows that stocks trading at high forward P/E levels are not simply bad investments; they are horrible investments.

Figure 12-2 Annualized return based on forward P/E (October 1987 to September 2002).

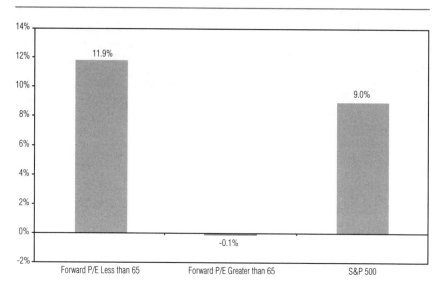

The lesson to be learned from the bar chart in Figure 12-2 is simple. Stocks with forward P/E levels above 65 tend to under-perform the market.

KEY POINT   You should actively avoid owning stocks that trade at a forward P/E multiple greater than 65.

The difference in returns between those stocks that trade at a P/E under 65 and those stocks that trade at over 65 is so great that it almost always makes sense not to buy stocks trading at a P/E level greater than 65. This is not such a hard guideline to follow, as roughly only 4–6% of those stocks that are expected to generate a profit have a forward P/E above 65.

Which Is Better: A Low P/E or PEG Ratio?

The chart in Figure 12-3 is based on the forward P/E ratio, while the chart in Figure 12-4 focuses on the PEG ratio. Both charts exclude companies that have negative consensus earnings estimates for the coming fiscal year, mainly because a negative P/E is meaningless. Figure 12-4 also excludes companies for which a consensus long-term earnings growth rate is not available.

As we discussed previously, companies that are expected to post losses do not, for the most part, make good investments and should be avoided.

The annualized returns in these charts are from the universe of the 3,300 largest companies sorted into five portfolios that are rebalanced on a monthly basis. Portfolio #1 contains stocks which have low PEG and P/E ratios, while Portfolio #5 contains stocks that have relatively high PEG and P/E ratios.

KEY POINT   Buying low P/E and low PEG stocks is definitely a winning strategy. Thus, the conventional wisdom appears to hold true—cheap stocks outperform over time, and it pays to hold value over growth. These results tend to hold true regardless of the value metric used, and other valuation metrics like Price-to-Book ratios show similar results.

Figure 12-3 Annualized return based on forward P/E levels (October 1987 to September 2002).

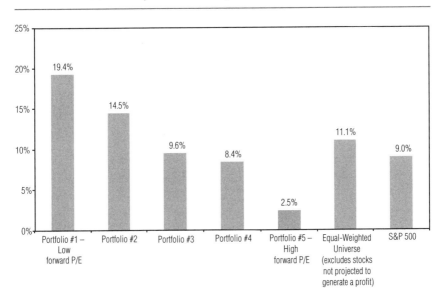

Figure 12-4 Annualized return based on PEG ratio (October 1987 to September 2002).

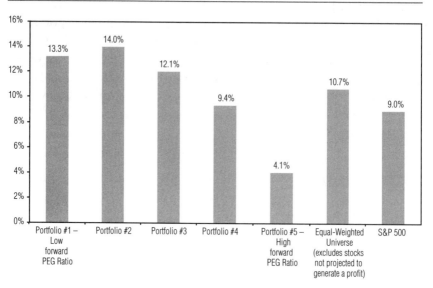

What Else Do These Charts Show?

- Very low PEG ratios—PEG ratios below 0.50, that place a stock in Portfolio #1—are not as great a signal as you might initially think. This is probably because analysts are often reluctant to adjust their long-term projected earnings growth rates downward. An overly optimistic projected earnings growth rate can result in an artificially low PEG ratio.

- The P/E ratio seems superior to the PEG ratio in identifying stocks that outperform. Again, this is partly due to the problem of analysts not quickly adjusting their long-term growth estimates that go into the calculation of the PEG ratio.

- If you are going to buy low P/E stocks, you must have patience and be willing to hear cocktail stories of friends buying stocks that appreciate massive amounts in a short time span. Low P/E stocks dramatically underperformed the S&P 500 from 1998 to 1999. Over this time period the S&P 500 was up 55.4% while a portfolio consisting of those stocks with the lowest P/E ratios actually fell. By the beginning of the millennium, value investors were a dying breed. But from mid–2000 onward, value stocks have dramatically outperformed the S&P 500. You win in the long run with value stocks, but the road is definitely a long, bumpy, and contrarian one.

How Do I Use P/E Ratios and PEG Ratios to Make Money?

- Avoid stocks with forward P/Es above 65.

- If you can bear several years of underperformance, search for stocks with forward P/E levels that are lower than the average P/E level for the S&P 500.

- When using PEG ratios, search for stocks with a lower-than-market-average PEG ratio. However, be wary of a stock that trades at an incredibly low PEG ratio: a PEG ratio below 0.75 should be looked at skeptically.

Earnings Uncertainty

In addition to calculating the consensus earnings estimate, we also can calculate the degree of uncertainty surrounding those projected earnings. This is important because stocks that show a low degree of earnings uncertainty tend to outperform those stocks that exhibit a high degree of earnings uncertainty.

In order to calculate the degree of earnings uncertainty, it is necessary to measure the dispersion of individual earnings estimates around the consensus. This is a fancy way of saying that you want to see if the earnings estimates issued by individual analysts are similar to or very different from one another.

Example of Earnings Uncertainty Calculation

In order to understand exactly what is meant by earnings uncertainty, consider the three stocks in Figure 12-5, each of which is followed by four analysts, with the individual earnings estimates shown.

The best way to measure earnings uncertainty is to calculate the standard deviation of the consensus earnings estimate by examining how much each individual analyst's earnings estimate differs from the consensus.

Figure 12-5 Example of earnings uncertainty.

	Acme Corp.	Big Corp.	Congo Corp.
Analyst #1	$ 1.05	$ 1.00	$ 3.00
Analyst #2	$ 1.13	$ 1.20	$ 3.20
Analyst #3	$ 1.11	$ 0.92	$ 2.70
Analyst #4	$ 1.09	$ 1.28	$ 3.45
Consensus	$ 1.10	$ 1.10	$ 3.09
St. Dev.	$ 0.03	$ 0.17	$ 0.32
St. Dev/ Consensus	3.12%	15.28%	10.27%

The higher the standard deviation of the individual earnings estimates, the more uncertainty there is among analysts. The best way to
find the standard deviation of the consensus is to go to the Zacks.com
website, where the standard deviation of the consensus is provided
under the "Estimate" report. (The standard deviation is really a way of
trying to quantify those histograms that we examined in Chapter
Five—a higher standard deviation means a histogram that is more
spread out.)

Divide the standard deviation by the consensus earnings estimate—
this is referred to as normalizing the standard deviation. This is done
because the standard deviation is measured in absolute terms. As a result,
you would expect a company that is projected to earn $5.00 per share
this coming year to have a higher standard deviation of analysts' earnings
estimates than a company that is expected to earn $0.50 per share.

The key in measuring earnings uncertainty is not how big the standard deviation is, but rather, how big the standard deviation is relative
to projected earnings.

For instance, in Figure 12-5, Congo Corp. has a standard deviation
of $0.32 while Big Corp. has a standard deviation of $0.17. However,
Big Corp. has a much greater degree of earnings uncertainty, because
its standard deviation of $0.17 is 15.3% of Big Corp.'s projected earn-
ings, while for Congo Corp., the standard deviation of $0.32 is only
10.3% of its projected earnings.

KEY POINT   In order to measure and compare earnings uncertainty, you must normalize the standard deviation of analysts' earnings estimates by dividing by the consensus earnings estimate itself.

Great, but So What?

Well, as a result we know that analysts are the most uncertain about the earnings prospects for Big Corp. and, as we will see, the stocks of companies that have uncertain future earnings prospects tend to underperform, while the stocks of companies whose future earnings prospects are more certain tend to outperform.

The chart in Figure 12-6 shows the returns generated by sorting the 3,300 largest companies that are also expected to generate a profit in the coming fiscal year into five portfolios based on the degree of earnings uncertainty in the current year's consensus estimate.

Portfolio #1 consists of those stocks with the least amount of uncertainty regarding earnings for the coming fiscal year and Portfolio #5 consists of those stocks with the greatest amount of uncertainty regarding earnings for the coming fiscal year.

Figure 12-6 Annualized returns based on earnings uncertainty (October 1987 to September 2002).

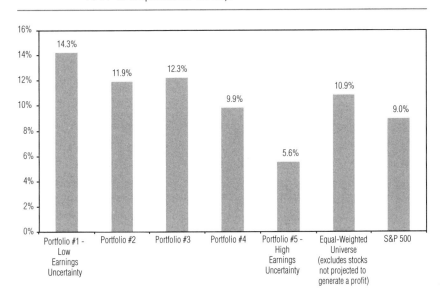

What Figure 12-6 Tells You

KEY POINT   Stocks that have a high degree of expected earnings uncertainty
tend to under-perform over time.

Over the last fifteen years, Portfolio #1—which consists of those
stocks with the least amount of earnings uncertainty—trounced
Portfolio #5, which consists of those stocks with the greatest amount
of earnings uncertainty by an annualized amount of almost 8% per
year. Again, this data suggests buying companies for which there is less
earnings uncertainty.

The reason that stocks with a high degree of earnings uncertainty
under-perform may simply be that the lower the degree of uncertainty
with respect to future earnings, the more "stable" a company's earnings
stream in fact may be.

Thus, low earnings uncertainty may actually be a proxy for a stable
earnings stream, and the market tends to reward stable earnings over
time.

How Do I Make Money Using Earnings Uncertainty?

Avoid companies whose earnings uncertainty places them in
Portfolio #5. This means avoiding companies whose earnings uncertainty is greater than 12% (the standard deviation of the consensus
earnings estimate for the current fiscal year divided by the consensus
estimate itself). This 12% level is not magical; it can change over
time.

KEY POINT   You should try to avoid stocks for which individual analysts'
earnings expectations are all over the map. When some ana-
lysts expect a company to produce earnings that are significantly different from what other analysts are expecting, it is
generally not a good sign for the stock's future price performance.

On the other hand, you should be on the lookout for companies whose earnings uncertainty is low, since companies with stable projected earnings tend to outperform over time.

The good thing about using earnings uncertainty to pick stocks is that earnings uncertainty is fairly stable over time. This means that if you build a portfolio based on earnings uncertainty, the turnover of the portfolio will be lower than some of the other strategies discussed.

The Fed Model—Using Earnings Estimates to Determine Your Asset Allocation

I do not want to mince words here: It never pays to time the market. If you try to time the market you will wind up losing money.

That being said, the Fed model is an excellent tool to try to gauge what your asset allocation should be. An asset-allocation model basically tells you how to split your assets between bonds and stocks. Obviously, you want to put more of your money in stocks when you think the market is going up.

The Fed Model Explained

You can get an unbiased back-of-the envelope read with respect to the valuation level of the S&P 500 by employing the Fed model detailed here.

Unlike many brokers and financial planners, the Fed model does not always signal that it is a "good time to be fully invested," mainly because the Fed model, unlike your broker, does not make more money the more fully you are invested in stocks.

Instead of listening to one of those macro or market analysts (who, as I indicated earlier, exist primarily to answer the often-asked question of what is going to happen to the market as well as to generate commissions and trades for the brokers who work at their firms), you should use the Fed model to independently provide you with some guidance with respect to the market's future direction.

The reason the model is referred to as the "Fed" model is that it was found buried in the back of a Federal Reserve report, supposedly by a market analyst at a large investment bank. It is not clear who exactly found the model, but it is widely used throughout Wall Street, mainly because it is one of the few market valuation models that seems to have worked.

The basic concept behind the Fed model is that when inflation and interest rates tend to be low, P/E levels for the S&P 500 tend to be high. As a result of this, the forward earnings yield of the S&P 500 should closely track the yield on the 10-year Treasury bond.

This correlation is demonstrated in Figure 12-7, which shows that when the yield on the 10-year Treasury note is high, so is the forward earnings yield on the S&P 500.

The forward earnings yield of the S&P 500 is calculated in two steps. Just as there are analysts who issue earnings estimates on individual companies, most of the macro-analysts also issue earnings estimates for the S&P 500 as a whole. These earnings estimates are generally calculated by the macro-analysts through a bottom-up aggregation of the consensus earnings estimates on the individual stocks that comprise the S&P 500.

Figure 12-7 Correlation between yield on 10-year Treasury note and the forward earnings yield of the S&P 500 (September 1987 to September 2002).

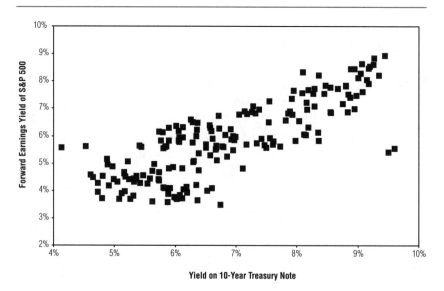

Yield on 10-Year Treasury Note

This consensus earnings estimate for the S&P 500 is then divided by the value of the S&P 500, generating the forward earnings yield of the S&P 500. Essentially, the earnings yield is the inverted forward P/E ratio for the S&P 500.

The way the Fed model calculates the fair value of the S&P 500 is by taking the projected earnings yield of the S&P 500 and dividing this number by the 10-year Treasury yield.[3]

KEY POINT   Since the 1980s, the forward earnings yield of the S&P 500 and the Treasury yield on the 10-year bond have been highly correlated; the result of this correlation is that the Fed model has proven to be fairly accurate as an indication of which way the market is heading.

The Fed model has had a few rather good calls. Prior to the October 1987 crash, the Fed model indicated that stocks were overvalued by about 40%.

The result of the high correlation is that when the earnings yield of the S&P 500 and the yield on the 10-year Treasury bond diverge, the Fed model implicitly indicates that the divergence is temporary and that the historically observed correlation will likely hold in the future. The assumption is that this will more likely occur through a change in stock prices than a change in rates or earnings estimates.[4]

Fed Model Equation

$$\text{“Fed Model” Fair Value for the S\&P 500} = \frac{\text{Projected Earnings per Share for the S\&P 500}}{\text{Yield on the Treasury Bond}}$$

The result of the equation, the "Fed Model" Fair Value, is the value that the S&P 500 is expected to trade at, assuming analysts' earnings estimates are not overly optimistic. You then compare the fair value to the actual value of the S&P 500 in order to determine whether the Fed model indicates the market is overvalued or undervalued.

Let's look at an example. As of the beginning of October 2002, the aggregate consensus earnings forecast for the next twelve months calculated from analysts following the S&P 500 is $50.58 per share. The current yield on a 10-year Treasury bond was around 4.0%. This gives a back-of-the-envelope "fair value" for the S&P 500 of around 1,200. With the S&P 500 trading around 800, this would imply the S&P 500 is substantially undervalued.

The Fed model itself is not exactly a market timing tool. An overvalued market can become even more overvalued for quite a while and vice versa. This is shown in Figure 12-8, which displays the signals the Fed model has issued since 1979.

What I find very attractive about the Fed model, though, is that among the chorus of bulls in the 1998–2000 period, the Fed model was one of the few lone voices of reason that indicated that the market was severely overvalued. However, a brief look back to 1979 should convince you that just because the Fed model indicates the market is over- or undervalued does not mean that the market will quickly correct the situation.

Nevertheless, the Fed model can be very useful in helping you determine your asset allocation strategy.

KEY POINT   If the Fed model shows the market is severely undervalued, you may want to increase your allocation to equities, while if the Fed model shows the market to be severely overvalued, you may want to increase your allocation to bonds and cash and away from equities.

Figure 12-8 S & P 500 valuation (monthly) (January 1979 to September 2002).

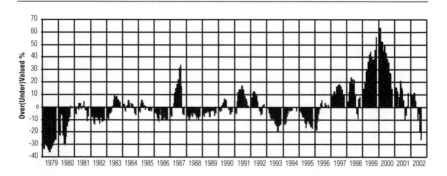

Source: Weijin Park

The key is not to use the Fed model to try to time the market. Instead an investor with a conservative outlook should follow the general asset allocation guidelines in Figure 12-9 after determining the reading of the Fed model.

At current readings, the Fed model indicates that now is one of the best times since the late 1970s to be invested in the stock market. Generally speaking, for a host of additional reasons, I tend to agree with the assessment of the Fed model.

As I write this book, the current bear market is the longest bear market in terms of length and the third-largest in terms of magnitude since the market crash of '29.

As of the third quarter of 2002, the S&P 500 is currently trading around 800, down roughly 47.6% from its March 2000 high of 1527.46, and within points of its most recent low. To put this in some perspective, during the 1973–1974 bear market, the S&P 500 index lost 48.2% before recovering ground. The absolute worst bear market since the '29 crash in terms of magnitude is the 54.34% decline during the bear market of 1937–1938. If history is any guide, we are probably closer to the bottom than we think.

KEY POINT   With the current bear market one of the worst the markets have ever seen, the blood is definitely running in the streets and now is probably one of the best times to be buying stocks since the mid-1970s.

Figure 12-9 Suggested asset allocation guidelines.

More than 30% overvalued	50% stocks, 50% bonds
20% to 30% overvalued	60% stocks, 40% bonds
10% to 20% overvalued	65% stocks, 35% bonds
Less than 10% overvalued or undervalued	70% stocks, 30% bonds
10% to 20% undervalued	75% stocks, 25% bonds
More than 20% undervalued	80% stocks, 20% bonds

Regardless of whether my prediction proves to be right, revisions to analysts' earnings estimates have been and will continue to be the best means of picking stocks that will beat the market. I am not sure what will happen in the future with the market; historical statistical analysis indicates the market has roughly an independent 70% chance of going up in any given year, while the Fed model indicates that this coming year will be a positive one. In any event, I remain totally convinced, based not only on my research but also on actual returns generated using the strategies detailed in this book, that revisions to analysts' earnings estimates are the best way for you to pick profitable stocks in any market and to get you "ahead of the market."

Summary

- Valuation—Buying low P/E and low PEG stocks is definitely a winning strategy. Thus, the conventional wisdom appears to hold true—cheap stocks outperform over time, and it pays to hold value over growth.

- If you are going to buy low P/E stocks, you must have patience.

- You should avoid companies that trade at forward P/E levels above 65.

- The P/E ratio is superior to the PEG ratio in identifying stocks that will outperform.

- Companies for which analysts project a low degree of earnings uncertainty tend to outperform stocks for which analysts project a high degree of earnings uncertainty.

- You should avoid owning stocks for which analysts' earnings estimates are all over the map.

- You can get an unbiased back-of-the-envelope read with respect to the valuation level of the market by employing the Fed model. To do this, divide the projected per-share consensus earnings estimate for the S&P 500 by the 10-year Treasury yield—this is the "fair value" of the S&P 500.

Figure 12-10 Analyst-related strategies from Chapters Eleven and Twelve.

Strategy	Turnover (level of trading necessary per month)	Investor Class
Neglect	Moderate	Hedge Fund
Valuation	Low	Buy & Hold Investor
Long-term Earnings Growth Rates	Moderate	Short Sellers
Earnings Uncertainty	Moderate	Buy & Hold Investor
Fed Model	Low	Market Timer and Asset Allocation

- Figure 12-10 displays the analyst-related strategies contained in Chapters Eleven and Twelve and provides their turnover (how much trading is required) and what type of investor implements the strategies.

Endnotes

[1] Some quantitative investors construct an EPS forecast for the next twelve months by combining the quarterly consensus estimates for the next four quarters.

[2] The universe used is the 3,300 largest companies, adjusted to exclude stocks with a consensus earnings estimate that is negative, since a negative P/E is somewhat meaningless.

[3] This comes from the valuation of a perpetuity using the 10-yr. Treasury yield as the discount rate.

[4] In order for the historically observed correlation to hold, it would be possible for either interest rates or earnings estimates to change as well. The assumption is, however, that these two elements of the Fed model are less prone to irrational optimism or pessimism.

Conclusion

So what do we know?

Analysts are paid a lot of money by brokerage firms to write research reports for investors. Many people think that analyst research is totally worthless. They are wrong. However, the research produced by analysts is sometimes very misleading.

Analysts are biased in their recommendations and even when you adjust for this bias you find that analysts are not exceptional stock pickers. You should never use the information from one individual analyst's research report to decide whether to buy or sell a stock.

In order to profit from analyst research you must do the following:

- Quantify the information contained in an analyst's research report.

- Focus on how this information changes over time and across multiple analysts.

By combining the research produced by many analysts and tracking how this information changes over time, you can effectively get "ahead of the market."

The past twelve chapters detailed several profitable investment strategies, all of which use the research produced by analysts in various ways. Here is a summary of the four main strategies and the supplemental investment strategies we have discussed in the book.

Strategy #1: Earnings Estimate Revisions

Basic Strategy

You want to buy stocks that are receiving upward earnings estimate revisions and sell stocks that are receiving downward earnings estimate revisions.

Reasoning

Buying stocks that are receiving upward earnings estimate revisions works because of two reasons:

- *"Analyst Creep."* Stocks that received upward earnings estimate revisions in the last month are more likely to receive upward earnings estimate revisions in the coming month.

- *Delayed Price Response.* As analysts raise their earnings estimates, institutional investors are more likely to buy the stocks and, as a result, stock prices rise gradually over time. There tends to be a slight institutional delay between earnings estimate revisions and price movement, so it pays to buy stocks quickly that have been receiving upward earnings estimate revisions.

Implementation

How the consensus earnings estimate has changed over time can be found on any of the websites listed in Appendix III.

- Calculate the percentage change to the current year's consensus earnings estimate over the past month. A buy signal has historically occurred when the consensus earnings estimate for the current year has increased by over 3% in the past month.

- Limit yourself to companies that are expected to generate a profit on a per-share basis in both the coming and next fiscal year.

- Make sure that the earnings estimate revisions are due to "organic growth"—that is, they come from top-line revenue growth and not cost savings or accounting changes. In order to determine this, it makes sense to read a few analysts' research reports.

- Sell the position whenever analysts actually lower earnings estimates, or the company reports earnings weaker than expectations.

- Give preference to companies that have earnings estimate histograms where the Os are to the right of the Xs and where the 30-day consensus earnings estimate is above the standard consensus earnings estimate. (For instructions on where to find the histogram, please see Appendix III.)

Strategy #2: Earnings Surprises

Basic Strategy

You want to buy companies that are reporting earnings better than expectations and avoid companies that are reporting earnings worse than expectations.

Reasoning

This strategy works for the following two main reasons:

- *Post-Earnings Announcement Drift.* Companies that report positive earnings surprises tend to outperform the market over the next three months.

- *"Cockroach Effect."* Companies that have a history of reporting positive earnings surprises are more like to report positive earnings surprises in the future.

Implementation

- You want to buy stocks that report positive earnings surprises or pre-announce positive earnings and sell stocks when they report earnings that fall short of the quarterly consensus earnings estimate. The larger the earnings surprise is, the greater is the price response.

- When a company reports earnings, in order to determine whether it should be bought you should immediately go through the following checklist:

    1. Determine the true extent of the earnings surprise. The best way to do this is to make sure that the reported earnings beat not only the consensus earnings estimate but also the most recent analysts' earnings estimates, as determined by the Os in the earnings estimate histogram (see Appendix III).

       You also want to make sure that the company did not warn about an earnings shortfall for future quarters, did not warn prior to announcing earnings, did not announce extraordinary or non-recurring charges in order to beat analysts' earnings estimates, and that the earnings surprise was not already expected by the market.

2. Determine the quality of the earnings. You want the company to be beating earnings through top-line revenue growth rather than through accounting changes or cost savings. Thus, to determine the quality of earnings, you should investigate the Sales Surprise™, the degree to which the company beat sales estimates.

Earnings Surprise

		Positive	Negative
Sales Surprise ™	**Positive**	Highest Quality— Action: Buy the stock	Poor Quality— Action: Sell the stock on some strength
	Negative	Decent Quality— Action: Hold the stock	Horrible Quality— Action: Sell the stock aggressively

3. When buying a stock following a high-quality earnings surprise, you should not buy immediately following the surprise but should instead wait a couple of days. You should buy stocks that report earnings better than analysts' expectations a few days after the earnings announcement, hold the stocks for a three-month period, and sell them prior to next quarter's earnings report. However, when selling a stock on a negative earnings surprise, you should sell immediately.

4. In addition to the cockroach effect, there are four good ways to predict an earnings surprise: examining where the most accurate analysts have issued their earnings estimates, seeing where the most recent earnings estimates are coming in relative to the consensus, looking for pre-earnings announcement price movement, and most importantly, focusing on multiple revisions to analysts' earnings estimates prior to a company reporting earnings.

Strategy #3: The Zacks Rank

Basic Strategy

The Zacks Rank combines the two previous strategies. The Zacks Rank is unbiased and has proven to be a very accurate indicator of how stocks will perform over the next one to three months.

Reasoning:

The theory behind the Zacks Rank is that upward earnings estimate revisions and positive earnings surprises ratchet up expectations for a stock, prompting institutional investors to funnel more money into it. Zacks #1 Ranked stocks are more likely than average to report a positive earnings surprise and/or have analysts raise their earnings estimates for the company, while Zacks #5 Ranked stocks are more likely than average to report a negative earnings surprise and/or have analysts lower their earnings estimates for the company.

Implementation

The Zacks Rank is updated on a daily basis as part of the free one-month subscription to the premium zacksadvisor.com website that you received when you bought this book. The instructions on how to access your free subscription are included in Appendix I. Using your free trial, you can view all stocks that have a Zacks #1 Rank, as well as receive daily e-mail updates for any stock in your portfolio.

Once you have access to the Zacks Rank, the next step is to implement the six-step process detailed at the end of Chapter Nine.

- Step One: Make sure to hold enough positions in order to keep commission costs below 2% annually.

- Step Two: Set sector exposure to match the sector exposure of the Zacks #1 Ranked portfolio. This is available in the portfolio section of the Zacks.com website and at zacksadvisor.com.

- Step Three: You should buy Zacks #1 Ranked stocks that are reasonably valued and have

- recently been added to the Zacks #1 Ranked list
- been growing earnings organically
- recently received analyst recommendation upgrades
- recently reported good earnings or raised guidance
- recently increased their dividend payment
- experienced some degree of insider buying or issued share buy-backs

- Step Four: Instead of trying to time the market, decide how much you want to be invested in the market and dollar-cost-average into the market over a period of time. Once invested, try to stay fully invested, which means that when you remove a position you add another position.

- Step Five: Sell a stock if after three months the Zacks Rank falls to a 3 (Hold) or below. Sell a stock prior to three months if the Zacks Rank falls to 4 or 5 or if a stock announces a negative earnings surprise, or lowers earnings guidance.

- Step Six: Rebalance positions after three months.

Strategy #4: Piggybacking on Recommendation Changes

Basic Strategy

If you simply buy the stocks that are the most highly recommended by analysts you will outperform in bull markets but substantially under-perform in bear markets. Instead, in order to use analysts' recommendations effectively in your investment strategy, you must focus on changes in analysts' recommendations over time. The way to do this is by focusing on changes to the consensus recommendation score over time.

Reasoning

Due to the sales activity of brokerage firms, stocks for which analysts have recently raised their recommendations—and thus stocks that have a more positive consensus recommendation score than one month ago—tend to outperform the market over the next three months.

Implementation

How analysts' recommendations have changed over the past few months is available on any of the websites listed in Appendix III.

Step One: Calculate the difference in the consensus recommendation score over the past month. Take this month's consensus recommendation score and subtract from it last month's consensus recommendation score. The consensus recommendation score may be referred to as the "mean" or "average" recommendation.

Step Two: Determine whether the change in the consensus recommendation score is strong enough to signal a "Buy" for the stock. To be considered a buy candidate, you want the change in the consensus recommendation score over the past month to be in the top 10% of all stocks covered by analysts. The most current threshold levels are available at zacksadvisor.com.

Step Three: One month after buying the stock, recalculate the change in the stock's consensus recommendation score. Sell a stock if after one month there are no additional upward recommendation changes.

Because of the high turnover of a piggybacking strategy you should implement the strategy on only a few stocks, not on a full portfolio.

These are the four main stock selection strategies. Additionally, there were four secondary investment strategies we talked about.

These strategies were as follows:

- *Neglect.* You can generate slight excess returns by buying stocks that are receiving increasing analyst coverage and avoiding stocks that are receiving decreasing analyst coverage.

- *Long-term Earnings Growth.* It makes sense to buy stocks whose consensus long-term earnings growth estimate has increased over the past month. However, you want to avoid stocks that analysts collectively project will grow earnings at greater than 30% per year—these stocks tend to exhibit poor price performance and to not grow earnings nearly as fast as anticipated.

- *Valuation.* It pays to buy stocks that are trading at relatively inexpensive valuation levels as determined by forward P/E ratios and PEG ratios. If a stock is trading at a forward P/E level greater than 65, it usually makes sense to avoid the stock. You must have patience if you are going to be a value investor.

- *Earnings Uncertainty.* Companies for which analysts project a low degree of earnings uncertainty tend to outperform stocks for which analysts project a high degree of earnings uncertainty. You should avoid owning stocks for which analysts' earnings estimates are all over the map.

Of the four major strategies discussed, the two that generate the best returns are the Zacks Rank and Earnings Estimate Revisions.

How hard is it to implement these strategies? Can I do it on my own?

Yes, you absolutely can; that is why I wrote this book. For the first time in nearly twenty years you have access to analyst earnings estimates, earnings surprises, and analyst recommendations for free from a variety of web sources. Additionally, transaction costs have fallen to the point where it is now affordable, through a discount brokerage firm, for an individual investor to implement the strategies discussed, most of which require a substantial amount of trading.

However, in implementing these strategies, you must make absolutely sure you have enough money to bear the relatively high transaction costs that come with high portfolio turnover, even if you are paying under $10 per trade.

Through the strategies mentioned here, you can ensure that the billions of dollars brokerage firms collectively spend each year on research analysts will help, rather than hurt, your portfolio. Good luck and good returns.

Free Subscription to zacksadvisor.com

CONGRATULATIONS! BY BUYING THIS BOOK you have acquired a one-month subscription to the full range of recommendations, information, and investment tools available on Zacks' premium website—www.zacksadvisor.com. Thousands of investors pay $299 per year for access to the information contained on the zacksadvisor.com website.

In fact, zacksadvisor.com is the most widely used stock newsletter available on the web and was selected by Forbes from 1998 to 2002 as "Best of the Web" in the Investment Newsletter category.

Money Magazine called the Zacks Advisor the "Best Fee-Based Web Site for Picking Stocks." Additionally, recent surveys have indicated that the Zacks Advisor is the most popular premium Internet service among professional investors. Included with the Zacks Advisor free subscription is access to the Zacks Rank, updated on a daily basis.

In order to access your Zacks Advisor subscription, please go to the website www.aheadofthemarket.com and proceed with the registration. The password necessary to activate the account is **AHEADJP3Z303**.

If you are an existing subscriber to zacksadvisor.com, you will receive a one-month extension to your subscription in exchange for registering.

What Is in the *Zacks Advisor*?

The Zacks Advisor offers you the Zacks Rank, updated on a daily basis, as well as several model portfolios, each based upon a unique stock-picking methodology that has historically outperformed the S&P 500.

Zacks Focus List

The Zacks Focus List is a diverse group of approximately fifty stocks selected to outperform the market over the next twelve months. The Focus List is a fully diversified portfolio and contains stocks from many different industries as well as market cap levels. It is designed to contain attractive investment opportunities to serve subscribers from the various schools of investing. The Focus List evolved because many of Zacks' individual clients wanted a traditional portfolio that had relatively low turnover. The Zacks Focus List is more of a "buy and hold" portfolio where the turnover is significantly lower than in the full-fledged Zacks #1 Ranked portfolio. In managing the Zacks Focus List, we tend to follow the strategy outlined at the end of Chapter Nine. Over the past five years ending in September 2002 the Zacks Focus List—as measured by Hulbert Financial (an independent auditor of newsletter returns)—appreciated 30.1% while the broad market fell 9.7% (as measured by the Wilshire 5000).

Zacks Timely Buys

The Zacks Timely Buys represent all the stocks from the Zacks Focus List that also currently have a Zacks Rank of 1 (meaning the stock should outperform the market over the next one to three months). When you add these two elements together (Focus List and Zacks #1 Rank), you have the makings of investment advice that is perfect for both long-term as well as short-term investors.

Zacks #1 Ranked Stocks

The Zacks Rank is the proprietary quantitative model based on trends in earnings estimate revisions and earnings surprises that I discussed in Chapters Eight and Nine. The Zacks #1 Ranked portfolio contains the daily updated list of the approximately 200 stocks with a Zacks Rank of 1. These stocks can be displayed alphabetically, by sector, or by the date the stock first became a Zacks #1 Rank.

These are the two ways to use zacksadvisor.com to improve the performance of your portfolio:

- *Pick some stocks you like.* You can find attractive stocks by selecting from among those stocks that are on the Focus List and have a Zacks Rank of 1 or 2, or selecting from among stocks that are in the Zacks #1 Ranked portfolio. You should sell the stock from your portfolio when the stock is deleted from the Focus List or, as I mentioned in Chapter Nine, when the Zacks Rank of the stock falls to a 4 or below. Because at any point in time you may own only a few stocks from the Focus list or the Zacks #1 Ranked portfolio, I cannot say anything about the performance that you should expect from this strategy. The preceding Focus List performance numbers assume that you would have been fully diversified and have owned all of the stocks that are on the Focus List, with each stock comprising an equal portion of your portfolio.

- *Own all the stocks on the Focus List.* If you structure your own portfolio to shadow or track the Focus List portfolio, you should be able to achieve the same returns we do in the Focus List (less transaction costs).

The Zacks Advisor website also provides you with daily commentary regarding the stocks on the Focus List. The morning call summarizes analyst research on the stocks that are on the Focus List and, before the market opens, it provides you with the current Zacks Rank for all Focus List companies. Additionally, during the day the headline for the morning call will be updated if a trade is made to the Focus List. The "Stock of the Day" profiles a stock in the Focus List that Zacks expects to be moving up during the day, usually due to news or technical factors. The closing commentary analyzes the news and price movement for selected stocks on the Focus List and provides directed advice as to what you should do about existing positions.

Additionally, with your Zacks Advisor free subscription you will receive the following:

Daily E-mail Updates

This daily updated e-mail contains any changes to the Zacks Rank, Earnings Estimate Revisions, Broker Recommendation Changes, or Earnings Surprises for the stocks in your portfolio. Additionally, the daily e-mail will contain any additions and deletions to the Focus List and Timely Buys portfolio. Changes to the Focus List and Timely Buys are also posted directly to the website during the day.

You can also select any of the following additional events you want to have included in the email alerts:

- Sales Surprises™
- New brokerage report issued
- New filing with SEC
- News stories about the company
- Insider trading
- Unusual price and volume activity

Company Research

Investment information for 6,000 companies. Clearly organized to help you make the best investment decisions.

Screening

We have one of the most powerful screening tools on the Internet. It allows you to select stocks in any combination based upon over ninety different criteria and is the only tool that lets you use the Zacks Rank in your screens.

Zacks' Market Outlook

Our market outlook is posted at the website on a biweekly basis. Over the past few years, we were able to direct investors to stay away from the tech sector and avoid significant losses. The market commentary also provides insight into economic data and market trends.

Biweekly Newsletter

The Zacks Advisor newsletter is available every two weeks and can be downloaded directly off of the website. The newsletter contains a detailed description of the stocks that are Timely Buys, as well as the current Focus List.

Finally, zacksadvisor.com contains all the data needed to implement any one of the four main strategies or the four supplemental strategies discussed in the book.

Overview of the Zacks Snapshot Report

THE ZACKS SNAPSHOT REPORT, which contains the Zacks Rank and is an excellent means of accessing the Zacks Rank, is updated on a weekly basis for free. If you choose not to use the one-month zacksadvisor.com subscription included with this book but you still want to have access to the Zacks Rank, your best bet is to go to www.zacks.com and select the "PDF Snapshot" report for a stock you are researching from the pull-down menu at the upper left-hand side of the home page, as shown here:

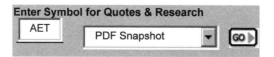

The PDF snapshot report provides a condensed overview of the data and metrics used by equity analysts to evaluate companies for the purpose of providing investment advice. The Zacks Rank appears at the top right of the snapshot report.

Figure AII-1 is a sample snapshot report, and in this appendix I will explain how best to interpret the data contained in it.

The one-page Zacks PDF Snapshot Report is a detailed graphical report featuring Broker Recommendations, Actual and Estimated EPS, Company versus Industry comparison, Fundamental Data, and Price Charting, as well as several other key financial statistics.

This report has been designed to help retail investors select stocks using data that, until recently, was only readily available to institutional investors. Each report contains hundreds of data points in critical metrics formatted to help you create a more informed investment decision.

Figure AII-1 Sample snapshop report.

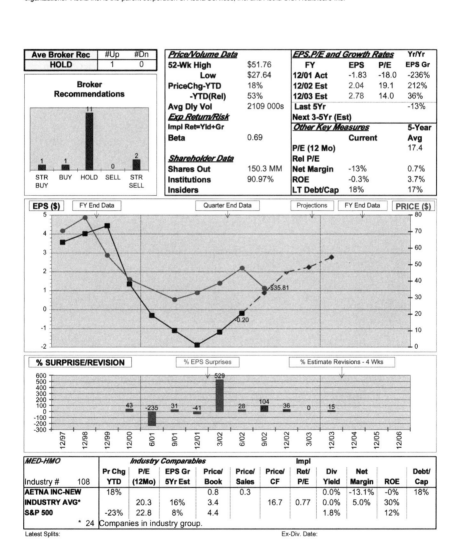

Zacks Company Report as of 10/18/02   Next EPS Report Date: 10/31/02

AETNA INC-NEW		AET	NYSE	Industry: *MED-HMO*			Type:	*Large*	*Value*
Rec Price	**P/E**	**Mkt Cap**	**Div Rate**	**Yield**	**Sales (12Mo)**	**Sls Gr**	**EPS Gr**	**Div Gr**	**Zacks Rank**
$38.95		$5856 MM	$0.00	0.0%	$22553 MM	9%	-13%	-44%	Strong Buy

Aetna Inc. is one of the nation's largest health benefits companies and one of the nation's largest insurance and financial services organizations. Aetna Inc. is the parent corporation of Aetna Services, Inc. and Aetna U.S. Healthcare Inc.

Latest Splits: Ex-Div. Date:

Summary Information at the Top of the Report

The most commonly referred to pieces of data on a stock are located near the top of the report for easy reference. Items here include Company Name, Ticker, the exchange on which the stock is traded; Price; P/E ratio (trailing twelve months); PEG (Price/Earnings divided by Growth Rate), Market Capitalization; current Dividend Rate and Dividend Yield; Annual Sales, EPS and Dividend Growth rates.

On the far right of the report is the weekly updated Zacks Rank. The Zacks Rank is presented as a "Strong Buy," "Buy," "Hold," "Sell," or "Strong Sell."

Also included is a brief business profile describing the primary revenue-driving divisions. The growth rates at the top are all historical growth rates over the past five years and the P/E ratio is based on trailing twelve-month earnings.

Broker Recommendations

The Average Broker Recommendation is highlighted and the number of analysts who have revised their opinion of the stock up or down in the past four weeks is noted. The recommendations, which are updated continuously based on information Zacks receives from brokerage firms, are broken into five categories: Strong Buy, Buy, Hold, Sell, and Strong Sell (corresponding with the Zacks Ranks of 1–5). The convenient bar chart format allows the investor to get a quick feel for both the number of analysts actively following the stock and their opinions about the stock's relative attractiveness.

Price/Volume Data

This section of the report includes data indicating the stock's price range over the last fifty-two weeks, as well as year-to-date price performance for the stock and its performance relative to the S&P 500. The average daily trading volume for the last twenty trading days is also provided. This is helpful in providing insight into the liquidity of the stock.

Expected Return/Market Risk

The Implied Return is calculated by adding a stock's current dividend yield plus its estimated long-term EPS growth rate. The Implied Return is a handy performance measure that could approximate the total annual return (including dividends and capital appreciation) an investor might achieve over the next several years, provided the projected growth in EPS actually materializes and the P/E ratio does not change. A stock's beta is a statistical measure of its sensitivity to past market movements. A stock with a beta of 1.5 has historically seen its price move (up or down) one and one-half times the percentage change in the broader equity market.

Shareholder Data

This section includes data on the number of shares outstanding and the percentage owned by inside management and institutional investors. Some institutional sponsorship is desirable because these large investors typically trade large blocks of stock that can result in significant upward price movements. However, too high a level of institutional ownership can increase a stock's downside risk because these large shareholders represent potential sellers if something goes wrong at the company. Significant ownership by corporate insiders is considered favorable because management's interests are then more closely aligned with other shareholders.

EPS, P/E, and Growth Rates

This section summarizes the company's recent actual and estimated EPS, P/E, and year-to-year EPS growth rates, consensus EPS estimates for the current and next fiscal year, and the estimated long-term EPS growth rate. The year/year earnings growth rates are calculated by comparing projected consensus earnings estimates against actual earnings. Below the projected yr/yr expected growth is the historical earnings growth and the consensus projected earnings growth rate over the next five years.

Other Key Measures

This section includes five key measures as they stand currently versus historically (average of the last five years). The measures are: P/E ratio (trailing 12 months), P/E ratio relative to the S&P 500, Net Margin, Return-on-Equity (ROE), and the long-term debt to capitalization ratio—a key indicator of financial risk. Stocks trading below (above) their historical P/E and relative P/E ratios may be cheap (expensive) unless there have been fundamental changes in the company's growth prospects. Similarly, changes in a company's profitability or capital structure from previous norms are important to note.

Price Chart

The chart at the center of this report plots the stock price versus the consensus earnings estimate. Price is plotted in green with circles, while earnings per share are plotted in black with rectangles. The chart includes fiscal year-end data going back five years and quarter-end data for the last four and next two quarters. Additionally, estimated earnings are projected out several years into the future. While not intended for use as a technical analysis tool, the price chart provides a visual representation of how the stock has been trading relative to its past growth in earnings, and of how Wall Street perceives the stock's future earnings growth prospects.

EPS Surprises and Estimate Revisions

A plot of the EPS surprises for the last four quarters and twelve-week earnings estimate revisions for the current and next fiscal year are shown in a bar graph below the price chart. Earnings surprises are the percentage by which a company's earnings exceed or fall short of the consensus estimates for the period. Estimate revisions are the percentage change in the consensus earnings estimates for a company over a particular period of time.

Industry Comparables

The table at the bottom of the report provides an overview of how a company stacks up against its industry peers and the overall market on a number of key measures including year-to-date price change, P/E ratio, estimated 3–5 year growth rate, price/book, yield, and return on equity. Also included in the table is the Implied Return to P/E ratio. This measure provides an indication of how expensive a stock is trading relative to a combination of its yields and long-term earnings growth.

The Industry Comparable data is most useful for relatively homogeneous industries such as banks and electric utilities. Still, Zacks' large number of industry classifications, roughly 200 in all, helps to insure comparability between companies.

Where to Find Analyst-Related Research

HERE ARE FOUR SOURCES OF ANALYST-RELATED RESEARCH. For each source, the web page is listed, as well as a sample of the earnings estimate revision data, recommendation data, and earnings surprise data that is available.

Source #1: Microsoft/CNBC

Step One: Go to http://moneycentral.msn.com/investor.

Step Two: Type in the ticker of the stock you are researching in the blue shaded box labeled "Get Quote" on the upper right-hand side of the page.

Step Three: On the left-hand side of the screen you should then see the following research options:

On the left-hand side of the screen, click on the link labeled "Earnings Estimates." Then click on the link in the middle of the page labeled "Consensus EPS Trend." A table similar to the following one should appear. This table enables you to implement the estimate revision strategy discussed in Chapters Four and Five.

Sara Lee Corporation: Consensus EPS Trend

Consensus EPS Trend	Qtr(9/02)	Qtr(12/02)	FY(6/03)	FY(6/04)
Current Estimate	0.35	0.42	1.58	1.73
7 Days Ago	0.35	0.42	1.58	1.71
30 Days Ago	0.28	0.40	1.48	1.62
60 Days Ago	0.28	0.40	1.48	1.61
90 Days Ago	0.29	0.41	1.48	NA

Zacks data updated daily.

In order to find earnings surprises on CNBC/MSN Money, on the left-hand side of the screen click on the link labeled "Earnings Estimates." Then click on the link in the middle of the page labeled "Earnings Surprise." Data similar to that contained in the table below should become available. This data indicates what earnings surprises historically have been so that you can implement the cockroach effect and the post-earnings announcement drift strategies discussed in Chapters Six and Seven.

Sara Lee Corporation: Earnings Surprise

Earnings Surprise	6/02	3/02	12/01	9/01	6/01
Estimate	0.42	0.30	0.39	0.24	0.36
Actual	0.42	0.31	0.37	0.26	0.37
Difference	NA	0.01	0.02	0.02	0.01
% Change	0.00%	3.33%	−5.13%	8.33%	2.78%

Zacks Industry: FOOD-MISC/DIVE

For analyst recommendations, click the link on the left-hand side of the screen labeled "Analyst Ratings." A table similar to the following one will then be displayed. This table enables you to implement the piggybacking strategy discussed in Chapter Ten by noticing how the consensus recommendation score has changed over the past month, as well as the neglect strategy detailed in Chapter Eleven by noticing how the number of covering analysts has changed over time. The consensus recommendation score is labeled as the "Mean Rec."

Sara Lee Corporation: Analyst Ratings

Recommendations	Current	1 Month Ago	2 Months Ago	3 Months Ago
Strong Buy	2	1	1	1
Moderate Buy	2	2	2	1
Hold	7	6	7	11
Moderate Sell	0	2	1	0
Strong Sell	1	1	1	0
Mean Rec.	2.67	3.00	2.92	2.77

For Long-term Earnings Growth Rates, on the left-hand side of the screen click on the link labeled "Earnings Estimates." Then click on the link in the middle of the page labeled "Earnings Growth Rates." A table similar to the following one should come up. You can use this table to determine the forward P/E level (labeled "03 P/E") and long-term earnings growth estimate (labeled "Next 5 Yrs."). This data will help you implement the strategies discussed in Chapter Twelve on valuation and in Chapter Eleven on the long-term earnings growth estimate.

Sara Lee Corporation: Earnings Growth Rates

Earnings Growth Rates	Last 5 yrs.	FY 2003	FY 2004	Next 5 yrs.	03 P/E
Company	6.50%	15.90%	9.30%	8.70%	14.60
Industry	6.00%	20.30%	19.30%	11.00%	16.60
S&P 500	−1.10%	30.20%	12.40%	8.00%	17.60

Zacks Industry: FOOD-MISC/DIVE

Source #2: Quicken

Step One : Go to http://www.quicken.com.

Step Two: Type in the ticker of the stock you are researching in the box labeled "Quotes & Research" on the left-hand side of the page.

Step Three: On the left-hand side of the screen you should then see the following:

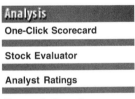

Click on the link labeled "Analyst Ratings."

For Earnings Estimate Revisions, look in the center of the page; you should see a section labeled "Analyst Estimate Trend" that resembles the following table. This table enables you to implement the estimate revision strategy discussed in Chapters Four and Five.

AAPL (Apple Computer Inc.) 14.67 –0.03

Analyst Estimates Trend	This Qtr 12/2002	Next Qtr 03/2003	This Fiscal Year 09/2003	Next Fisca Year 09/2004
Current	$0.05	$0.06	$0.35	$0.25
7 days ago	$0.09	$0.08	$0.45	$0.35
30 days ago	$0.11	$0.10	$0.48	$0.35
60 days ago	$0.12	$0.11	$0.49	$0.35
90 days ago	$0.14	$0.12	$0.55	$0.35

For earnings surprise data, look directly below the "Analysts Estimate Trend" section; there will be a section labeled "Qtrly EPS History." The section should resemble the following table. The "Qtrly

EPS History" section shows you what earnings surprises have historically been so that you can implement the cockroach effect and the
post- earnings announcement drift strategies discussed in Chapters Six
and Seven.

AAPL (Apple Computer Inc.) 14.67 -0.03

Qtrly EPS History	09/2001	12/2001	03/2002	06/2002	09/2002
Estimate EPS	$0.17	$0.11	$0.10	$0.09	$0.03
Actual EPS	$0.19	$0.11	$0.11	$0.09	$0.02
Difference	$0.02	-$0.00	$0.01	$0.00	-$0.01
% Surprise	11.8%	0.0%	10.0%	0.0%	-33.3%

Near the top of the page there is a section labeled "Analyst
Ratings." This section contains a a table similar to the following one.
The "Analyst Ratings" section enables you to implement the piggybacking strategy discussed in Chapter Ten by noticing how the consensus recommendation has changed over the past month, as well as the
neglect strategy discussed in Chapter Eleven by noticing how the
number of covering analysts has changed over time. The consensus recommendation score is labeled as the "★★★ Average Rating.★★★"

AAPL (Apple Computer Inc.) 14.67 -0.03A

Analyst Ratings	Today	1 month ago	2 months ago	3 months ago
1 - Strong Buy	3	3	3	2
2 - Buy	2	2	2	4
3 - Hold	12	11	13	12
4 - Sell	1	1	0	0
5 - Strong Sell	0	0	0	0
*** Average Rating ***	2.57	2.55	2.48	2.48

See top rated stocks releasing earnings today

For Long-term Earnings Growth Rates, a section near the bottom of the screen is labeled "Earnings Growth." A table similar to the following one is there. You can use this table to determine the forward P/E labeled "P/E (FY 2003)" and long-term earnings growth estimate labeled "Avg Est Next 5 years." The data in this section will help you implement the strategies discussed in Chapter Twelve on valuation and in Chapter Eleven on the long-term earnings growth estimate.

Earnings Growth	Last 5 years	This Fiscal Year	Next Fiscal Year	Ave Est Next 5 years	P/E (FY 2003)	PEG ratio
AAPL Industry Rank: 3 of 8	N/A	10.1% (09/2003)	−27.6% (09/2004)	11.1%	41.91	3.78
Industry (comp-micro)	27.3%	17.4%	15.4%	22.2%	12.91	.88
Sector (computer and technology)	−73.6%	207.0%	66.8%	22.6%	7.83	.42
S&P 500	−1.1%	30.2%	12.4%	8.0%	17.49	2.19

Source #3: Morningstar

Step One: Go to www.morningstar.com.

Step Two: On the front page in the section labeled Quicktake reports, type the ticker of the stock you are investigating. Next click on the link labeled EPS estimates. You should then be presented with one page containing the relevant information.

For earnings estimate revisions look in the center of the page where you will see a section labeled "Annual Earnings Estimates" that resembles the following table. This table enables you to implement the estimate revision strategy discussed in Chapters Four and Five. At the bottom of the table is the long-term earnings growth rate labeled "Five-Year Growth Forecast."

International Business Machines Corporation (IBM)

Annual Earnings Estimates

	12-02		12-03	
	$	**Growth %**	**$**	**Growth %**
High	4.20	−3.4	4.80	21.2
Low	3.84	−11.7	4.15	4.8
Mean	3.96	−9.0	4.41	11.4
30 Days Ago	3.97	−8.7	4.51	13.6
60 Days Ago	4.00	−8.0	4.54	13.5
90 Days Ago	4.02	−7.6	4.61	14.7
Number of Estimates	19		18	

Five-Year Growth Forecast: 11.3 %
Industry Average: 21.9 %

For Earnings Surprises, look directly above the "Annual Earnings Estimates" section; there will be a section labeled "Earnings Surprises %." The chart in the "Earnings Surprises %" section should resemble the following. This chart shows you what the earnings surprises have historically been, so that you can implement the cockroach effect and the post-earnings announcement drift strategies discussed in Chapters Six and Seven.

International Business Machines Corporation (IBM)

Earnings Surprises %

Did the company beat consensus analyst earnings estimates?

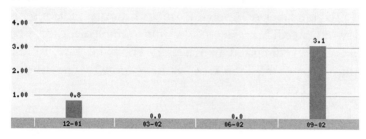

EPS estimates provided by Zacks.

At the bottom of the page, in a section labeled "Analyst Opinions," you will find a table similar to the one shown. This table enables you to implement the piggybacking strategy discussed in Chapter Ten by calculating how the consensus recommendation has changed over the past month. The consensus recommendation score is labeled as the "Average Rating."

International Business Machines Corporation (IBM)

Analyst Opinions

Number of Analysts

Average Rating	Last Month	Industry Average	S&P 500 Average
2.1	2.2	1.5	2.4

1=Strong Buy 5=Strong Sell
Data through last Friday.
EPS estimates provided by Zacks.

Source #4: Zacks Investment Research

Step One: Go to www.zacks.com.

Step Two: On the front page, at the top left of the screen, you can input the ticker of the stock you are researching and select the "Estimates" report.

Following is the "Estimates" report available for Ford (F). A similar report is available for any stock you are researching.

Ford (F)

Reported Earnings   Detailed Report

	09/2002	06/2002	03/2002	12/2001	09/2001
Reported	0.12	0.31	−0.06	−0.48	−0.28
Estimate	0.04	0.25	−0.14	−0.50	−0.28
Difference	0.08	0.06	0.08	0.02	0.00
Surprise	200.00%	24.00%	57.14%	4.00%	0.00%

Analyst EPS Estimates   Detailed Estimates

Current Year	Current Quarter (12/2002)	Next Quarter (12/2003)	Current Year (12/2002)	Next Year (03/2003)
Average Estimate	0.13	0.25	0.41	0.65
High Estimate	0.25	0.27	0.57	1.20
Low Estimate	0.04	0.22	0.15	0.10
# of Estimates	13	2	18	18

Consensus EPS Trend & Revisions   Detailed Report

Current Year	Current Quarter (12/2002)	Next Quarter (03/2003)	Current Year (12/2002)	Next Year 03/2003)
Consensus 7 Days Ago	0.14	0.25	0.39	0.67
Upward Revisions	2	0	5	1
Downward Revisions	3	0	1	3
Consensus 30 Days Ago	0.13	0.25	0.36	0.71
Upward Revisions	3	0	8	1
Downward Revisions	3	0	1	6

The last section on the page is labeled "Consensus EPS Trend & Revisions." Click on the link labeled "Detailed Report" in the upper right-hand corner of the section. A page labeled "Consensus EPS Trends & Revisions—Detailed Report," which is similar to the one displayed here, will then become available.

Ford (F)

Consensus EPS Trends & Revisions – Detailed Report

6-Month Perspective

	Current Quarter (12/2002)	Next Quarter 03/2003)	Current Year (12/2002)	Next Year (12/2003)	Long Term Earnings Growth Estimate (%)
Mean – Current	0.13	0.25	0.41	0.65	5.43
Mean – 7 Days Ago	0.14	0.25	0.39	0.67	5.43
Mean – 30 Days Ago	0.13	0.25	0.36	0.71	4.83
Mean – 60 Days Ago	0.12	0.25	0.26	0.79	4.57
Mean – 90 Days Ago	0.12	0.25	0.26	0.82	4.57
Mean – 6 Months Ago	0.14	0.28	0.15	0.88	6.00
% change in Mean from 6 months Ago	−9.25	−11.45	181.83	−30.49	−11.11

30-Day Perspective

	Current Quarter (12/2002)	Next Quarter 03/2003)	Current Year (12/2002)	Next Year (12/2003)	Long Term Earnings Growth Estimate
30-day consensus mean	$0.12	$0.24	$0.46	$0.53	7.00%
# of estimates in 30-day consensus	7	1	10	8	2
# of estimates added in last 30 days	1	0	1	1	1
# of estimates removed in last 30 days	0	0	0	0	0

(continued)

30-Day Perspective

	Current Quarter (12/2002)	Next Quarter 03/2003)	Current Year (12/2002)	Next Year (12/2003)	Long Term Earnings Growth Estimate
# of estimates unchanged in last 30 days	6	2	8	10	6
# of estimates revised UP in last 30 days	3	0	8	1	N/A
# of estimates revised DOWN in last 30 days	3	0	1	6	N/A

7-Day Perspective

	Current Quarter (12/2002)	Next Quarter 03/2003)	Current Year (12/2002)	Next Year (12/2003)	Long Term Earnings Growth Estimate
Current Consensus EPS Estimate	0.13	0.25	0.41	0.65	5.43
Mean of 3 most recent estimates	0.06	0.25	0.47	0.40	6.33
Age of 3 most recent est. changes	4 days	94 days	4 days	4 days	130 days
# of estimates added in last 7 days	0	0	0	0	0
# of estimates removed in last 7 days	0	0	0	0	0
# of estimates unchanged in last 7 days	8	2	12	14	7
# of estimates revised UP in last 7 days	2	0	5	1	N/A
# of estimates revised DOWN in last 7 days	3	0	1	3	N/A

In order to implement the earnings estimate revision strategies, look at the top of the "Consensus EPS Trends & Revisions—Detailed Report" at a section labeled "6-Month Perspective." This section enables you to implement the estimate revision strategy discussed in Chapters Four and Five. Additionally, the "6-Month Perspective" section describes how the long-term earnings growth estimate has been changing over time, as discussed in Chapter Eleven. Finally, the "Consensus EPS Trends & Revisions—Detailed Report" contains the 30-day consensus in a section labeled "30-Day Perspective," which can be used as discussed in Chapter Five.

At the top of the "Estimates" report is a section labeled "Reported Earnings." The section resembles what is shown below. The "Reported Earnings" section shows you what the earnings surprises historically have been, so that you can implement the cockroach effect and the post-earnings announcement drift strategies discussed in Chapters Six and Seven.

Ford (F)

Reported Earnings					Detailed Report
	09/2002	06/2002	03/2002	12/2001	09/2001
Reported	0.12	0.31	−0.06	−0.48	−0.28
Estimate	0.04	0.25	−0.14	−0.50	−0.28
Difference	0.08	0.06	0.08	0.02	0.00
Surprise	200.00%	24.00%	57.14%	4.00%	0.00%

By clicking on the link in this section labeled "Detailed Report," you will have access to the Earnings Estimate Histograms discussed in Chapters Six and Seven. The earnings estimate histogram should resemble what is shown here for Ford (F).

At the top of the "Estimate" report page is a link labeled "Analyst Recommendations." Clicking on this link will provide the information shown here, which can be used in implementing the piggybacking strategy discussed in Chapter Ten.

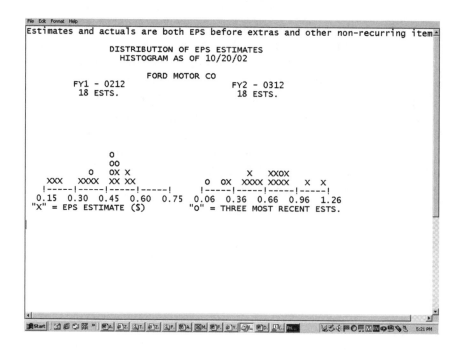

Ford (F)

Analyst Ratings

	Today	1 Month Ago	2 Months Ago	3 Months Ago
Strong Buy	2	3	4	4
Buy	3	3	2	2
Hold	7	7	10	11
Sell	2	1	0	0
Strong Sell	3	2	1	0
Consensus (mean)	3.06	2.75	2.53	2.41

Recent Research on F : FORD MOTOR CO

Additionally, from the "Estimates" report, by clicking on the "Detailed Estimates" link, you will be provided with the detailed analyst earnings estimates for Ford (F), as shown. This detailed report contains the forward P/E ratios based on the current and next fiscal year's estimates. Also, from the detailed estimates you can calculate the earnings uncertainty metric mentioned in Chapter Twelve and the valuation statistics in Chapter Eleven.

Zacks.com – Company News for: ' F '

Zacks Detailed Analyst Estimates for: FORD MOTOR CO

Ticker Symbol: F | Cusip: 345370860 | Fiscal Year End: December
Updated: 10/23/02

Broker	Recommendation	Fiscal Year EPS Estimates 12/02	12/03	Quarter EPS Estimates 09/02	12/02	5 year Growth Est(%)	Estimate Date
Insttn'l Broker	3.0 Hold	0.38	0.50	0.05	0.04	5.00	10/17/02
National Broker	5.0 Strong Sell	0.50	0.80	0.05	0.13	5.00	10/17/02
National Broker	3.0 Hold	0.46	0.29	0.03	0.06	4.00	10/17/02
Regional Broker	3.0 Hold	0.45	0.80	0.05	0.09	—	10/17/02
Insttn'l Broker	5.0 Strong Sell	0.40	0.65	—	0.14	—	10/01/02
National Broker	4.0 Moderate Sell	0.45	0.30	0.02	0.15	9.00	10/10/02
Regional Broker	2.0 Moderate Buy	0.55	0.75	0.05	0.25	—	10/01/02
Insttn'l Broker	3.0 Hold	0.35	0.50	0.02	0.08	—	09/30/02
Regional Broker	6.0 N/A	0.36	1.02	—	0.14	—	09/30/02
Regional Broker	2.0 Moderate Buy	0.48	0.70	0.05	—	5.00	09/17/02
Insttn'l Broker	4.0 Moderate Sell	0.15	0.55	—	—	—	09/03/02
National Broker	5.0 Strong Sell	0.23	0.87	—	—	5.00	07/31/02
Regional Broker	1.0 Strong Buy	0.30	0.85	—	0.15	—	07/19/02
Regional Broker	1.0 Strong Buy	0.20	1.20	—	—	—	07/10/02

(continued)

Zacks.com – Company News for: ' F ' (*cont*)

Zacks Detailed Analyst Estimates for: FORD MOTOR CO

Ticker Symbol: F | Cusip: 345370860 | Fiscal Year End: December
Updated: 10/23/02

	Fiscal Year EPS Estimates		Quarter EPS Estimates		5 year Growth Est(%)
	12/02	12/03	09/02	12/02	
30-Day Consensus					
Low Estimate	0.36	0.10	0.02	0.04	9.00
*Mean / Consensus Estimate	0.46	0.53	0.04	0.12	9.00
High Estimate	0.57	1.02	0.05	0.25	9.00
Number of Estimates	10	8	2	7	1
Indicated P/E for stock price on *10/21/02* of $9.55:	20.85	18.15			
120-Day Consensus (All Estimates)					
Low Estimate	0.15	0.10	0.02	0.04	4.00
*Mean / Consensus Estimate	0.40	0.69	0.04	0.13	5.38
High Estimate	0.57	1.32	0.05	0.25	9.00
Number of Estimates	19	19	12	13	8
Indicated P/E for stock price on *10/21/02* of $9.55:	24.03	13.88			

Total Number of Reporting Brokers: 19

NOTE: Earnings estimates are for diluted earnings per share from continuing operations before extraordinary earnings adjustments & discontinued operations.

NOTE: Quarterly estimates roll over 45 days after the quarter. Fiscal year estimates roll over 60 days after the fiscal year.

All information contained herein is based on data that has been provided to Zacks Investment Research, Inc., by contributing brokers and analysts. Zacks Investment Research, Inc. has used its best efforts in compiling and preparing data for inclusion in this report but does not warrant that the infomation herein is complete or accurate, and does not assume, and hereby disclaims any liability for errors or omissions whether caused by negligence, accident or any other cause. Reproduction of any portion of this publication without written consent of Zacks Investment Research, Inc. is strictly prohibited.

A Dow Strategy Based on Expected Earnings Uncertainty

THE INTERESTING THING ABOUT EARNINGS UNCERTAINTY is that it is fairly stable over time. This means that if you build a portfolio based on earnings uncertainty, the turnover of the portfolio will be relatively low.

The other strategies examined throughout the book generally have a time horizon of a quarter and are implemented on the entire universe of tradeable stocks. The Dow Strategy contained in this appendix, on the other hand, is a long-term buy and hold strategy that attempts to find the ten most promising stocks within the thirty stocks that comprise the Dow Jones Industrial Average.

The goal of the Dow Strategy is to select a portfolio of Dow stocks that is only re-balanced once a year but which over the year-long holding period outperforms the Dow Jones Industrial Average.

As shown in Chapter Twelve, stocks with low expected earnings uncertainty tend to outperform stocks with a high-degree of earnings uncertainty. Additionally, using earnings uncertainty as a stock-selection strategy provides a buy-and-hold approach, as those stocks with highly variable earnings streams tend to remain so over time. This is especially true among the blue-chip stocks that comprise the Dow Jones.

Strategy

The Dow Strategy invests in those ten stocks within the Dow Jones Industrial Index with the lowest degree of earnings uncertainty, and holds this portfolio of stocks for one year before re-balancing.

The Dow Strategy is a fairly straightforward strategy and its implementation is as follows.

Step One: For all the Dow component stocks an earnings uncertainty measurement is calculated. This earnings uncertainty measurement is simply the sum of the earnings uncertainty for both the current and next fiscal year as determined by the consensus earnings estimate and the standard deviation of this consensus earnings estimate for the current and next fiscal year.

Earnings Uncertainty Metric:

$$\left(\frac{\text{Std. Deviation of the Consensus Earnings Estimate for the Current Fiscal Year}}{\text{Consensus Earnings Estimate for the Current Fiscal Year}} \right) +$$

$$\left(\frac{\text{Std. Deviation of the Consensus Earnings Estimate for the Next Fiscal Year}}{\text{Consensus Earnings Estimate for the Next Fiscal Year}} \right)$$

Step Two: The thirty stocks within the Dow Jones are ranked according to the Earnings Uncertainty Metric. Those ten stocks with the lowest degree of earnings uncertainty—which would be those ten stocks for which the preceding metric has the lowest value—comprise the portfolio. These ten stocks are then equal-weighted and held in the portfolio.

Step Three: The portfolio is held without any rebalancing or selling for one full year. At the end of the year, the current portfolio is sold and the money is re-invested in a new portfolio.

The returns of the strategy are good but not nearly as good as those generated with a higher level of turnover through use of the Zacks Rank. The other problem with the strategy is that unlike the Zacks Rank, the Dow Strategy is a back-test. The strategy thus runs the danger that the results may be attributable to some degree to data mining. Data mining means that you have simply found a relationship that has historically existed without any guarantee that the relationship will continue to exist in the future.

There is no danger of data mining with the Zacks Rank because the returns due to the Zacks Rank are calculated from rankings that were actually published by Zacks over the past twenty years.

Nevertheless, I have included the strategy as an appendix, as it represents a novel approach to using analyst data to select a portfolio of stocks that will be held for a full-year time period and the strategy has generated historical excess returns over the Dow of approximately 4.5% per year. Additionally, the transaction costs because of the year-long holding period are practically non-existent.

Returns of the Dow Strategy

The returns of the Dow strategy are given below. Because turnover is limited to once a year, the transaction costs for the strategy are minimal.

Historical Returns

- Return figures in percentage(%). Returns include dividend re-investment.

- Yearly Rebalancing, Portfolio Selection occurs on last trading day of December in each year

- 2002 returns are through August 2002

Period	Dow Strategy	Dow Return	Excess Return
1988	17.16	16.14	1.01
1989	45.92	32.19	13.72
1990	10.90	−0.56	11.46
1991	46.02	24.19	21.83
1992	6.10	7.41	−1.30
1993	13.94	16.93	−2.98
1994	1.04	5.01	−3.97
1995	45.98	36.87	9.11
1996	26.16	28.89	−2.74
1997	26.69	24.94	1.75
1998	35.84	18.16	17.69
1999	30.74	27.21	3.54

(continued)

Period	Dow Strategy	Dow Return	Excess Return
2000	8.53	−4.71	13.25
2001	−8.97	−5.43	−3.54
2002	−15.41	−12.42	−2.99

On an annualized basis the Dow strategy outperforms the Dow by roughly 4.5% per year.

The stocks that would have been held in the portfolio over the last few years are given here:

(1995)	(1996)	(1997)	(1998)	(1999)	(2000)	(2001)	(Since Jan. '02)
GE	GE	CBS	AXP	AXP	AXP	AXP	C
GT	GT	GE	GE	GE	EK	JNJ	GE
HON	HON	HON	GT	HON	GE	MCD	HD
KO	KO	KO	HON	IBM	HON	MMM	IBM
MCD	MCD	MMM	JNJ	JNJ	MCD	MO	JNJ
MMM	MO	MO	MCD	MCD	MMM	MRK	KO
MO	MRK	MRK	MRK	MMM	MO	PG	MCD
MRK	PG	PG	PG	MRK	MRK	SBC	PG
PG	T	S	UTX	UTX	PG	UTX	SBC
T	UTX	UTX	WMT	WMT	UTX	WMT	WMT

What is encouraging is that when the strategy is tested with portfolios that have yearly holding periods but are constructed quarterly, as opposed to annually, the returns continue to look good. In fact, it seems that portfolios that are constructed mid-year tend to perform slightly better. The results are shown on the next page.

Performance of the Dow Strategy portfolios created quarterly.

Year	1-Yr Holding Period Excess Return for 10 Dow Strategy stocks relative to the Dow Jones Industrial Average for the portfolios purchased on			
	March 31st	**June 30th**	**September 30th**	**December 31st**
1987				1.01%
1988	1.26%	4.07%	3.97%	13.72%
1989	0.92%	16.56%	8.05%	11.46%
1990	16.83%	3.04%	5.60%	21.83%
1991	2.79%	3.09%	2.62%	−1.30%
1992	2.14%	3.97%	−1.50%	−2.98%
1993	−10.14%	−4.14%	3.09%	−3.97%
1994	6.36%	2.46%	4.26%	9.11%
1995	3.76%	6.17%	3.38%	−2.74%
1996	5.70%	3.71%	0.92%	1.75%
1997	4.38%	9.71%	3.90%	17.69%
1998	18.09%	−0.07%	6.62%	3.54%
1999	−17.72%	−2.20%	−3.66%	13.25%
2000	17.89%	6.15%	10.25%	−3.54%
2001	−0.84%	2.34%		

Year	Performance through August 31st, 2002 (less than 1-Yr holding period)			
2001			-4.55%	-2.99%
2002	0.03%	2.05%		

15: Number of Dow Strategy portfolios with Negative Excess Return (25.42%)

44: Number of Dow Strategy portfolios with Positive Excess Return (74.58%)

59: Total Number of Portfolios tested

Results seem to indicate that the underlying Diamonds of the Dow strategy is more likely to generate a negative excess return when applied at the beginning (end) of the year.

Index